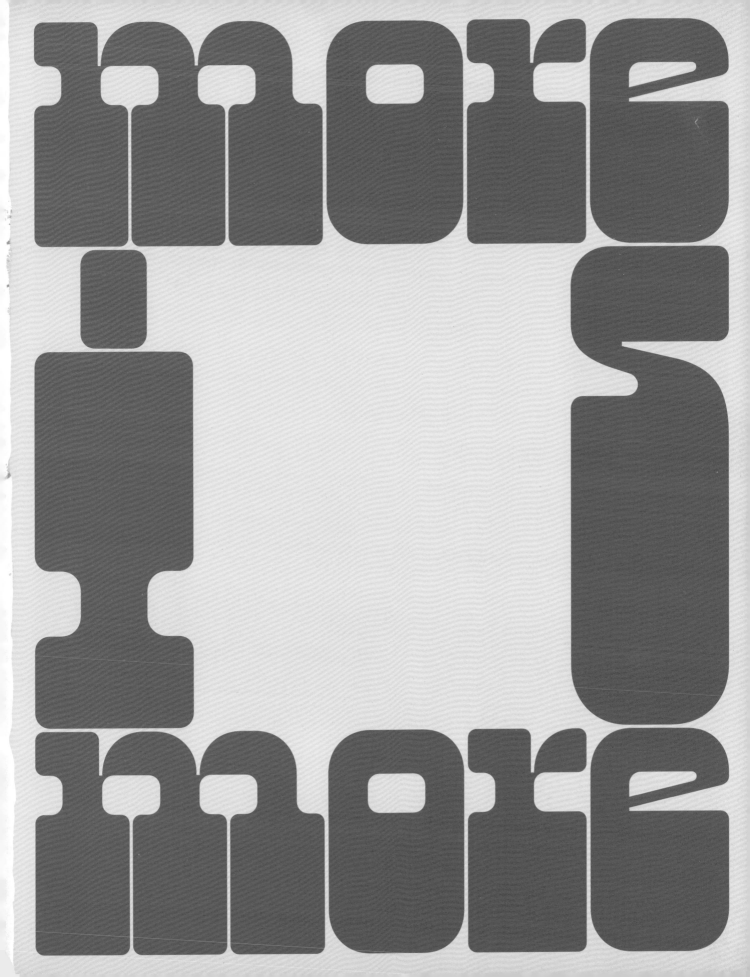

GET LOOSE IN THE KITCHEN

MOLLY BAZ

Photographs by
PEDEN + MUNK

Clarkson Potter/Publishers
New York

TO LOS ANGELES
AND ALL THE WACKY,
WONDERFUL PEOPLE
WHO MAKE THIS CITY
THE NOURISHING,
CREATIVE, AND LIFE-
ENRICHING PLACE
THAT I AM SO VERY
LUCKY TO CALL HOME

Copyright © 2023 by Molly Baz

Photographs copyright © 2023 by
PEDEN + MUNK

All rights reserved.
Published in the United States by Clarkson
Potter/Publishers, an imprint of the Crown
Publishing Group, a division of Penguin
Random House LLC, New York.

ClarksonPotter.com

CLARKSON POTTER is a trademark and
POTTER with colophon is a registered
trademark of Penguin Random House LLC.

Library of Congress Cataloging-in-Publication
Data
Names: Baz, Molly, author. | PEDEN + MUNK,
photographers.
Title: More is more / Molly Baz ; photographs
by Peden + Munk.
Identifiers: LCCN 2022055188 (print) |
LCCN 2022055189 (ebook) |
ISBN 9780593578841 (hardcover) |
ISBN 9780593578858 (ebook)
Subjects: LCSH: Cooking. | LCGFT: Cookbooks.
Classification: LCC TX714 .B384554 2023
(print) | LCC TX714 (ebook) | DDC
641.3—dc23/eng/20221122
LC record available at https://lccn.loc.
gov/2022055188
LC ebook record available at https://lccn.loc.
gov/2022055189

ISBN: 978-0-593-57884-1
Ebook ISBN: 978-0-593-57885-8
Barnes & Noble ISBN: 978-0-593-79665-8

Printed in China

Editor: Jennifer Sit
Editorial assistant: Bianca Cruz

Art direction and design: PlayLab, Inc.
Creative direction: Ben Willett
Photographs: PEDEN + MUNK

Production editor: Terry Deal
Production manager: Jessica Heim
Compositors: Merri Ann Morrell and
Hannah Hunt

Project assistant: Becky Gordon

Food stylist: Christopher St. Onge
Food stylist assistants: Jasmyn Crawford
  and Stephanie Gomez
Prop stylist: Elizabeth Jaime
Photo assistant: Jake Caminero
Wardrobe stylist: Joanie Del Santo
Makeup artist (cover photo): Matisse Andrews
Hairstylist (cover photo): Eddie Cook

Copyeditor: Deborah Weiss Geline
Proofreaders: Ivy McFadden and Kathy Brock
Indexer: Elizabeth T. Parson

Publicist: Jana Branson
Marketer: Stephanie Davis

10 9 8 7 6 5 4 3 2 1

First Edition

CONTENTS

RECIPES

✳ — Recipes with Video Cook-Alongs
✶ — Recipes with Audio Cook-Alongs

A COUPLE SNICK—SNACKS NEVER KILLED NOBODY 50

BE THE SALAD YOU WISH TO SEE IN THE WORLD

MY INTERESTS INCLUDE BUT ARE NOT LIMITED TO CARBS

THE USDA RECOMMENDS 9 SERVINGS OF VEG PER DAY

IF YOU SHOW ME YOUR SANDO I'LL SHOW YOU MINE

I THOUGHT YOU SHOULD KNOW THAT I RARELY EAT BREAKFAST

SWEETS

FOR SALT TOOTHS

BIG FAT THANKS

INDEX

It was a completely insignificant Saturday in September. The year was 2021. It was 9:30 a.m. and my husband, Ben, had dragged me to a dive bar off of Sunset Boulevard to watch a *very important* English Premier League soccer match.

Don't be fooled. This isn't a story about sports (I have very little to say on the matter); it's a story about calamari. . . . Cut to the top of the second half, an hour-ish or so later. It was far too early for lunch, I hadn't had breakfast, and there was nary a pancake in sight. The menu featured all the classic bar food hits, that magnificent category of rich and delicious foods you crave when you're at a dive—loaded nachos, Buffalo wings, potato skins, and, my personal weakness, fried calamari. I may or may not also have been two Bloody Marys deep at this point, though that is relevant to this story only insofar as to paint a picture of who I am. The game plan was clear: I was having calamari for breakfast.

Ten minutes and half a Bloody later, the calamari arrived. The diagnosis: golden brown, craggy crisp, unadorned, and served in a paper-lined red plastic basket, just as you'd expect. It looked like . . . calamari. Taste-wise, it wasn't bad, not rancid or anything—far from it. It was simply very whatevs. Underseasoned and just kinda plain.

For most people, that's where this story would end. They'd eat their perfectly fine breakfast squid and life would go on as it always does. Well, as I am about to make clear, I am not most people, and I happened to have some time on my hands. I took a look around me to see how I might remedy the sitch: right away I noticed a pepper grinder and a bottle of hot sauce on the table. There were lemon wedges perched on the rims of our Bloodys (I knew I'd ordered two for a reason). I always carry a tiny tin of Maldon flaky sea salt in my bag, so the seasoning element was on lock. I politely asked my server for a side of mayo and then determinedly got to work.

Within minutes, I had successfully transformed a perfectly fine and absolutely forgettable plate of fried calamari into a meal that will stick with me forever (just don't ask me who won the match or, for that matter, who was playing).

Here's how it went:

1 Squeeze the juice of 4 lemon wedges over the basket of calamari.

2 Season the calamari liberally with flaky sea salt.

3 Stir together a quick tableside spicy mayo for dipping by combining mayonnaise, hot sauce, a touch more lemon juice, salt, and pepper.

4 Wash down with another Bloody and enjoy one of the greatest plates of calamari of my life.

Willett (that's Ben) sat across from me eating his breakfast burger (a very delicious one, I will add), slightly horrified and yet entirely unfazed because, of course, he'd seen this whole on-the-fly doctoring routine go down at least a thousand times before.

But it was right then, in that seemingly insignificant moment, that this book was born. Sitting in that bar, I realized that what the calamari had needed was just a little *more*. Suddenly, everything became clear. What sets apart a good cook from a great one, an amateur chef from a professional, a true pursuer of good food from an apathetic one, can be summarized in a single phrase: **MORE IS MORE**.

When it comes to cooking, *More Is More* is an ideology to live by. It is a guiding principle to embrace boldness in the kitchen (or, in this case, at the table) in order to level up your food. It's a commitment to doing anything and everything in our power to land a delicious meal. It's about refusing to settle for something mediocre and instead figuring out how to transform that mediocrity into something stupendous. If your first reaction is to think I mean "more bacon, more salt, more cheese"—gluttonous excess is not what this book is about. It's about finding more confidence in the kitchen, gaining more trust in our own cooking ability, and having the nerve to go for bigger, bolder, more explosive flavor.

When I was a fine-dining line cook, I spent years being drilled with the mindset that less is always more. Single dots of sauce on a plate, a whopping two-ounce portion of fish, and three perfectly placed chive batons as garnish. But then I became a home cook and realized that in my kitchen, I am in charge. I call the shots. And what I actually crave is just the opposite. I don't know about you, but I want to cook and eat with ABANDON. We're on this planet only once, and gustatorily speaking (it's a word—trust me), I see no reason we shouldn't make the most of that time. I want to cook and eat BOLD food with BIG personality, especially if I'm going to go to the trouble of making it myself. Restraint, my friends, is overrated.

So what does this all mean, practically? It means I want you to crank up the dang heat! To grab a big-ass pinch of salt! To use every part of every ingredient to its fullest potential and then some. To cook with gumption, and personality, all in the service of building confidence and boldness and taking control of your home kitchen! I've seen the way my friends and fam reluctantly turn their heat to medium-high when a recipe calls for it and then

instinctively turn it down to medium-low for fear of burning. (We need that good browning!!) I've seen the way an amateur cook gingerly seasons a steak. (Nothin' worse than a bland piece of meat!) I've seen all of it and then some, and through my observations I've deduced that a little confidence, good technique, and a better understanding of ingredients can be the difference between the forgettable and the memorable—my calamari zhoozhing being just one everyday example.

"More is more" is that moment you recognize your salad needs an extra glug of vinegar, or your roasted carrots could really use a handful of chopped peanuts for texture. It's that first time you drizzle chili crisp on a fried egg and the stars suddenly align. It's about trusting yourself enough to leave the chicken thighs skin-side down on the heat, undisturbed, for fifteen whole minutes, only to then enjoy the crispiest dang chicken skin of your life. It's all the adjustments, big and small, that take your food from good to lights-out GREAT.

The recipes in this book will encourage you to break out of your comfort zone, to learn how to cook passionately, fearlessly, and, as always, in pursuit of something yumz. They'll leave some ingredients open-ended so that you can pick

your fave [insert herb here] for a salad, and quantities like generous handfuls, glugs, and pinches will be encouraged so you reach less for the tangled-up set of measuring spoons and connect more with the ones you've got attached to your body. To cook with a "more is more" mentality is to identify what the right amount of any given ingredient means to you, and the only way to gain that self-assuredness is to cook more—and more—and then probably a little more. Through some trial and error, and, I hope, a lil' help from this book, you'll soon become a cook who knows exactly when the "more" becomes "it's perfect, let's eat."

Okay! Enough preaching, you get the point. It's time to pick up your knives and clear your cutting boards. We're **MORE IS MORE** people, and we've got cooking to do.

I promise it's going to be fucking delicious.

PLAY BY THE

RULES

RULES

If the ultimate goal is to learn to cook without inhibition, here are a few rules of the road that will help as you navigate your way.

IF YOU'RE GONNA USE IT, USE IT

There's no point in calling for an ingredient if it's not going to make itself known in a dish. I'm sick and tired of recipes that call for one garlic clove. One garlic clove?!? Have you lost your marbles??? I wanna taste that garlic! It's also important to consider HOW each ingredient is being used and let that guide the quantity. Is the garlic raw? Okay fine, in that case, perhaps just a clove or two will do. Are you simmering it in a stew for three hours? Then you can probably afford ten to twelve of them because time will mellow their flavor. It's allll about context, people!

LOOSEN UP

Part of the "more is more" journey involves learning to cook intuitively and more comfortably so that you rely less heavily on recipes. A confident cook will rarely measure out a ½ cup of grated Parm before stirring it into pasta sauce. A confident cook will, however, grab a big ole handful and start adding it little by little, tasting as they go, until they deem the sauce sufficiently cheesy. Ultimately, I want you to cook that way and not be glued to the recipe. As you cook your way through this book, see if you can loosen up a bit. Think critically about each ingredient you're adding. Consider its purpose and then GO FOR IT. Screw the measurements. Cook with abandon. Never stop tasting. Always be tweaking. And most of all, do not freak out if things don't turn out as planned. You will mess some shit up along the way; I can absolutely guarantee it. You don't see all of the fails and flops that happen in my home kitchen before these recipes hit the page, but rest assured, they happen. (Ask me about the coconut custard–filled corn bread someday.) Does that stop me from picking right back up, walking back into the kitchen, and trying something different? HELLLL NO. Do I learn a lot along the way about what I don't like, and what does and doesn't work? HELLLL YES.

YOU'RE PROBS NOT USING ENOUGH

One of the greatest dishes I've ever eaten was a plate of potatoes, seasoned liberally with salt and pepper, showered with fresh herbs, doused in olive oil, and swimming in lemon juice. These foundational ingredients will enhance almost anything you cook, and you'll encounter them often in this book. If I've done my job correctly, they'll end up as staples in your kitchen, too.

Salt

kosher salt, flaky sea salt

Fat

olive oil, ghee, butter, coconut oil, coconut milk, schmaltz

Fresh Herbs

cilantro, dill, parsley, chives, basil, mint, tarragon

Acid

vinegar, fresh citrus, pickle brine

ONE INGREDIENT, MANY WAYS

One of the most effective ways to coax a range of textures and flavors from a single ingredient is to treat it several different ways. Take a head of cauliflower: you can eat it raw, and you can eat it cooked, so why not combine the two in one dish? A skillet of charred cauliflower steaks topped with a pile of shaved raw cauliflower becomes a multidimensional eating experience using only one ingredient. (Check out Raw & Roasted Cauli Salad with Creamy, Dreamy Vegan Ranch, page 82.) A bunch of celery or a bulb of fennel can be used as the base of a braise, while their tender, herbaceous leaves can be used as a garnish. (See Fennel on Fennel on Fennel Tortilla, page 212, for the ultimate multiuse scenario.) Pickles are great, but have you ever stirred pickle brine into a vinaigrette or used it as a marinade for chicken? Look at an ingredient's potential for both flavor and texture, and challenge yourself to use it in as many ways as you can imagine.

IF IT AIN'T YUMMY, FIX IT

This is where the whole "not settling" thing comes into play and where you'll hone your zhoozhing skills. You deserve to eat something that you find truly delicious, especially if you spent your own highly valuable time cooking it. As in the mediocre-calamari-turned-phenom example I shared with you in the intro (you did read that, didn't you?), if you get to the end of a recipe, whether it's mine, your own, or someone else's, and you're not LOVING how it tastes, FIX IT, Y'ALL! I won't be offended. Actually, I'll be thrilled, as my mission here will have been accomplished. Ask yourself: "What is it missing?" "What would make this meal better?" "What do I already have in the pantry that might remedy this?" "What don't I like about this dish and what could I add that would make me like it more?" Then go make it happen!

TURN YA BURNERS UP (LET'S BURN SOME SHIT)

Charring, crisping, and blistering are all essential to building deep, nuanced flavor, but you'll never brown anything over moderate heat. (Mom, I am lookin' at you.) To properly brown whatever you're cooking, you gotta CRANK that heat to drive enough moisture off its surface to do so. If you're searing a steak, you need a ripping-hot skillet to achieve that coveted charred exterior, and the only way to get a ripping-hot skillet is to turn ya burners up. And maybe open some windows. Similarly, a tray of beautifully caramelized roasted vegetables can be achieved only when the oven is hot enough to evaporate all the water from the surface of the vegetables. Vegetables are high in water, which means that the oven will need to be REAL HAWT or they'll end up soggy and bland. The only time you should set your oven to a low or moderate temperature (< 375°F) is when baking, slow-braising, or reheating. So don't be scared to crank that oven to 475°F or 500°F. You can check out some of my high-heat faves in the book to get yourself acquainted: Spicy Coconut-Smothered Green Beans (page 225) and Skirt Steak with Juicy Tomatoes & Salsa Macha (page 141).

IT'S ALL IN THE SAUCE

I'm going to let you in on a little (open) secret that most chefs holds true: EVERYTHING TASTES BETTER WITH SAUCE. Sauceless food is . . . dry, and a sauce will not only add flavor to a dish but texture and moisture, too. Would you ever eat a salad without dressing or a bowl of cereal without milk??? You'll notice that most of the dishes in this book contain some kind of sauce, dressing, marinade, or vinaigrette, and that's largely what makes them so delicious. Sauces don't have to be complicated, they just need to be thoughtful, meaning the sauce element contains flavors that will enhance whatever it's saucing. As you peruse these recipes, take note of which sauces speak to you most and then keep them on hand as quick fixes for other dishes.

MORE RULES

THOU SHALT NOT WASTE HERBS

I really mean this, you guys. How many times have you purchased an entire bunch of parsley for a recipe that calls for 2 tablespoons and then let the rest of it wilt away in your crisper drawer? Not in this kitchen. Not for a second. You can never have too many tender herbs (basil, parsley, cilantro, chives, mint, dill, tarragon), which is why when they're called for in this book, you'll use the whole dang bunch (and sometimes even multiples!). Wanna try me? See Olive Oil–Drowned Potatoes with Lemony Onions & Herbs (page 222), Dilly Beans & Burrata (page 218), or Shells, Peas & Buttermilk (page 104)!

(Woody herbs are the exception here as they can really overpower things if not deployed in moderation.)

CONDIMENTS ARE YOUR BFFL

A fridge full of condiments is a surefire way to ensure a great meal. Condiments can be reimagined and recombined into many different sauces and marinades with very little effort at all. I keep an arsenal of eight or ten different spicy condiments, three or four mustards, and several jars of pickly things on hand at all times so there's always something appropriate for the job. A plate of grilled sausages dragged through homemade Dijonnaise (Dijon mustard plus mayo is all it takes!) is the ultimate grilling level-up, whereas a lonely blob of ketchup might be totally forgettable. A pot of buttered rice, speckled with chopped pickles and seasoned with pickle brine—wayyy more fun than buttered rice alone. A turkey sandwich slathered in a quick spicy condiment of mayo and sambal: a game changer. "More is more" doesn't have to mean more ingredients. The thing that's great about condiments is that they're already packed with ingredients, so they handle the heavy lifting.

WHEN IN DOUBT, REFRY

Burritos are good, but you know what's even better? A burrito that's crisped up in a pan with a little oil before serving. Banana bread is yummy, but picture this: a slice of banana bread that's been sizzled in butter until caramelized like French toast. A slice of meat loaf, but just take three extra minutes to throw it in a skillet and sear until crisp and golden at the edges. My point here is to see the potential in the dish before you. Texture is a huge part of our enjoyment of food, and one way to quickly add texture to a dish is to give it one last moment of crisping. Refrying also creates roasty-toasty caramelized flavors—it's the same reason a slice of toasted bread is almost always more delicious than an untoasted one.

ENOUGH IS ENOUGH

Part of the "more is more" mentality involves taking the driver's seat, and knowing when to call it. There's only so much salt a dish can take, only so many condiments you can pile on, only so much charring any vegetable can handle before you go overboard. Luckily, that threshold is likely a lot further than you think, but it is up to you to decide when it's time to eat. Challenge yourself and then trust your instincts. The more meals you cook, the easier it will become to know when enough is enough.

WHEN LESS IS MORE

Sometimes a peak-season tomato needs nothing more than a sprinkle of flaky salt to take it to an otherworldly level. That's a call you'll need to make, and as long as you're constantly tasting your food, you'll be able to do so. "More is more" is not about dumping piles of ingredients onto one another and hoping for the best. It's about thinking about what ingredients, if any, will take a meal from good to great, and acting on it. If it's only a squeeze of lemon over your roasted broccoli, so be it. You made that brocc more delicious, and that's precisely the point.

I STILL LOVE

SALT

If you own *Cook This Book* (that's my other cookbook, and you can find it right here!), you already know how much I fuck with salt. Salt is the spice of life. But before we get any further down this road, I'd like to reiterate one last time that I do NOT care for salty food. I like properly seasoned food, and there's a big difference. As with heat, I encourage you to really explore your personal limitations in the salt and seasoning department, 'cause I bet you'll realize that your food can take a few more three-finger pinches than you once thought. People say that restaurant food tastes better because of all the butter, but I've had lots of delicious butterless meals out in the world, and they were delicious because they were seasoned properly with salt.

COOK THIS BOOK

THREE FINGER PINCH

Many commonly used pantry ingredients are inherently salty, so you'll end up needing less actual salt to go along with them—anchovies, capers, olives, fish sauce, feta cheese, soy sauce, miso paste, to name just a few, are all great, dynamic ways to season your food and add flavor at the same time.

Here's the TL;DR: if you salt from the beginning, salt often, taste as you go, and remember that there's more than one way to add salt, you'll have properly seasoned food in no time.

THE SALTVILLE SPECTRUM

← LEAST SALTY

(A)
KIMCHI
(141 MG)

(B)
SAUERKRAUT
(187 MG)

(C)
BLACK OLIVES
(209 MG)

(D)
CASTELVETRANO
OLIVES (246 MG)

(E)
FETA CHEESE
(316 MG)

(F)
DILL PICKLES
(342 MG)

(G)
COTIJA CHEESE
(397 MG)

(H)
PARMIGIANO
REGGIANO CHEESE
(433 MG)

(I)
BACON
(485 MG)

(A)

(B)

(G)

(C)

(I)

(D)

(E)

(F)

(H)

A SCOVILLE SPECTRUM FOR SALT (MG SODIUM PER OUNCE)

SALTIEST $\longrightarrow$

(J)
PECORINO ROMANO CHEESE
(556 MG)

(K)
CAPERS IN BRINE
(635 MG)

(L)
MISO PASTE
(1,057 MG)

(M)
OIL-CURED BLACK OLIVES
(1,204 MG)

(N)
LOW-SODIUM SOY SAUCE
(1,557 MG)

(O)
OIL-PACKED ANCHOVY FILLETS
(1,822 MG)

(P)
FISH SAUCE
(2,225 MG)

(Q)
KOSHER SALT
(11,151 MG)

SET UP

SHOP

SET UP SHOP

Here's the thing: there are certain pieces of equipment that ya simply cannot successfully cook without. And then there's the stuff that's nice to have and will make your life easier but is not strictly necessary. I've separated those two groups of tools here. As long as you can check off most of the MUST-HAVES, you're in good shape. If you're committed to doing this whole cooking thing on the regs, you miiiiight wanna consider the NICE-BUT-NOT-NEC ones as well.

Naturally, after many years of experimenting, I've become partial to specific brands and items for each of these categories. If you want to get the exact tools that I keep on hand in my home kitchen, they can all be found here:

SET UP SHOP

MUST-HAVES

- Chef's Knife (8 to 10 inch)
- Cutting Board (large)
- Pots (S, M, L)
- Dutch Oven (6 to 8 quart)
- Nonstick Skillet
- Cast-Iron Skillet (12 inch)
- Mixing Bowls
- Tongs, Whisk, Wooden Spoon, Spatula
- Microplane Grater
- Box Grater
- Oven Thermometer
- Large Fine-Mesh Sieve
- Loaf Pan (9 x 5 inch)
- Measuring Cups and Spoons
- Digital Scale
- Large Rimmed Baking Sheets (18 x 13 inch)

NICE-BUT-NOT-NEC

- Meat Thermometer
- Citrus Juicer
- Bench Scraper
- Mandoline
- Potato Masher
- Rolling Pin
- Pastry Brush
- Mini and Large Offset Spatulas
- Spice Grinder or Mortar and Pestle
- Blender
- Food Processor
- Mini Food Processor
- Springform Cake Pan (9 or 10 inch)
- Baking Dish (9 x 13 inch)
- Grill or Grill Pan

STOCK YA BAR!

You don't need much to twist up a yummy cocktail, but there are a few tools that make measuring, pouring, stirring, and shaking feel really right, if you're interested in stepping up your game.

○ Jigger for measuring alcohol

○ Large cocktail shaker with strainer

○ Long-handled cocktail spoon

○ Toothpicks, for garnish

○ Mix of glasses, such as rocks, collins, martini

○ Lots and lots and lots of ice

COOK

SMARTER, NOT HARDER

COOK SMARTER, NOT HARDER

(A) PREP DRAWERS
Within grabbing distance of wherever you're choppin' and mixin': mixing bowls, measuring cups and spoons, cutting boards (Plastic for alliums and meat! Wood for the rest!), storage containers, frequently used prep tools (veg peeler, citrus press, etc.)

(B) COOKWARE
Separated by type (nonstick, cast-iron, stainless), stacked biggest to smallest for visibility and as close to the oven as possible

(C) EVERY-SO-OFTEN DRAWER
Stuff you use often, but not quite often enough: mandoline, can opener, bench scraper, peelers

(D) CADDY
Daily-use pantry staples: olive oil, 2 or 3 vinegars, pepper grinder, hot sauce, soy sauce, sesame oil, etc. (everyone's caddy looks a lil' diff!)

(E) KNIFE DRAWER
As close to your cutting board as poss!

Kitchen organization is as important as a well-stocked pantry, and knowing how and where to store your gear will make your cooking a lot more graceful in the long run. Storing your tools right where they need to be when you need them the most reduces the fumble factor tremendously. And nothing makes a home cook feel less swaggy than a fumble.

(F) CROCK
Most frequently used tools live here: tongs, wooden spoons, whisks, spatulas, Microplane, ladle

(G) VEG BASKET
For room-temp-storage veg only! Sweet pots, pots, garlic, onions, shallots, avocados

(H) FRUIT BOWL
For room-temp-storage fruit only! Stone fruit, tomatoes, bananas, melons, pineapple, citrus (3 or 4 days max)

(I) SALT CELLARS
One for kosher, one for flaky sea salt, don't get it twisted

(J) WHACKY DRAWER
For things that have no other home: phone chargers, labeling tape, pens, candy, Chapstick, birthday candles, lighters, hair ties

(K) Baking sheets of all sizes, close to your oven or cutting board, where you'll use them the most

RAID MY

PANTRY

A PIE CHART

Math happened. We counted the pantry ingredients used most often in the 105 recipes in this book and wow, were there a lot of lemons. So I guess what I'm sayin' is, load the fuck up on lemons, keep your pantry stocked with everything below, and you'll be croozin' through *More Is More* in no time.

Lemons (32)

Parmigiano Reggiano (19)

Sesame Seeds (13)

Dill (12)

Capers (9)

Hot Sauce/Chili Oil (9)

Miso Paste (9)

Sour Cream (8)

Yogurt (8)

Dill Pickles (8)

Peanuts (8)

Buttermilk (8)

Smoked Paprika (7)

Anchovies (6)

Morty-d (4)

Pepperoni (1—NOT enough)

Chocolate (1—don't love the stuff)

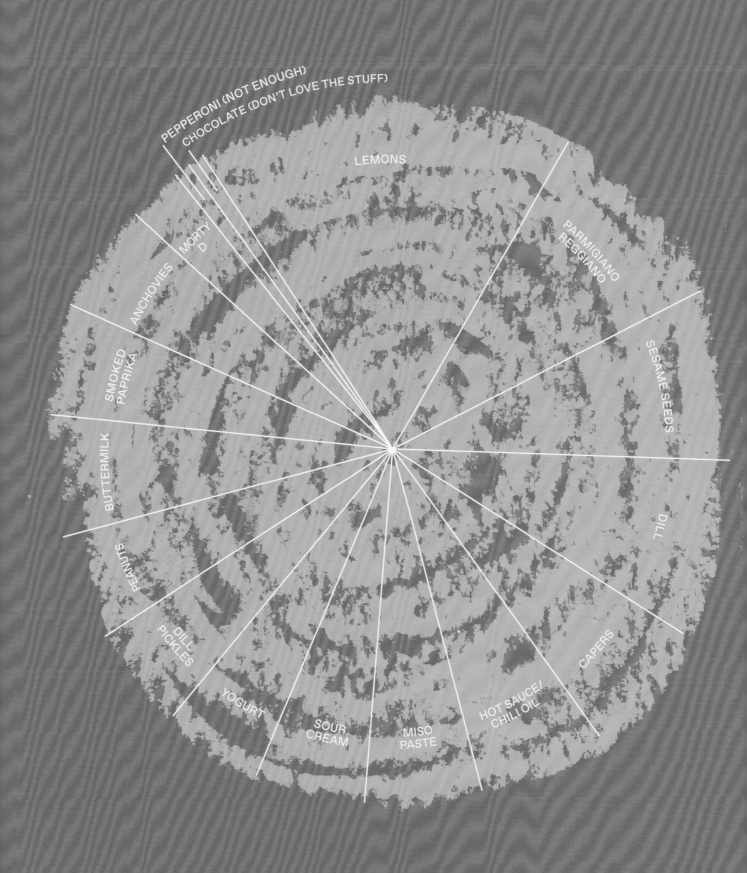

PEPPERONI (NOT ENOUGH)
CHOCOLATE (DON'T LOVE THE STUFF)
LEMONS
PARMIGIANO REGGIANO
MORTY D
ANCHOVIES
SMOKED PAPRIKA
SESAME SEEDS
BUTTERMILK
DILL
PEANUTS
DILL PICKLES
CAPERS
YOGURT
HOT SAUCE/CHILI OIL
SOUR CREAM
MISO PASTE

USE THIS

BOOK

USE THIS BOOK

I've BOLDED INGREDIENTS within the recipe methods to make it easy to jump to them on the page. That way, you can use the ingredient lists (categorized by department in your grocery store) to shop from, and the recipe steps themselves to remind yourself how much you'll need of any given ingredient. In the case of baking recipes, where precision is king, I've included weights measurements (in grams) for amounts ¼ cup and higher, as using a scale is the most accurate way to bake.

Whenever it's necessary, I've also called out any SPECIAL EQUIPMENT (think blenders, cake pans, and food processors) that you may need for a recipe below the ingredient lists, so you won't get halfway through and realize you don't own a springform pan. In most cases, there are options and substitutes.

As much as I love the physicality of a cookbook, there are things that a jumble of written words cannot easily express, like where to probe a chicken to get the proper temp, or how to knead focaccia dough. To overcome this, I've included two different types of QR CODES to bring the pages of the book to life digitally. (When you see a QR code, hover your phone's camera over it to open the video or audio that goes along with it.)

AUDIO COOK-ALONG CODES will take you to an audio recording of the recipe (narrated by yours truly) so that you can close the book, roll up your sleeves, and just COOK. I'll walk you through every step, from explaining the inspiration for the recipe to measuring the ingredients, to starting your prep and getting you to the recipe's completion, in more depth than what's on the page. By the end of the recording, you'll be at the dinner table with a meal in front of you.

LAST-MEAL SCALLOPS

SERVES 4

QUICK AS HECK!

GOES WITH: TABLESIDE TARTARE (PAGE 166), MARTINI THRICE (PAGE 144), FAUX FRENCH ONION SOUP (PAGE 207)

I first tasted a version of these scallops at a big, vibe-y, bustling French restaurant called Les Vapeurs on the coast of Normandy. It was as fancy as it sounds. And when I tell you I nearly died and went to heaven . . . I knew it was my responsibility to come up with a recipe that would come close. The key is a garlicky, lemony herb butter that melts into each scallop after you've given them a caramelized crust. You may have more garlic-parsley butter than you need—rub the leftovers on a whole chicken before roasting, or toss it with hot boiled potatoes and tell me that's not your idea of a good time.

PRODUCE
- 1 bunch of flat-leaf parsley
- 8 garlic cloves
- 1 lemon

DAIRY
- 10 tablespoons (1¼ sticks) unsalted butter, at room temperature

PROTEIN
- 1½ pounds dry-packed sea scallops (size U10 or U15)[1]

PANTRY
- Kosher salt
- Extra-virgin olive oil
- Crusty bread, for serving

SPECIAL EQUIPMENT
- Food processor

1 MAKE THE GARLIC-PARSLEY BUTTER:

- If it's not already quite soft and malleable, cut **10 tablespoons unsalted butter** into small pieces and set out at room temperature or pulse in the microwave in 10-second increments until soft but not melted.

- Pick the leaves of **1 bunch of flat-leaf parsley** and either very finely chop them by hand or add them to a **food processor**. If mixing by hand, add the parsley to a medium bowl.

- Finely grate **8 garlic cloves** and the zest of **1 lemon** into the bowl or food processor and mix or pulse to combine.

- When the butter is soft, add it to the bowl or food processor, along with **a big pinch of salt**, and mix or pulse well to combine, scraping the sides of the bowl as necessary to be sure it's all incorporated.

2 COOK THE SCALLOPS:

- Position a rack in the top of the oven. Preheat the broiler.

- Pat dry **1½ pounds dry-packed sea scallops** with a paper towel. Season all over with salt.

- Heat a large cast-iron skillet over high heat. Add enough **olive oil** to coat the skillet. Once you see smoke emanating from the surface of the pan, add the scallops in a single layer and cook, undisturbed, moving them only if they seem to be burning in some areas, until a deep, golden brown crust forms, about 3 minutes. Don't rush this process! It's crucial to the flavor development of the scallops—they cook VERY quickly, so high heat, and no touching, are musts to establish that golden crust. TURN YA BURNERS UP (PG 21)

- Momentarily transfer the scallops to a plate, seared-side up. Tip out and discard the oil that remains in the skillet.

- Schmear a generous dollop of garlic-parsley butter on top of each scallop (½ tablespoon or so each) and then return them to the skillet, butter-side up. Place the skillet under the broiler and broil until the butter melts and the scallops have firmed up but still have considerable bounce (they shouldn't be tough), 1 to 2 minutes.

3 SERVE:

- Squeeze the juice of the zested lemon over the scallops and serve right out of the skillet, with **lots of crusty bread** for soaking up all the buttery juices.

[1] Scallops are sold by their quantity per pound, so, for example, U10 scallops means there will be 10 scallops to the pound. The lower the number, the bigger the scallops. Always look for dry-packed scallops because they are not treated with preservatives. The wet ones will never caramelize properly.

COOK ALONG!
C
AUDIO

COOK ALONG!
D
VIDEO

My only dream in life, aside from acquiring a baker's dozen of weenie dogs, is to make it as easy as possible for you, the cook, to go from grocery store to recipe to plate. The recipes in this book have been painstakingly designed to make that happen.

As always in my recipes, I've incorporated all the prep steps into the recipes themselves, so you don't have to worry about when to chop the onions, or how far in advance to start picking herbs. I figured all that out so you can just crooooooooz through the recipes and COOK.

D VIDEO COOK-ALONG CODES are found in some recipes that are better understood visually, and for each of those, I've shot instructional step-by-step cooking videos to show you how it's done. Use the camera on your phone to pull up the video to watch me do it first, then jump in and tackle it on your own. Or you could just pop some popcorn and watch for the hell of it.

E You'll encounter FOOTNOTES throughout the recipes, which contain important related bits of info, none of which is absolutely crucial to the success of the recipe but will certainly make you a better, more informed cook.

F Because I know your time is valuable, whenever a recipe can be accomplished in forty minutes or less, you'll see a QUICK AS HECK! callout, for nights when you've got limited time on your hands but still want to land yourself a bangin' meal.

G I've included suggested recipe pairings to go along with each recipe, as signified by the GOES WITH tag. This way, if you're throwing a dinner party, or cooking for your friends and fam, and know for certain you want to make the Mollz Ballz (page 142), I'll be right there with ya to suggest what dishes I think will best round out the meal.

H I refer to the "Play by the Rules" chapter (pages 18–23) when I think you'll need a fully fleshed out explanation of a *More Is More* rule. Look for the wavy guys in the method text.

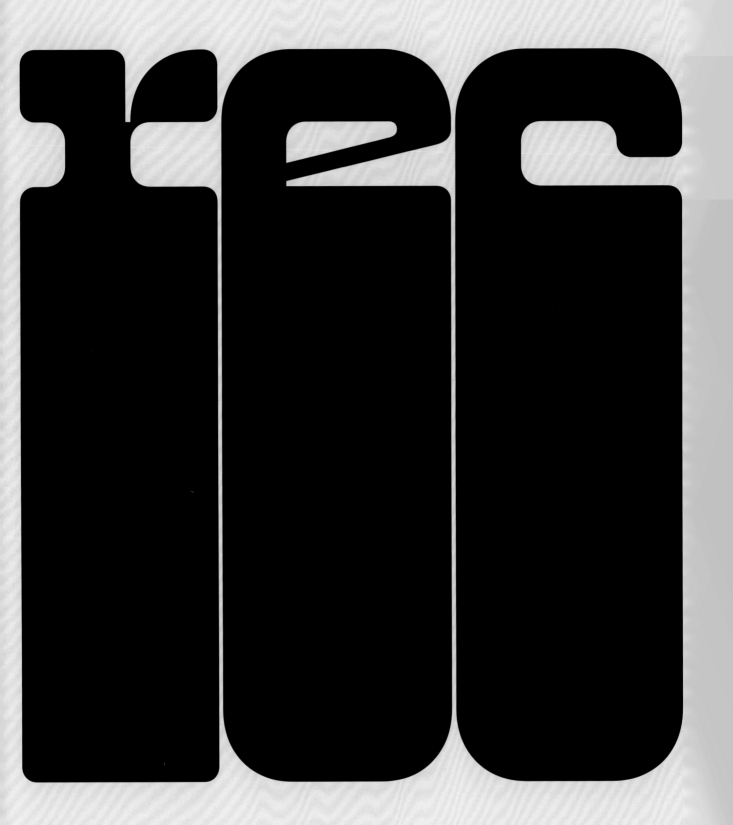

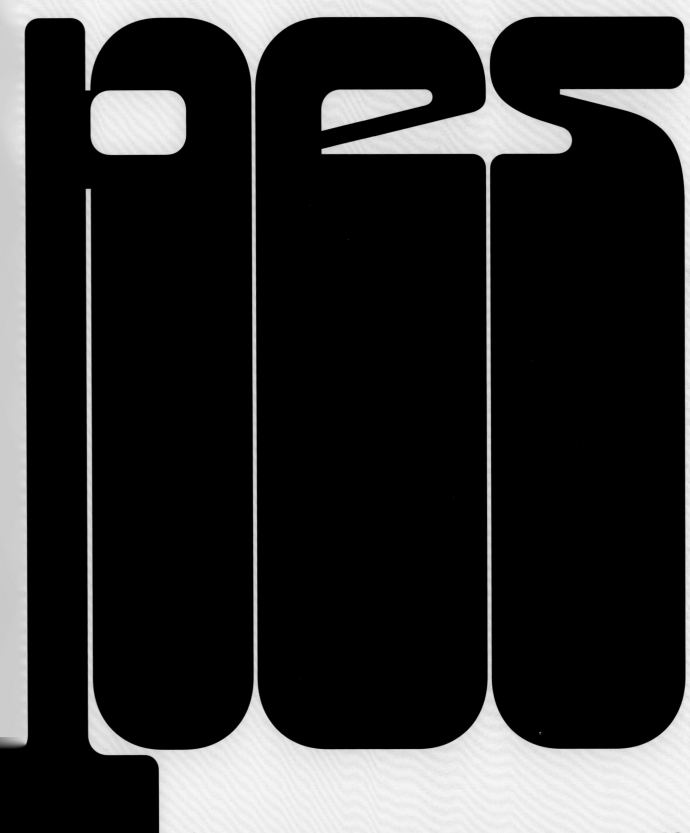

MORTADELLA -WRAPPED GRISSINI

GOES WITH: MARINATED ZUCCH & MOZZ WITH FRIED SUNFLOWER SEEDS (PAGE 90), RIGATONI WITH CREAMED LEEKS & CHIVE-Y BREAD CRUMBS (PAGE 108), MOLLZ BALLZ (PAGE 142)

MAKES 16

QUICK AS HECK!

The only thing more decadent than starting a meal off with a platter of mortadella is starting a meal off with a platter of breadsticks rolled in spicy chile butter and then wrapped in mortadella. I first had a mortadella-wrapped breadstick at Nancy Silverton's Osteria Mozza and haven't stopped thinking about it since. My version features a super-simple compound butter with funky, spicy Calabrian chiles and lemon zest (to really live, try it on roast chicken and baked potatoes). The citrus and spice help cut through the fatty morty-d and bring harmony to what may be the world's easiest and most impressive snack.

PRODUCE

- ½ lemon

DAIRY

- 5 tablespoons unsalted butter

PROTEIN

- 16 thin mortadella slices (about ⅓ pound)

PANTRY

- 2 tablespoons chopped jarred Calabrian chiles
- Flaky sea salt
- 16 grissini or breadsticks

1

MAKE THE CHILE BUTTER: CONDIMENTS ARE YOUR BFFL (PG 22)

- Cut **5 tablespoons unsalted butter** into 1-inch pieces, transfer to a small bowl, and let sit at room temperature until soft and malleable.

- Once the butter is soft, add **2 tablespoons chopped jarred Calabrian chiles** and **a big pinch of flaky sea salt** and mix together with a fork until bright orange and well combined. Schmear on a large plate.

- Finely grate the **zest of ½ lemon** over the butter.

2

ASSEMBLE AND SERVE:

- Roll each **grissini** in the chile butter, season with flaky sea salt, and then wrap in **a slice of mortadella**, or set the grissini, chile butter, and sea salt out and let people wrap them themselves.

SIZZLED DOLMAS WITH YOGURT & BROWN-BUTTERED PINE NUTS

GOES WITH: PICKLE-MARINATED FETA (PAGE 65), HALLOUMI, CUKE & WALNUT SPOON SALAD (PAGE 81), KIELBASA & CABBAGE PITAS WITH CURRY MUSTARD (PAGE 162)

SERVES 4

QUICK AS HECK!

Dolmas (rice-stuffed grape leaves) are a snack I rely on heavily to get me through the peckish moments of my day, and I love to doctor them up. You'll find them either alongside other canned goods or in the olive bar, if your grocery has one. Take five extra minutes to sizzle the dolmas in a skillet until caramelized and brown, then drench them with golden, turmeric-stained brown butter and toasty pine nuts for an incredible snack or party play. If you're looking for a way to "more is more" your snack game, sizzling stuff in brown butter is probably the answer.

PRODUCE

- 2 garlic cloves
- 1 lemon

DAIRY

- 2 tablespoons (¼ stick) unsalted butter
- ½ cup whole-milk yogurt

PANTRY

- 10 dolmas
- 2 tablespoons extra-virgin olive oil
- 3 tablespoons raw pine nuts
- ¾ teaspoon ground turmeric
- Kosher salt and freshly ground black pepper

 SIZZLE THE DOLMAS:

- Pat **10 dolmas** dry with paper towels.

- In a large nonstick skillet, heat **a couple glugs of olive oil** over medium heat. Add the dolmas and cook, turning once halfway through, until crisp and browned on both sides, about 3 minutes total.

- Remove to a plate, reserving the skillet.

TOAST THE NUTS:

- To the same skillet, add **2 tablespoons unsalted butter** and **3 tablespoons pine nuts**. Cook over medium heat, stirring and constantly swirling, until the pine nuts are roasty-toasty all the way through and the butter is browned, about 3 minutes.

- Remove the skillet from the heat and finely grate **2 garlic cloves** right into it. Stir in **¾ teaspoon ground turmeric, a big pinch of salt**, and **a few big cranks of pepper.**

SERVE:

- Schmear **a few generous spoonfuls of whole-milk yogurt** in a serving vessel. Top with the sizzled dolmas and spoon the pine nuts and brown butter all over them.

- Squeeze the **juice of 1 lemon** over the top and serve warm.

BRING BACK BRUSCHETTA

SERVES 2

GOES WITH: MOLLZ BALLZ (PAGE 142), DRUNKEN CACIO E PEPE (PAGE 96)

QUICK AS HECK!

If you're like me, you may associate bruschetta with watery, flavorless versions passed around a party ad infinitum (and in this place, curly kale is still a garnish on salad bars). What if we made bruschetta with only the plumpest, juiciest, sweetest summer tomatoes? Could bruschetta be esteemed as highly as the beloved tomato toast, which is pretty much what it is? So here we're using Sungold tomatoes at the peak of their late-summer ripeness, dripping in juices and spooned over a tangy swoosh of cottage cheese, which lends fat and creaminess to an otherwise lean dish. Fried garlic chips and basil top it off, and suddenly it's the bruschetta we deserved all along.

PRODUCE

- 4 garlic cloves
- ¾ pound Sungold or cherry tomatoes
- 1 small bunch of basil and/or chives

DAIRY

- ½ cup full-fat cottage cheese

PANTRY

- Extra-virgin olive oil
- Kosher salt
- Any grape-based vinegar, such as red, white, balsamic, or sherry
- Sugar
- Red pepper flakes
- 2 (1-inch-thick) crusty, sturdy bread slices

1 FRY THE GARLIC:

- Thinly slice **3 garlic cloves**.
- Line a plate with paper towels.

- In a large nonstick skillet, combine the sliced garlic with **several glugs of olive oil**—the garlic should be swimming in a shallow pool of it—and set it over medium heat. Cook, stirring to separate the slices, until just lightly golden brown (watch closely, they burn very easily), 3 to 4 minutes. Transfer to the paper-towel-lined plate with a slotted spoon to drain. Season lightly with **salt**. Don't discard the oil in the skillet! We're gonna get into that shortly.

2 MARINATE THE TOMATOES:

- Cut **¾ pound Sungold tomatoes** in half. Toss in a medium bowl with **a splash of vinegar, a few big glugs of olive oil, a big pinch each of salt** and **sugar**, and some **red pepper flakes** to taste. Taste and adjust the seasoning to your liking.

- Chop or tear **1 small bunch of basil** and toss through the tomatoes.

3 FRY THE BREAD:

- Place **2 (1-inch-thick) crusty bread slices** in the garlic oil remaining in the skillet and set over medium heat. Cook until deeply golden brown and fried to a crisp on both sides, flipping once, about 6 minutes total.

- Transfer the toasts to a cutting board and rub all over with the remaining whole **garlic clove**—the craggy nature of the bread will act as an abrasive to grate the garlic. Season with salt.

4 ASSEMBLE:

- Cut each toast in half. Spoon some of the tomato juices over the toasts.

- Schmear **a big spoonful of cottage cheese** on each toast. Spoon the tomatoes over the top and garnish with the fried garlic and a drizzle of olive oil.

CRICK-CRACKS!

SERVES 6 TO 8

GOES WITH: PICKLE-MARINATED FETA (PAGE 65), MARTINI THRICE (PAGE 145), PURPLE SALAD (PAGE 71)

QUICK AS HECK!

If you've ever had frico, a lacy cheese cracker (like the crispy edges of a grilled cheese) that's often served as a garnish on soups/salads, and thought to yourself, *I wish there were more of this,* welcome to crick-cracks—my word for crispy sheets of melted cheese loaded with nuts and seeds. These are the easiest DIY crackers you can imagine. (Hat tip to Carla Lalli Music, a fellow frico freak.) This recipe makes one tray of crick-cracks, but you might as well double it for your general happiness and well-being. They'll last several days stored in an airtight container at room temperature, although LBH, crick-cracks don't tend to stay around!

DAIRY

● 4 ounces sharp or nutty cheese, such as extra-sharp cheddar, Parmesan, Piave, or Gruyère (in wedge form)

PANTRY

● ½ cup raw nuts, such as pistachios, walnuts, almonds, hazelnuts, or pecans

● 2 tablespoons mixed whole spices, such as cumin, fennel, and/or coriander

● Extra-virgin olive oil, for drizzling

● Flaky sea salt and freshly ground black pepper

1 **DO SOME PREP:**

● Preheat the oven to 350°F. Line a rimmed baking sheet with parchment paper.

● Grate **4 ounces sharp or nutty cheese** on the small holes of a box grater, right over the prepared baking sheet. Spread the cheese in an even layer across the whole sheet of parchment.

● Chop **½ cup raw nuts** into lentil-size pieces. Sprinkle the nuts over the cheese.

● Coarsely chop **2 tablespoons mixed whole spices** (or grind in a mortar and pestle). Scatter them evenly over the baking sheet. Lightly drizzle with **olive oil**. Season with **freshly ground black pepper**.

2 **BAKE:**

● Bake, rotating the baking sheet once halfway through to ensure even cooking, until the cheese has melted and turned light golden brown, 10 to 15 minutes.

● Lightly season with **flaky sea salt** when the baking sheet is just out of the oven.

● Let cool completely on the pan before breaking into large pieces. (If making ahead, store in an airtight container at room temperature for up to 5 days.)

CAESAR-ED OEUF MAYO

GOES WITH: TABLESIDE TARTARE (PAGE 166), CRICK-CRACKS! (PAGE 58), LE GRAND GREEN GRILLED AIOLI (PAGE 221)

MAKES 12

QUICK AS HECK!

PRODUCE

- 1 small garlic clove

PROTEIN

- 7 large eggs

PANTRY

- 1 tablespoon white wine vinegar, plus more for serving
- 2 teaspoons Dijon mustard
- 2 oil-packed anchovy fillets
- Kosher salt and freshly ground black pepper
- ½ cup vegetable oil
- Flaky sea salt

SPECIAL EQUIPMENT

- Blender

This recipe takes three of my favorite ways to consume eggs—deviled, smashed into egg salad, and in Caesar dressing—and combines them into one perfect snack. Oeuf mayo is a traditional French appetizer of boiled eggs topped with mayonnaise. To *oomph* it up, I've made the mayo topping a mustardy Caesar dressing instead, and that's all you need to know about that. Put these out at your next dinner party and let the rave reviews flow in.

1 COOK THE EGGS:

- Bring a medium saucepan of water to a boil. Once the water is boiling, gently lower **6 large eggs** into the pot. Set a timer for 6½ minutes.

- While the eggs are cooking, fill a large bowl with ice and water. When the timer rings, plunge the eggs into the ice bath and allow them to cool completely before peeling.

2 MAKE THE CAESAR MAYO:

- Into a **blender**, crack the remaining **1 egg**. Add **1 tablespoon white wine vinegar**, **2 teaspoons Dijon mustard**, **1 finely grated garlic clove**, **2 oil-packed anchovy fillets** (leave 'em whole), and **a pinch of kosher salt**. Blend to combine. You could also do this by hand, using a medium bowl and a whisk (but you'll need to finely chop your anchovies first).

- In a thin steady stream, blend or whisk in **½ cup vegetable oil**. Season with salt to taste. You don't want this emulsion to get too hot or it will break, so if you're using a blender and it starts to feel very warm, throw in a tiny splash of ice-cold water to cool the mayo down before proceeding with the rest of the oil.

3 ASSEMBLE:

- Spread a pool of the Caesar mayo on a serving plate.

- Cut the boiled eggs in half. Season each yolk with **flaky sea salt** and a tiny dash of white wine vinegar, and place on the mayo. Spoon some more mayo over each serving and finish with **lots of freshly ground black pepper**.

MASHED POTATO ARANCINI

GOES WITH: UMAM LASAGN! (PAGE 116), DRUNKEN CACIO E PEPE (PAGE 96), MARTINI THRICE (PAGE 145)

MAKES 16

PRODUCE

- 4 medium Yukon Gold potatoes (about 1¼ pounds)
- 1 lemon

DAIRY

- 1 ounce grated Parmigiano Reggiano (¼ cup)
- 3 ounces mozzarella or fontina cheese

PROTEIN

- 2 large eggs

PANTRY

- Kosher salt and freshly ground black pepper
- 2 tablespoons extra-virgin olive oil
- 28 small pitted green olives
- Canola oil, for frying
- 1 cup all-purpose flour
- 1½ cups panko bread crumbs

You might already be familiar with Italian arancini, the crispy, molten rice ball street snacks that hail from Sicily. These little cuties are kinda like those, except that instead of being made with leftover risotto, they're made with mashed potatoes—a potato croquette of sorts! You could get resourceful and use the leftover potato innards from the Crispy Potato Skins with Fried Herb Aioli on page 226 (eh? eh?). These are lighter and fluffier than traditional arancini and stuffed with olives and mozzarella, which makes them the quintessential drinking snack. IMO, they're best paired with a Martini Thrice (page 145).

1 COOK THE POTATOES:

- Peel **4 medium Yukon Gold potatoes** and cut them in half. Place the potatoes in a medium pot and cover with 2 inches of cold water. Season with **lots of salt**—it should be saltier than the sea.[1]

- Bring to a boil over medium-high heat. Once the water boils, reduce the heat as needed to maintain a simmer and cook the potatoes until very tender when pierced with a fork, 15 to 18 minutes. Drain and let cool slightly.

2 MAKE THE POTATO MASH:

- Once the potatoes are cool enough to handle, transfer them to a medium bowl, add **a few glugs of olive oil**, and mash with a fork.

- Finely chop **12 small pitted green olives** and add to the potato mixture, along with **1 ounce grated Parmesan cheese**, the **zest of ½ lemon**, and the **juice of the entire lemon**. Season the mixture with salt and **lots of freshly ground black pepper** and mash well to combine.

3 STUFF THE ARANCINI:

- Dice **3 ounces mozzarella cheese** into sixteen ¾-inch cubes.

- Working with 2 heaping tablespoons (about 1½ ounces) of the mixture at a time, roll the mixture into a ball and then flatten it in your palm into a ¼-inch-thick pancake. Place **1 of the remaining olives** and 1 mozzarella cube at the center.

- Fold the edges up around the fillings and reroll into a ball, making sure no olive or mozz is poking out. Repeat until all the potato mixture is used up.

4 BREAD THE ARANCINI:

- Fill a medium pot with enough **canola oil** to reach a depth of 1½ inches. (The amount will vary depending on the size of your pot.) Set over medium heat.

- In a medium bowl, lightly beat **2 large eggs**.

- In another medium bowl, place **1 cup all-purpose flour**. Season with salt and pepper.

- In a third medium bowl, place **1½ cups panko bread crumbs**.

- Working with one or two at a time, roll the balls in the flour, then dip them in the eggs, and finally roll them in the bread crumbs. Transfer to a large plate.

5 FRY:

- Set a wire rack inside a rimmed baking sheet.

- Once the oil reaches 375°F, working in batches, use a slotted spoon to gently lower 5 or 6 arancini balls at a time into the oil. Cook, flipping occasionally, until deep golden brown all over, 3 to 4 minutes per batch.

- Transfer the balls to the prepared baking sheet and season all over with salt. Repeat with the remaining arancini and serve immediately, so the cheese stays oozy!!

[1] Most of that salt will ultimately get discarded when you drain the potatoes anyway, and this is how we ensure properly seasoned pohtates!

PICKLE-MARINATED FETA

SERVES 4 TO 6

GOES WITH: KIELBASA & CABBAGE PITAS WITH CURRY MUSTARD
(PAGE 162), SALTED CITRUS SHANDY (PAGE 229)

QUICK AS HECK!

Sure, maybe you've seen feta marinated in herbs and olive oil before, but do you know what feta actually wants—no, needs—more than both of those things? PICKLES. Feta is salty and creamy, and pickles are crunchy and acidic. They belong together. Serve this at your next dinner party with some big hunks of warm crusty bread for schmearing and I guarantee no one will be mad about the roast chicken taking too long.

PRODUCE

- 1 medium shallot
- 4 garlic cloves

DAIRY

- 12 ounces feta cheese

PANTRY

- 6 baby dill pickles, plus ⅓ cup pickle brine
- ½ cup extra-virgin olive oil
- 1 tablespoon capers, plus their brine
- 1 tablespoon cumin seeds
- 2 teaspoons smoked paprika
- Red pepper flakes

WARM THE AROMATICS:

- Thinly slice **1 medium shallot** and **4 garlic cloves.**

- Quarter **6 baby dill pickles** lengthwise (into spears), then chop them crosswise into ¼-inch pieces.

- In a small saucepan, combine the shallot and garlic, along with **½ cup olive oil** and **a big spoonful of capers**. Set over medium heat and cook, occasionally swirling, until the oil is bubbling and the shallots and garlic are soft but not browned, 3 to 4 minutes.

- Stir in **1 tablespoon cumin seeds,** **2 teaspoons smoked paprika**, and **a couple pinches of red pepper flakes**. Cook for 30 seconds to bloom the aromatics.[1] Remove from the heat.

ASSEMBLE:

- Break **12 ounces feta cheese** into large, irregular chunks and arrange in a small bowl or glass mason jar.

- Stir the chopped pickles and **⅓ cup pickle brine** into the infused oil, then pour the oil over the feta, gently stirring and turning the feta to combine. Season with **a big splash of caper brine**—taste and adjust as needed. Let sit at room temperature for at least 1 hour or in the fridge for up to 3 days so the flavors can marry.

- Serve at room temperature with things to schmear it on—bread, crackers, pita chips, etc., or spoon it over some simple roasted veggies.

[1] Blooming is a process in which you cook spices in fat in order to extract their flavor/aroma.

BE THE SALAD YOU WISH

10 FLAGS TO SEE IN THE WORLD

PEACH & PICKLED PEPPER PANZANELLA

SERVES 4

GOES WITH: CHICKEN PICCATA WITH SWEET CORN, CHILES & BUTTERMILK (PAGE 181), CRISPY CUTLETS WITH GIARDINIERA SLAW (PAGE 154)

QUICK AS HECK!

While panzanella is traditionally made with stale bread and ripe tomatoes, the formula works for a range of juicy fruits. Combining spicy pickled peppers with sweet, ripe stone fruit nods to the acidity and sweetness of tomatoes but with bigger flavor all around. Make it your own: any combo of stone fruit and pickled pepps will work (peperoncini people, I see you). The real star of this show, however, is the olive oil–fried bread, which is, objectively speaking, more satisfying than stale bread can and will ever be. It still soaks up the fruits' juices, plus you get that good crunchetty crunch.

PRODUCE

- 1½ pounds peaches or nectarines (about 4 large)
- 1 small shallot
- 1 garlic clove
- 1 bunch of flat-leaf parsley

DAIRY

- ¾ cup fresh whole-milk ricotta cheese

PANTRY

- Extra-virgin olive oil
- Kosher salt and freshly ground black pepper
- ½ cup spicy pickled peppers, such as jalapeños, banana peppers, or peperoncini, plus their brine
- 2 (1-inch-thick) sourdough bread slices
- Flaky sea salt

1 SEASON THE RICOTTA:

- In a medium bowl, whisk together **¾ cup ricotta cheese and a glug of olive oil.** Season with **kosher salt and lots of freshly ground black pepper.**

2 MARINATE THE PEACHES:

- Cut **1½ pounds peaches** into wedges, discarding the pits.

- Thinly slice **1 shallot.** In a large bowl, toss the peaches and shallot with **½ cup pickled peppers, 2 or 3 big splashes of their brine,** and **a couple generous glugs of olive oil.** Season with kosher salt. Taste and adjust the seasoning—it should be bright and vibrant! YOU'RE PROBS NOT USING ENOUGH ... ACID (PG 20)

3 FRY THE BREAD:

- In a large skillet, add **a couple more glugs of olive oil.** Place **2 (1-inch-thick) bread slices** in the skillet and turn to coat all over in the oil. Set the skillet over medium heat and cook until deeply crispy and golden on both sides, flipping halfway through, 3 to 4 minutes per side.

- Rub both sides of the toast with **1 garlic clove.** Season with kosher salt.

4 ASSEMBLE:

- Tear or cut the bread into bite-size pieces and add to the bowl of peaches, along with the **leaves of 1 bunch of parsley**—you heard me! The whole bunch! Toss everything several times to encourage the bread to start soaking up all the liquid. Season with kosher salt. THOU SHALT NOT WASTE HERBS (PG 22)

- Spoon the ricotta into a shallow serving bowl and pile the salad atop it. Drizzle generously with more olive oil and season with **flaky sea salt** and pepper.

PURPLE SALAD

SERVES 4

GOES WITH: TANGLED LEEK 'ZA (PAGE 121), SPICED LENTIL BURGER WITH A VERY SPECIAL SAUCE (PAGE 245)

QUICK AS HECK!

This is a moody, monochromatic winter salad (a sibling to the Monochromatic Melon Salad on page 85), wherein almost every ingredient is purple. Just because it's fun, it's a very "more is more" way to really lean into a singular color palette, and I am a fan of monochromatic anything. However, should you not be able to find purple sweet potatoes, purple basil, or blood oranges (I know, I know), everything will be fine with their non-purple counterparts. This is all about that spicy tahini-maple vinaigrette, anyway.

PRODUCE

- 2 medium sweet potatoes (purple)
- 1 garlic clove
- 1 large head radicchio (10 ounces)
- 2 oranges (blood, if possible)
- 1 bunch of basil (purple, if avails)

PANTRY

- Extra-virgin olive oil
- Kosher salt and freshly ground black pepper
- ¼ cup tahini
- 3 tablespoons unseasoned rice vinegar
- 1½ teaspoons fish sauce (optional)
- 1½ teaspoons maple syrup
- Red pepper flakes
- Flaky sea salt
- Lots of toasted sesame seeds, for sprinkling

1 ROAST THE SWEETIE P'S:

- Preheat the oven to 450°F.

- Cut **2 medium sweet potatoes** in half lengthwise. Place on a small rimmed baking sheet, drizzle generously with **olive oil**, and season with **kosher salt**. Place cut-side down and roast until deeply golden on the bottom and very soft and tender throughout, 25 to 35 minutes (this will vary, depending on how fat they are, so stay nimble!).

2 MAKE THE DRESSING:

- In a large bowl, whisk together **¼ cup tahini, 3 tablespoons rice vinegar, a couple tablespoons olive oil, 1½ teaspoons fish sauce (if using), 1½ teaspoons maple syrup, 1 grated garlic clove**, and **a big pinch of red pepper flakes**. It will be very thick and pasty—slowly whisk in a little bit of water until it reaches a nice drizzle-able consistency. Season with **kosher salt and freshly ground black pepper**.

3 PREP THE OTHER STUFF AND TOSS INTO THE BOWL OF DRESSING:

- Separate the leaves of **1 large head radicchio** and tear them into bite-size pieces.

- Cut away the peel and pith of **2 oranges** and cut the flesh into irregular shapes (truly doesn't matter!).

- Pick the leaves from **1 bunch of basil**.

4 ASSEMBLE:

- Tear the warm sweet potatoes into 2-inch pieces and add to the bowl of dressing and salad stuff.

- Season with **flaky sea salt** and liberally sprinkle with **lots and lots of toasted sesame seeds**—like, really go for it. Toss gently with your hands to ensure all elements are coated in the dressing. IF YOU'RE GONNA USE IT, USE IT (PG 20)

- Transfer the salad to a serving platter and top with even more sesame seeds! Serve immediately.

BRUSSELS SPROUTS
WITH SHALLOTS & STICKY FISH SAUCE

SERVES 4

GOES WITH: RAMEN NOODLES WITH SHROOMS & SOY BUTTER (PAGE 128), CRISPY SALMON WITH COCONUT RICE & CRACKLE SAUCE (PAGE 146)

PRODUCE

- 1½ pounds Brussels sprouts
- 1 large shallot
- 3 garlic cloves
- 1 serrano or Fresno chile
- 1 bunch of cilantro

PANTRY

- ¼ cup unseasoned rice vinegar, plus more to taste
- Kosher salt and freshly ground black pepper
- 3 tablespoons sugar, plus a pinch
- 3 tablespoons extra-virgin olive oil
- 1 tablespoon fish sauce
- 3 big handfuls of roasted, salted peanuts (about ½ cup)

You know how when you roast Brussels sprouts, their leaves fall off and burn on the baking sheet? I have a solution, and it recognizes those lost leaves and celebrates them for who they are. All we're going to do is set the leaves aside while the sprouts roast. They'll get tossed in toward the end and dressed with a punchy, caramel-y, Vietnamese-inspired fish sauce vinaigrette and a ton of chopped peanuts. The contrast of the fresh leaves with the roasted sprouts is *chef's kiss*, so If you're looking for something fun and spesh to bring to the Thanksgiving table this year, I got you.

1 DO SOME PREP:

- Place a large rimmed baking sheet on a rack in the bottom third of the oven. Preheat the oven to 450°F.

- Trim ½ inch off the ends of **1½ pounds Brussels sprouts**, pulling off a couple of outer leaves from each sprout (they'll naturally fall off as you trim). Halve the sprouts and set the leaves aside (you should have about 2 cups of leaves).

- Thinly slice **1 large shallot**. Place it in a small bowl and cover with **¼ cup rice vinegar** and **a pinch each of salt** and sugar. Let sit and pickle while you prep the rest.

- In a large bowl, toss the halved Brussels sprouts with **a few generous glugs of olive oil**. Season with salt and **freshly ground black pepper**. Once the oven has preheated, carefully remove the hot baking sheet and dump the Brussels onto the sheet, using tongs to arrange them cut-side down.[1] Return the pan to the oven and roast until the Brussels are soft in the center and charred all over, 20 to 25 minutes.

2 MAKE THE FISH SAUCE VINAIGRETTE AND PREP THE REST:

- Firmly smash **3 garlic cloves** with the side of your knife, discarding their skins.

- Thinly slice **1 serrano chile**.

- While the Brussels roast, in a small saucepan, add **3 tablespoons sugar**, shaking the pan to distribute the sugar evenly. Set

it over medium-low heat and cook without stirring (I mean it! NO touch!) until the sugar turns a deep caramel color, 8 to 10 minutes. If you notice that certain parts of the pan are turning brown quicker than others, move the pan around and rearrange it on the burner to avoid hot spots. Keep an eye on things, as the sugar will get very dark very quickly toward the end. Once you achieve a deep caramel color, remove the pan from the heat and stir in the liquid from the pickled shallots, holding the shallots back (they'll get added to the sprouts later on). The liquid will sputter a bit when it hits the caramel—that's okay! Stir in the smashed garlic and sliced chiles.

- Return the saucepan to medium heat and simmer, stirring, until slightly reduced, 2 to 3 minutes. Remove from the heat and stir in **1 tablespoon fish sauce**.

3 TOSS AND FINISH:

- Add the Brussels leaves to the now-vacant bowl along with the pickled shallots. Add another glug or two of rice vinegar and season well with salt. Use your hands to scrunch the leaves, encouraging them to break down a bit and become well seasoned.

- Coarsely chop or crush **3 BIG handfuls of roasted, salted peanuts** and chop the leaves and tender stems of **1 bunch of cilantro**. Add them to the bowl of Brussels.

- Once the roasting sprouts are well browned, add them to the bowl as well, along with the fish sauce caramel, and toss well to coat evenly. Serve immediately!

[1] Roasting on a preheated baking sheet ensures quick charring and avoids soggy steamed Brussels sprouts—the worst!

COOK ALONG!

AUDIO

SIZZLED SEEDY TOMATO SALAD

SERVES 4

GOES WITH: CHICKEN PICCATA WITH SWEET CORN, CHILES & BUTTERMILK (PAGE 181), KIELBASA & CABBAGE PITAS WITH CURRY MUSTARD (PAGE 162)

QUICK AS HECK!

I was once told that this cookbook should have been named "Sizzled Seeds and Spices." And the truth is, I thought about it. I love a sizzled seedy moment because it's a way to add texture and a bright burst of flavor. Whole toasted spices sizzled in fat (or, as it is known in India, *chhonk* or *tadka*) take only two minutes to prepare, and you don't have to chop a damn thing. Take this technique and use it with your favorite spices (mustard seeds, anyone?), then spoon it on anything you're cooking that needs a little something-something.

PRODUCE

- 2 ripe, juicy large tomatoes (20 ounces)[1]
- 1 small garlic clove

DAIRY

- ⅔ cup plain whole-milk or Greek yogurt

PANTRY

- Kosher salt
- 3 tablespoons extra-virgin olive oil
- 2 tablespoons mixed whole spices and seeds, such as fennel, cumin, mustard, coriander, sesame, poppy, or nigella[2]
- Flaky sea salt
- Red pepper flakes
- Toasted or grilled bread, for serving (optional)

1 PREP THE TOMATOES AND YOG:

- Cut **2 ripe, juicy large tomatoes** into large, irregularly shaped pieces, discarding the stems.

- In a shallow serving bowl, combine **⅔ cup whole-milk yogurt** and **1 finely grated garlic clove**. Stir well and season with **kosher salt**.

2 TOAST THE SPICES:

- In a medium saucepan, combine **3 tablespoons olive oil** and **2 tablespoons mixed whole spices and seeds**—they should be swimming in the oil. Cook over medium heat, stirring and swirling occasionally, until the spices begin to pop, sizzle, and turn fragrant,

about 2 minutes. Remove from the heat and immediately stir in the chopped tomatoes—they will sizzle and sputter. That's okay, just be careful! Stir gently to coat the tomatoes in the spices and oil and allow them to warm through. We are not looking to cook the tomatoes, just warm them and infuse them with the flavors of the spices. Season with **flaky sea salt**.[3]

- Spoon the tomatoes and their juices on top of the yogurt. Season with **red pepper flakes** and more flaky sea salt. Serve warm with bread, if desired.

[1] Storing tomatoes in the fridge turns their flesh from juicy to mealy, so they should always, always, always be left out on the counter as they ripen. And, yes, that means no grape tomatoes in the fridge either!

[2] Not all seeds and spices are created equal in terms of the intensity of their flavor. Bear this in mind when choosing—you'll want to use more sesame, poppy, and nigella, which are mild in flavor, than fennel, cumin, mustard, or coriander, which are quite strong. A mix of all is great!

[3] This is very important in carrying flavor through all that fat. Without it, the oil won't taste like much.

CRISPY, CRUNCHY BROCC & GRAINS WITH SO. MUCH. MINT.

GOES WITH: FENNEL ON FENNEL ON FENNEL TORTILLA (PAGE 212), SKIRT STEAK WITH JUICY TOMATOES & SALSA MACHA (PAGE 141)

QUICK AS HECK!

This salad is my late-in-the-game response to nearly every piece of broccoli I was forced to eat as a kid. I hated it. So much. It was mushy and overcooked or, worse, not cooked at all. But as I now know, there's a lot to love about broccoli, and this is one of my favorite ways to eat it. In this recipe you'll be asked to place your tray of vegetables on the oven floor. Don't freak out! That's the hottest part of the oven, which means the bottoms will be charred crisp wayyy faster. This salad is a study in textures—tender charred broccoli gets tossed with crisp-chewy bits of panfried farro, nuggets of crumbled cheddar cheese, sliced chiles, and lots and lots of fresh mint (though you could also use basil or cilantro—as long as there's lots of herbs, you'll be in good shape).

PRODUCE

- 1½ pounds broccoli (2 to 3 heads)
- 1 Fresno chile or jalapeño
- 1 large shallot
- 1 bunch of mint, basil, or cilantro

DAIRY

- 2 ounces smoked cheddar or other hard smoked cheese

PANTRY

- Kosher salt and freshly ground black pepper
- ½ cup grains, such as farro, wheatberries, or barley
- Extra-virgin olive oil
- 3 tablespoons white wine vinegar or champagne vinegar

1 DO SOME PREP & COOK THE FARRO:

- Set two oven racks in the lower third of the oven and preheat it to 450°F.

- Bring a medium pot of **salted** water to a boil. Add **2 big handfuls of grains (about ½ cup)** and cook until tender but not mushy, 10 minutes (cook time may vary if using a different grain!). Drain and let cool to room temp.

2 CHAR THE BROCCOLI:

- Cut **1½ pounds broccoli** into 2-inch pieces, separating the florets from the stems and discarding just the woodiest tough ends.[1]

- Divide the broccoli between 2 large rimmed baking sheets, drizzle generously with **olive oil**, and season with **salt and freshly ground black pepper**. Place one baking sheet on the bottom of the oven, if it is available to you, and the other on the lowest rack.[2]

- Roast, switching the baking sheets halfway through, until the bottoms are well charred, 18 to 24 minutes, depending on the heat of your oven.

3 MAKE THE DRESSING:

- Finely chop **1 Fresno chile**, discarding the seeds.

- Thinly slice **1 large shallot**.

- In a large bowl, whisk together **3 tablespoons white wine vinegar, a couple tablespoons of olive oil**, and **a pinch of salt**. Add the Fresno and shallot.

4 CRISP THE FARRO:

- In a medium nonstick skillet, heat **a few good glugs of olive oil (about 2 tablespoons)** over medium heat. Add the drained and cooled grains and cook, undisturbed, until crisped and chewy on the bottom, 2 to 3 minutes. Give it a stir and continue to crisp for 1 to 2 minutes longer, until lightly golden and crisp but chewy. Season with salt and transfer to the bowl of dressing.

5 ASSEMBLE:

- Coarsely chop or crumble **2 ounces smoked cheddar cheese** into bite-size pieces (you'll have about ⅓ cup). Add to the bowl, along with the **leaves from 1 bunch of mint**. YOU'RE PROBS NOT USING ENOUGH ... HERBS (PG 20)

- Add the broccoli. Toss everything together, season with salt and pepper, and serve!

[1] The stems are as delicious as the florets, and because you can create flat sides as you cut them, they get super caramelized and crispy as they cook.

[2] If it seems like your oven is running really hot and the broccoli is charring too quickly before it's tender, you can always move the broccoli up to a higher rack.

HALLOUMI, CUKE & WALNUT SPOON SALAD

SERVES 4

QUICK AS HECK!

PRODUCE

- 3 Persian cucumbers

- 2 small bunches of tender herbs, such as dill, parsley, and/or mint

- 4 scallions

DAIRY

- 8 ounces halloumi cheese

PANTRY

- ¾ cup walnuts

- 3 baby dill pickles, or 1 regular dill pickle

- ½ cup pickled jalapeños, plus ⅓ cup of their brine

- 5 tablespoons extra-virgin olive oil

- 1 teaspoon cumin seeds

- Kosher salt and freshly ground black pepper

GOES WITH: KIELBASA & CABBAGE PITAS WITH CURRY MUSTARD (PAGE 162), ONE-POT CHICKEN MUJADARA (PAGE 194), SPICED LENTIL BURGER WITH A VERY SPECIAL SAUCE (PAGE 245)

What is a spoon salad, you ask? Commonly found in Turkey, where it's served piled high with tomatoes, this type of salad is so finely chopped that you can eat it with a spoon. This one features every texture imaginable: squeaky griddled halloumi cheese, crisp cucumbers, tender dill pickles, and crunchy walnuts. I will happily spoon this on its own, but I could also see it alongside grilled chicken or fish. You choose!

1 TOAST THE WALNUTS:

- Preheat the oven to 325°F. Place **2 big handfuls walnuts** on a small rimmed baking sheet. Roast in the oven until deeply golden throughout and fragrant, 10 to 12 minutes.

- Let cool, then finely chop.

2 PREP THE SALAD INGREDIENTS AND PLACE IN A LARGE BOWL:

- Dice **3 Persian cucumbers** and **3 baby dill pickles** into ½-inch cubes.

- Finely chop **½ cup pickled jalapeños**.

- Finely chop **2 small bunches of mixed herbs**.

- Thinly slice **4 scallions**.

- Put the cukes, dill pickles, jalapeños, herbs, and scallions in a large bowl. Add **¼ cup olive oil** and **⅓ cup pickled jalapeño brine** and toss to combine.

3 SEAR THE HALLOUMI AND ASSEMBLE:

- Cut **8 ounces halloumi cheese** into ½-inch cubes.

- In a large nonstick skillet, heat another **glug of olive oil** over medium-high heat. Once the oil is hot, add the halloumi and cook until golden and crispy, 1 minute. Use a spatula to flip the halloumi and break it up if it's clumping together. Cook on the second side until golden and melty, 1 minute more. Add the halloumi to the salad.

- Add **2 fat pinches of cumin seeds** to the skillet and toast until fragrant, 30 seconds. Stir into the salad, along with the toasted walnuts, and mix well to combine. Season with **salt and freshly ground black pepper**.

RAW & ROASTED
CAULI SALAD WITH CREAMY, DREAMY VEGAN RANCH

SERVES 4

GOES WITH: GRANDMA PIE WITH MORTY-D & PEPERONCINI PESTO (PAGE 100),
CHILE-BASTED HALF CHICKEN WITH CAPER CHIMICHURRI (PAGE 182)

PRODUCE

- 2 large heads of cauliflower (4 pounds)
- 1 bunch of dill
- 1 bunch of flat-leaf parsley
- 1 large garlic clove
- 1 lemon
- 1 jalapeño

PROTEIN

- 8 ounces silken tofu (half a 16-ounce package)

PANTRY

- Extra-virgin olive oil
- Kosher salt and freshly ground black pepper
- ⅓ cup plus 3 tablespoons vegetable oil
- 6 tablespoons unseasoned rice vinegar
- 3 tablespoons white miso paste

SPECIAL EQUIPMENT

- Blender

In this texture-wonderland salad, we've got cauli two ways, plus the world's creamiest, dreamiest ranch dressing (tofu ftw!). The sweet, caramelized craggy bits of roast cauliflower are always going to do it for me, but pairing it with some raw cauli for contrast is even better. Take this to a potluck, or serve it warm for dinner and enjoy the cold leftovers the next day for lunch. This dish is simply never not thriving.

1 PREP AND ROAST THE CAULI:

- Preheat the oven to 450°F.

- Coarsely chop **2 large heads of cauliflower** (stems and all) into 1½-inch pieces. Divide about two-thirds of the chopped cauli between 2 large rimmed baking sheets, keeping the remaining one-third aside. Drizzle with **olive oil** until generously coated and season with **salt and freshly ground black pepper.**

- Roast, stirring after 25 to 30 minutes, until deeply brown and crisp all over, 40 to 50 minutes total.

- While the cauliflower roasts, chop the reserved raw cauliflower into smaller bite-size pieces (about ½ inch). ONE INGREDIENT, MANY WAYS (PG 21)

2 MEANWHILE, MAKE THE VEGAN RANCH:

- In a **blender**, combine **8 ounces silken tofu**, **⅓ cup plus 3 tablespoons vegetable oil**, **6 tablespoons rice vinegar**, **a big ole handful of dill**, **a big ole handful of parsley leaves**, **3 tablespoons miso paste**, **1 large garlic clove**, and the **zest of 1 lemon**. Blend on high until bright green

and very creamy. Taste and season with salt as needed, bearing in mind that miso can be very salty! If you don't have a blender, finely chop the dill and parsley, grate the garlic clove, and then vigorously whisk the remaining aforementioned ingredients together in a large bowl, breaking the silken tofu up as much as possible. The dressing won't be as smooth, but it'll still be tasty.

3 COMBINE AND SERVE:

- Thinly slice **1 jalapeño**.

- Once the cauliflower is roasted, in a large bowl, combine it with the reserved raw cauli and sliced jalapeño (start by adding only half, if you are spice averse), then pick and toss in the **remaining leaves from the bunches of dill and parsley.**

- Add about half of the dressing, toss well to coat, and continue to add more as needed until the salad is very well dressed—you choose just how saucy you like it! IT'S ALL IN THE SAUCE (PG 21)

- Squeeze the **juice of the zested lemon** into the salad, taste, and add more salt and pepper if needed. Serve warm, room temp, or cold.

MONOCHROMATIC MELON SALAD

GOES WITH: TANGLED LEEK 'ZA (PAGE 121), SHELLS, PEAS & BUTTERMILK (PAGE 104), STUFFED FOCACCIA WITH SPICY GREENS & CHEESE (PAGE 134)

SERVES 4

QUICK AS HECK!

PRODUCE

- 2 medium fennel bulbs (about 1 pound)
- ½ small ripe honeydew or cantaloupe melon (¾ pound)[1]
- 2 lemons

DAIRY

- 5 ounces Parmigiano Reggiano (in wedge form)

PANTRY

- ⅓ cup roasted, salted pistachios
- ⅓ cup extra-virgin olive oil
- Flaky sea salt and freshly ground black pepper

SPECIAL EQUIPMENT

- Food processor

[1] The most effective way to suss out a ripe, sweet melon is to smell it. It should immediately smell ripe and sweet and . . . like melon. The fainter the smell, the less ripe the melon. But beware, the sniff test works on all melons except for watermelon.

This salad is all about letting peak summer melon shine. You'll make a nutty, green pistachio oil to drench it in, then toss the fruit with thinly shaved fennel and tons and tons of thick shards of Parmigiano Reggiano. It's sweet, it's salty, it's crunchy and soft simultaneously; it is THE summer salad moment.

1 MAKE THE PISTACHIO OIL:

- If **fennel fronds** are attached to your fennel bulbs, chop up **about ¼ cup** of them. Add them to a **food processor**, along with **⅓ cup roasted, salted pistachios**, and pulse until coarsely ground. Stream in some **olive oil** until it reaches a nice drizzle-able, loose-pesto-ish consistency (⅓ cup-ish). Season with **flaky sea salt**.

2 PREP THE SALAD:

- Remove the tough outer layers of **2 medium fennel bulbs**. Trim the root ends, and then thinly slice.

- Cut **½ small ripe melon** into 2-inch wedges, then cut the rind away from the flesh. Thinly slice the melon (you should have about 10 ounces of sliced fruit at the end of the day).

- In a large bowl, combine the fennel and melon. Season with flaky sea salt and squeeze the **juice of 2 lemons** over, depending on how juicy they are—use your judgment. Toss gently to combine.

- Using a sharp knife or vegetable peeler, shave **5 ounces Parm** into large shards and add them to the bowl. If you have some **fennel fronds** left, add them to the bowl and very gently toss the salad so as not to break up the shards of Parm too much.

3 PILE AND SERVE:

- Pile the salad onto a plate in a tall tower, drizzling the pistachio oil over every handful you stack so it gets to the lower parts of the tower as well as the top. Finish with more flaky sea salt and **black pepper**.

CHICKEN SALAD WITH COCONUT CRUNCH

SERVES 4

GOES WITH: SPICY COCONUT-SMOTHERED GREEN BEANS (PAGE 225), CUCUMBER BAG SALAD WITH MISO-POPPY DRESSING (PAGE 93)

PRODUCE

- 2 limes
- 1 (½-inch) piece of fresh ginger
- 1½ pounds mixed crunchy vegetables, such as snap peas, carrots, Broccolini, radishes, cucumbers, daikon, kohlrabi, and/or celery
- 1 bunch of cilantro

PROTEIN

- 1 large egg
- 2 cups picked rotisserie chicken meat or other leftover cooked protein

PANTRY

- 3 tablespoons plus 1 teaspoon brown sugar
- 4 teaspoons toasted sesame oil
- 1 teaspoon curry powder
- Kosher salt and freshly ground black pepper
- ½ teaspoon cayenne pepper
- 1½ cups nuts, such as raw cashews, roasted peanuts, and/or raw almonds[1]
- 1½ cups unsweetened coconut flakes
- 2 tablespoons white and/or black sesame seeds
- ⅓ cup full-fat coconut milk
- ¼ cup creamy peanut butter
- 1 tablespoon vegetable oil

Consider this your anything-goes, nothing-planned, clean-out-the-fridge mome. I bet most of us could open our refrigerators right now and find at least three or four random, on-their-way-out vegetables in need of a purpose. This is their destiny. The salad is inspired by Indonesian gado-gado, a mix of crunchy vegetables tossed together with a creamy peanut-coconut dressing. You'll also make a big ole tray of coconut crunch, a sweet-salty-spicy-crunchy savory granola that you can and shall sprinkle on anything and everything that comes your way.

1 MAKE THE COCONUT CRUNCH:

- Preheat the oven to 325°F. Line a rimmed baking sheet with parchment paper.

- Separate **1 egg**. Place the white in a large bowl (reserve the yolk for future aioli!) and vigorously whisk until fluffy, foamy, soft peaks form.

- Add **3 tablespoons brown sugar, 3 teaspoons toasted sesame oil, 1 teaspoon curry powder, ¾ teaspoon salt**, and **½ teaspoon cayenne pepper**. Whisk to incorporate.

- Add **1½ cups nuts, 1½ cups unsweetened coconut flakes, 2 tablespoons sesame seeds**, and the **zest of 1 lime**. Fold with a rubber spatula until thoroughly coated.

- Scrape the mixture onto the prepared baking sheet and spread in an even layer. Transfer to the oven and bake, stirring halfway through, until the coconut is lightly golden, 20 to 25 minutes. Let cool slightly, then use your hands to break up into large chunks.

2 MAKE THE PEANUT-COCONUT DRESSING:

- Finely grate a **½-inch piece of fresh ginger** into a large bowl. Add **⅓ cup coconut milk, ¼ cup peanut butter, 1 tablespoon vegetable oil**, the **juice of 1 lime**, the remaining **1 teaspoon toasted sesame oil**, and the remaining **1 teaspoon brown sugar**. Whisk until smooth. Season with salt to taste.

3 MAKE THAT SALAD:

- Chop, slice, julienne, trim, shave, and/or dice **1½ pounds mixed crunchy vegetables**.[2] Add all the veg to the bowl of dressing.

- Coarsely chop the leaves and tender stems from **1 bunch of cilantro** and add to the bowl.

- Add **2 cups picked chicken meat** to the bowl. Season with **salt** and **freshly ground black pepper** to taste. Add a few handfuls of coconut crunch and toss to combine. Add more **lime juice** as needed to taste.

- Divide the salad among plates and top with more coconut crunch.

[1] Nuts and seeds last a lot longer when stored in the fridge than they do at room temperature. That said, they can still last up to a couple months in the pantry. If you blow through seeds and nuts like I do, room-temperature storage is fine, but if not, your fridge or your freezer is a safer bet.

[2] The shapes don't really matter, as long as everything is more or less bite-size, so get creative with your cuts!

DRINK
BREAK

PIÑACILLIN

GOES WITH: CHICKEN SALAD WITH
COCONUT CRUNCH (PAGE 86), PARTY
CHIX (PAGE 185)

SERVES 4

- 1 (3-inch) piece of fresh ginger

- 12 ounces fresh-cut pineapple
  (from ½ pineapple)[1]

- 9 juicy limes

- Kosher salt

- 4½ ounces Coco López cream of
  coconut

- 9 ounces tequila blanco

- Ice

- Mezcal, for floating

What happens when you cross a piña colada (the world's greatest tropical drink) with a Penicillin (a smoky, ginger-flecked classic cocktail)? A Piñacillin! This is your summer party drink when you don't want to deal with a blender. (Mix everything in a pitcher before people come over, then add ice and stir when they walk in.) Fresh pineapple, freshly grated ginger, lime, and tequila get combined with sweet Coco López and a whisper of mezcal. Your friends will never know what hit 'em. Just kidding, they will. It's friggin' tequila.

● In a pitcher, combine a finely grated **3-inch piece of fresh ginger, 12 ounces fresh-cut 1-inch chunks of pineapple**, the **juice of 9 limes**, and **a big pinch of salt**. Add a couple of the spent lime halves to the pitcher and muddle and mash (use the back of a wooden spoon if you have to!) until all of the pineapple has broken down into a pulp.

● Stir in **4½ ounces Coco López** and **9 ounces tequila blanco** and fill with **ice**. Stir vigorously until well combined and chilled, 1 to 2 minutes.

● Fill 4 glasses with some more fresh **ice** and pour the Piñacillin over it, allowing all that muddled pulp to flow into the glass.

● Float **a splash of mezcal** on top of each glass and garnish with more pineapple, lime wedges, and pineapple leaves, if you've got 'em!

[1] People mistakenly think that pineapples will continue to ripen on the counter, but that's not the case! When shopping for pineapple, smell the outside—if it's fragrant and smells like . . . pineapple, you've got a good one. If not, move on—it's not going to get any riper.

MARINATED ZUCCH & MOZZ  WITH FRIED SUNFLOWER SEEDS

GOES WITH: CHICKEN PICCATA WITH SWEET CORN, CHILES & BUTTERMILK (PAGE 181), RIGATONI WITH CREAMED LEEKS & CHIVE-Y BREAD CRUMBS (PAGE 108)

SERVES 4

QUICK AS HECK!

I've done a lot of hating on zucchini in my day, but I'm capable of personal growth, and I've come around, okay? You've heard the rant: it's a watery, bland, flavorless bore-snore. Here's the thing: if you know how to treat it right, zucchini is a sponge for flavor. If you don't, it's blah-dee-blah. In this recipe, you'll use zucchini (or summer squash!) in two ways: raw and pan-seared. As the zucch sits in a vibrant, garlicky, tangy, minty marinade, allll that flavor is absorbed into its flesh. The fried sunflower seeds on top add a necessary salty crunch.

PRODUCE

- 3 pounds zucchini or summer squash (3 or 4 medium)
- 1 garlic clove
- 1 bunch of mint

DAIRY

- 6 ounces fresh whole-milk mozzarella cheese

PANTRY

- Kosher salt and freshly ground black pepper
- ¼ cup white wine vinegar
- 5 tablespoons extra-virgin olive oil, plus more as needed
- A pinch of sugar
- 3 tablespoons raw sunflower seeds, pepitas, or sesame seeds

1 PREP THE ZUCCH AND MOZZ:

- Slice **½ medium zucchini** crosswise as thinly as possible. Place in a large bowl.

- Cut **all the remaining zucchini** (including the other half of the sliced zucchini) in half lengthwise. Using the tip of a sharp knife, score the zucchini flesh in a crosshatch pattern. Season all over with **salt**.

- Tear **6 ounces mozzarella cheese** into bite-size pieces.

2 MAKE THE MARINADE:

- To the bowl of sliced zucchini, add **¼ cup white wine vinegar, 3 tablespoons olive oil, 1 finely grated garlic clove, a pinch of sugar, a big pinch of salt**, and some **freshly ground black pepper**.

- Firmly whack about **half of the bunch of mint** against your cutting board to release some of its essential oil. Add the whacked mint (stems and all) to the marinating zucchini and stir well to combine—the mint will flavor the marinade as it sits. Add the torn mozzarella and let marinate.

3 COOK THE ZUCCH:

- In a large cast-iron skillet, heat **a few big glugs of olive oil** over medium-high heat until smoking. Pat the zucchini halves dry (they will have expelled some liquid by now) and arrange in the skillet, cut-side down. If it doesn't all fit, work in 2 batches. Cook, undisturbed, until well caramelized on the cut side, 5 to 6 minutes.

- Flip and continue to cook until lightly browned, 2 minutes longer. Transfer to a cutting board to cool.

- Reduce the heat to medium-low. If there's no oil remaining in the skillet, add another glug, along with **3 tablespoons sunflower seeds**, and cook, constantly stirring, until well toasted, about 1 minute. Remove from the heat. Season with salt and transfer the seeds to a plate to cool.

4 ASSEMBLE:

- Once the cooked zucch are cool enough to handle, tear or cut them into large pieces, adding them to the marinated sliced zucchini, along with allll the rest of **what remains of your bunch of mint**. THOU SHALT NOT WASTE HERBS (PG 22) Toss well, taste, and adjust the seasoning, then transfer to a serving platter. Top with the sunflower seeds and a drizzle of olive oil and serve.

CUCUMBER BAG SALAD WITH MISO-POPPY DRESSING

GOES WITH: PARTY CHIX (PAGE 185), HOT SAUCE–BRAISED SHORT RIBS WITH WINTER SQUASH (PAGE 149), RED CURRY HOT WINGS ROLLED IN PEANUTS (PAGE 191)

SERVES 4

QUICK AS HECK!

PRODUCE

- 2¼ pounds Persian cucumbers (about 10)
- ½ orange
- 1 bunch of cilantro

DAIRY

- ¼ cup buttermilk

PANTRY

- Kosher salt
- ¼ cup extra-virgin olive oil
- 3 tablespoons white miso paste
- 3 tablespoons unseasoned rice vinegar
- 1 heaping tablespoon poppy seeds

Refreshing, crisp cucumbers are the perfect complement to heavy, fatty, meaty dishes, of which there are many in this book. This is a "bag salad" because you'll halve your cukes and then smash them to pieces in a resealable bag, reducing splatter and mess. It is also a bag salad because you can take it out of the kitchen and into the world in its bag (just make sure the bag's not ripped!). Perfect for picnic transport or showing up to a party with a salad in your purse. The dressing is inspired by the phenom wedge salad at Kismet Rotisserie, which is smothered in a miso-poppy vinaigrette in place of ranch. Sarah and Sara, this one goes out to you. <3

1 SMASH AND SALT THE CUKES:

- Cut 2¼ pounds Persian cucumbers in half lengthwise. Transfer them to a resealable bag, season with a few big pinches of salt, press out the air, and seal tightly. Whack the bag with a rolling pin or heavy skillet to break the cucumbers into irregular, bite-size pieces.

- Line a rimmed baking sheet with a double layer of paper towels. Pour the cucumbers out onto the paper towels and distribute them evenly; reserve the bag. Let them sit while you make the dressing.[1]

2 MAKE THE MISO-POPPY DRESSING:

- In a large bowl, whisk together ¼ cup buttermilk, ¼ cup olive oil, 3 tablespoons miso paste, 3 tablespoons rice vinegar, the zest and juice of ½ orange, and 1 heaping tablespoon of poppy seeds until smooth.

3 PAT DRY AND COMBINE:

- Pat the cucumbers dry, wicking away as much moisture as possible, and then add them to the bowl of dressing, along with the leaves and tender stems of 1 bunch of cilantro—this salad is essentially equal parts cukes and herbs and that's what makes it so refreshing. YOU'RE PROBS NOT USING ENOUGH ... HERBS (PG 20) Taste and season with more salt if needed. Serve immediately or return the contents of the salad to the bag (make sure there are no holes!) and store in the refrigerator for later, or take on the go to a picnic or potluck.

[1] The salt will draw moisture out of the cukes, which will get absorbed by the towels, leaving the cucumbers extra crispy and crunchy.

DRUNKEN CACIO E PEPE

GOES WITH: MASHED POTATO ARANCINI (PAGE 63), MOLLZ BALLZ (PAGE 142), TRIPLE THREAT GARLIC BREAD (PAGE 99)

SERVES 4

QUICK AS HECK!

This pasta is so impressive-looking, you'd never guess how easy it is to make (the best kind of pasta dish). You're romancing classic cacio e pepe with a deep, dark, shmoody red wine sauce, a technique I learned from the amazing Montreal pizza and natty wine joint Elena. You'll reduce an entire bottle of wine (!!!), along with lots of garlic and black pepper, until it's thick and fragrant and devoid of any astringency, and then add boatloads of salty cheese. I like to use a fifty-fifty mix of Pecorino Romano (salty, sheepy) and Parmigiano Reggiano (nutty, sweet), but you could use one; just know that pecorino is a supremely salty cheese, so you might want to hold back on the salt elsewhere in the recipe.

PRODUCE

- 8 garlic cloves

DAIRY

- 3 ounces Pecorino Romano and/or Parmigiano Reggiano, plus more for serving
- 8 tablespoons (1 stick) unsalted butter

PANTRY

- Kosher salt
- 2 tablespoons black peppercorns
- 1 (750 ml) bottle full-bodied red wine, such as zinfandel or cabernet[1]
- 1 tablespoon extra-virgin olive oil
- 1 pound spaghetti

1 DO SOME PREP:

- Put a large pot of water on the heat to boil. **Salt** it generously.

- Thinly slice **8 garlic cloves**.

- Coarsely grind enough **black peppercorns** to measure a scant 2 tablespoons. The grind should be very large! If your pepper mill doesn't make a large grind, use a mortar and pestle or resealable plastic bag and crush them with the bottom of a heavy skillet.

- If it's not already, finely grate **3 ounces Pecorino Romano**.[2]

- Cube **6 tablespoons unsalted butter**. Keep chilled in the fridge.

2 MAKE THE BASE OF THE SAUCE:

- Crack open **1 (750 ml) bottle full-bodied red wine**.

- In a large Dutch oven, heat the remaining **2 tablespoons butter** and **a glug of olive oil** over medium-high heat (the olive oil raises the smoking point of the butter, allowing you to cook over medium-high heat without burning it). Add the sliced garlic and ground peppercorns, season with **salt**, and cook, stirring, over medium heat until the garlic is softened but not browned, 1 to 2 minutes.

- Pour the whole bottle of wine into the pot, raise the heat to high, and bring to a boil.

Cook until the liquid reduces to ¾ cup, 16 to 20 minutes. IF YOU'RE GONNA USE IT, USE IT (PG 20)

3 MEANWHILE, COOK YOUR PASTA:

- Once the wine has been reducing for 10 minutes or so, add **1 pound spaghetti** to the pot of boiling water. Give it a stir and cook until very al dente, 2 to 3 minutes less than the package directions. Scoop out a cup or so of the pasta water and drain the pasta.

4 FINISH IT UP:

- Once the wine has adequately reduced, reduce the heat to low and add the cold cubed butter, a few pieces at a time. Shake the pot back and forth, while stirring, to emulsify the butter and wine into a silky homogeneous sauce.

- Add the drained pasta to the pot. Using a pair of tongs, coat the noodles in the sauce. And here comes the cacio: add the 3 ounces grated cheese, along with **a big splash of the reserved pasta water**. Continue stirring and coating the pasta with the sauce, adding more of the reserved pasta water, a splash at a time, until a loose, silky sauce is formed (you may not use all the pasta water). Give a final seasoning of salt.

- Divide the pasta among serving bowls and eat immediately, with more grated cheese on top.

[1] I don't like to use super-high-quality, expensive wine when cooking. Of course, it's got to be something you like the taste of, so find your balance. A lot of the nuance of flavor will get cooked off, but the essence will remain.

[2] If using a Microplane, you'll want a few BIG piles; if using store-bought grated cheese, you'll need a few big handfuls (about ¾ cup).

COOK ALONG!

AUDIO

TRIPLE THREAT GARLIC BREAD

SERVES 6 TO 8

GOES WITH: MOLLZ BALLZ (PAGE 142), DRUNKEN CACIO E PEPE (PAGE 96)

PRODUCE

- 2 garlic heads
- 1 large or 2 small bunches of chives

DAIRY

- 12 tablespoons (1½ sticks) unsalted butter
- 1½ ounces grated Parmigiano Reggiano (heaping ⅓ cup)

PANTRY

- Extra-virgin olive oil
- Kosher salt
- Red pepper flakes
- 1 loaf challah bread (12 to 16 ounces)
- Flaky sea salt

This garlic bread goes beyond the call of garlic bread duty. The way I see it, if you're gonna make garlic bread and commit to the wrath of garlic breath, you might as well REALLY make some garlic bread. One whole head of roasted garlic, twelve grated garlic cloves, and tons of sliced chives (that's the triple threat!) go into the supercharged garlic butter that you'll slather over a big loaf of challah bread, inside and out, for what may be the most extra garlic bread of all time. ONE INGREDIENT, MANY WAYS (PG 21)

1 ROAST THE GARLIC:

- Preheat the oven to 375°F.

- Cut ½ inch off the top of **1 garlic head**, or just enough to expose the tops of the cloves. Place the head on a square of aluminum foil, drizzle with **olive oil**, season with **kosher salt**, and enclose.

- Place on a small rimmed baking sheet and bake until the garlic is very soft and lightly golden, 45 to 55 minutes. Unwrap the foil and let the garlic cool.

- Raise the oven temperature to 400°F.

2 MEANWHILE, MAKE THE GARLIC BUTTER:

- Lightly smash and peel **12 raw garlic cloves**. Finely grate the cloves. Yes, this recipe calls for a tonnnn of garlic. IF YOU'RE GONNA USE IT, USE IT (PG 20)

- In a small saucepan, melt **12 tablespoons unsalted butter** over medium-high heat. When the foaming subsides, add the grated garlic and **2 big pinches of red pepper flakes**. Stir and let cook until you see the slightest hint of golden on the garlic, 30 seconds. Immediately remove from the heat and season with kosher salt.

- Squeeze the cloves from the roasted garlic head into the garlic butter, add any leftover oil in the foil, and mash to combine. It's okay if the mixture is a little chunky.

3 ASSEMBLE:

- Line a rimmed baking sheet with parchment paper.

- Thinly slice **1 large bunch of chives**.

- Place **a loaf of challah** on a cutting board and, with your knife parallel to the surface, carefully slice it nearly in half horizontally so the loaf opens like a book.

- Transfer the challah to the prepared baking sheet. Brush the insides of the loaf with half of the garlic butter.[1] Scatter with half of the chives and **a big handful of grated Parmesan**. Close the bread.

- Brush the remaining garlic butter over the top, separating the braids of the bread to brush butter in the crevices.

- Bake until the challah is lightly golden and the butter is fully soaked into the bread on the inside, 14 to 16 minutes.

- Remove the challah from the oven and immediately shower the outside with the remaining **chives**, remaining **Parmesan**, and **flaky sea salt**. Cut crosswise into slices and serve hot!

[1] If your loaf is small (that is, 12 ounces or less), you may have more garlic butter than you need. Save it for another use! There's nothing that doesn't benefit from garlic butter.

GRANDMA PIE WITH MORTY-D & PEPERONCINI PESTO

SERVES 4 TO 6

GOES WITH: MARINATED ZUCCH & MOZZ WITH FRIED SUNFLOWER SEEDS (PAGE 90), DILLY BEANS & BURRATA WITH FRIZZLED SHALLOTS (PAGE 218), PURPLE SALAD (PAGE 71)

PRODUCE

- 2 garlic cloves
- ½ small red onion
- 1 small bunch of basil

DAIRY

- 10 ounces fresh whole-milk mozzarella cheese
- ½ cup fresh whole-milk ricotta cheese
- 1 ounce grated Parmigiano Reggiano (¼ cup), plus more for serving

PROTEIN

- 6 ounces thinly sliced mortadella

PANTRY

- 2 (1-pound) balls store-bought pizza dough
- Kosher salt and freshly ground black pepper
- ½ cup extra-virgin olive oil, plus more for drizzling
- ¼ cup roasted pistachios, shelled
- ¾ cup peperoncini, plus 3 tablespoons brine
- ½ cup pitted Castelvetrano olives

I gotta tell you, this pizza recipe is more impressive than it ought to be, given that we're using store-bought dough and baking it in a conventional home oven. Mortadella, ricotta, and a bang-a-langin' pistachio and pickled pepper pesto do some seriously heavy lifting. This recipe yields a half sheet pan of pizza (your standard rimmed baking sheet), so you'll need two 1-pound balls of dough to fill it. You could also halve this recipe and bake it in a quarter sheet pan or a 9 × 13-inch baking dish. But if you ask me, it's worth going for the full shebangy. There's really nothing worse than running out of 'za, especiallly when there's morty-d involved.

1. DO SOME PREP:

- Remove **2 pounds pizza dough** from the fridge.

- Knead both balls together to form one large, taut ball of dough. Return the dough to one of the bags it came in and let it come to room temperature. This can take up to 90 minutes from when you pull it from the refrigerator, so plan ahead!

- Tear **10 ounces mozzarella cheese** into bite-size pieces (the size of a quarter) and transfer to a medium bowl. Add **½ cup ricotta cheese**. Finely grate in **2 garlic cloves**, tossing to combine evenly. Season with **salt and freshly ground black pepper**.

- Thinly slice **½ small red onion** through the root end.

2. STRETCH THE DOUGH:

- Position a rack on the lowest rung of the oven. Preheat the oven to 500°F. Generously grease a 13 × 18-inch baking sheet with **about 3 tablespoons olive oil** and coat well.

- Place the pizza dough in the center of the baking sheet and use your hands to dimple and stretch it toward the edges, working from the middle outward. If the dough feels tight and won't stretch to the edges, cover with plastic wrap and let rest a few minutes more. Repeat this process until the dough stretches to the edges of the pan without springing back.

3. BUILD AND COOK THE PIZZA:

- Scatter the mozzarella mixture and red onions evenly over the dough.

- Drizzle with more **olive oil** and season with salt and pepper.

- Bake for 10 minutes. Remove the pizza from the oven. Tear **6 ounces sliced mortadella** and scatter the pieces in mounds on the pizza (to increase the potential for crispy edges).

- Return to the oven (rotate the pan when doing so) and bake until the crust is deeply golden brown at the edges and the mortadella is crisp on top, 6 to 10 minutes.

4. MEANWHILE, MAKE THE PESTO:

- Finely chop **¼ cup roasted pistachios** and **¾ cup peperoncini**.

- Coarsely chop **½ cup pitted Castelvetrano olives**.

- Stir everything together in a medium bowl with the remaining **⅓ cup olive oil, a handful of grated Parmesan (about ¼ cup)**, and **3 tablespoons peperoncini brine**.

5. TOP AND SERVE:

- Once the pizza is cooked, let cool for a few minutes before spooning the pistachio pesto over the top.

- Scatter the **leaves from 1 bunch of basil** over the pizza—it's a lot of basil, and that's what makes it special—really cover that 'za. It will lend a spicy, fresh element to a very rich, indulgent pie. YOU'RE PROBS NOT USING ENOUGH ... HERBS (PG 20)

- Sprinkle with more grated Parm and cut into squares.

COOK ALONG!

AUDIO

PEPPERONI FRIED RICE

GOES WITH: SIZZLED SEEDY TOMATO SALAD (PAGE 75), MARINATED ZUCCH & MOZZ WITH FRIED SUNFLOWER SEEDS (PAGE 90)

SERVES 4

QUICK AS HECK!

I am an absolute freak for pepperoni, and will never understand why it isn't a more popular ingredient beyond a pizza topping. With any luck, this recipe will begin to change that narrative for pepperoni everywhere. Notice I call for ten garlic cloves in this recipe. I agree it's a lot. But I don't see the point in using just one or two when we all love garlic and it comes in a bulb with so many cloves anyway. "More is more," bay-bee.

PRODUCE

- 10 garlic cloves
- 1 large shallot
- 1 bunch of basil

PROTEIN

- 4 ounces sliced pepperoni

PANTRY

- 1 cup mayonnaise
- Kosher salt
- 3 tablespoons sherry vinegar, plus more to taste
- 4 tablespoons extra-virgin olive oil
- 4 cups cooled cooked white rice
- Red pepper flakes

1. DO SOME PREP:

- Cut **4 ounces sliced pepperoni** in half, creating half-moons.

- Smash and thinly slice **8 garlic cloves** (grate and reserve the remaining 2). That's a lot of garlic! That's why it's so good! IF YOU'RE GONNA USE IT, USE IT (PG 20)

- Thinly slice **1 large shallot**.

- Pick the leaves from **1 bunch of basil**.

2. MAKE A QUICKIE AIOLI:

- In a small bowl, whisk together **1 cup mayonnaise**, **2 grated garlic cloves**, and **a big pinch of salt**. Season with **sherry vinegar** to taste—it will take a tablespoon or so before it starts to taste really bright and delicious.

3. FRY THE RICE:

- In a large nonstick skillet, heat **3 glugs of olive oil** over medium heat. Add the pepperoni and cook, stirring often, until about half of the pepperoni has crispy edges, 4 to 5 minutes.[1] Using a slotted spoon, transfer the cooked pepperoni to a plate.

- Add **4 cups cooled cooked rice**, season with salt, and pat into a single layer. Cook, undisturbed, until the rice is very crispy and evenly golden brown underneath, 6 to 8 minutes.

- Using a heatproof rubber spatula, fold the rice pancake in half (like an omelet) so that it occupies only half of the skillet. If it doesn't easily fold over, just scoot the rice over to one half of the skillet to make some room.

- Add **another glug of olive oil** to the bare spot in the skillet, along with the garlic, shallots, and **a few pinches of red pepper flakes**. Reduce the heat to medium-low and cook until the shallots are softened but not browned, 1 to 2 minutes.

- Add the pepperoni back into the skillet and break up the rice, stirring the pepperoni and aromatics into the rice as you break it up.

- Once the ingredients are incorporated, remove the pan from the heat and stir in **a few glugs of sherry vinegar** and the basil leaves. They will wilt with the heat, and that's what we want! Taste and adjust the seasoning with salt.

4. SERVE:

- Generously schmear the aioli on the bottom of a serving bowl (you may not need all of it—save the rest in the fridge for up to 7 days). Pile the pepperoni rice on top and serve hot.

[1] We're going for lots of textures here, so not every slice of pepperoni has to be the same—some can be chewy, others crispy, etc. It's all part of the fun.

SHELLS, PEAS & BUTTERMILK

GOES WITH: STUFFED FOCACCIA WITH SPICY GREENS & CHEESE (PAGE 134); MASHED POTATO ARANCINI (PAGE 63); CRISPY, CRUNCHY BROCC & GRAINS WITH SO. MUCH. MINT. (PAGE 78)

SERVES 4

QUICK AS HECK!

Things that I think were meant to be together: mint, peas, and pecorino cheese. Pasta shapes that I think are underrated: small shells, medium shells, big shells, and jumbo shells. Something I think about a lot regarding shells: They deserve the kind of press bucatini gets, just look at the way they swim around in that sauce! This recipe celebrates all of the above in one very simple spring pasta dish. You'll use buttermilk as the base of the sauce to keep it light and tangy. But be warned . . . heating buttermilk too aggressively can cause it to split, so never let it come to a simmer!

PRODUCE

- 3 garlic cloves
- 2 lemons
- 1 bunch of mint

DAIRY

- 2 cups buttermilk
- 1 ounce grated Pecorino Romano cheese (¼ cup), plus more for serving

PANTRY

- Kosher salt and freshly ground black pepper
- ¼ cup extra-virgin olive oil, plus more for serving
- 1 pound medium pasta shells

FROZEN

- 2½ cups frozen peas

SPECIAL EQUIPMENT

- Blender

1
- Bring a large pot of **heavily salted water** to a boil.

2
BLEND THE BUTTERMILK SAUCE:

- Rinse **2 cups frozen peas** under cold water until they are thawed, about 1 minute. Drain. Add to a **blender**, along with **2 cups buttermilk**, **3 garlic cloves**, the **zest of 2 lemons**, **¼ cup olive oil**, **a few very big cranks of black pepper**, and the leaves from **1 bunch of mint**. Blend on high until very smooth. Season the sauce with **salt** and set aside.

3
COOK THE PASTA AND SAUCE:

- Stir **1 pound pasta shells** into the pot of boiling water. Cook until al dente according to the package directions. One minute before the pasta is done cooking, add the remaining **½ cup frozen peas** to the pasta pot. Drain the pasta and peas, reserving a big scoop of pasta water.

- To a large Dutch oven, add the buttermilk sauce and set over medium-low heat. Add the hot pasta to the buttermilk sauce and very gently warm the sauce through (the heat from the pasta will do a lot of this for you), taking care to never boil or simmer the sauce. Remove from the heat and stir in **a small handful of grated pecorino**—this isn't a cheese sauce, so don't go too crazy here. We want to really taste the peas and mint—the cheese is there more as seasoning. The buttermilk sauce should still be quite loose and brothy. If it looks thick, add **a splash of your reserved pasta water**. Season with salt and pepper.

4
SERVE:

- Among shallow serving bowls, divide the pasta and add a couple big spoonfuls of the sauce to each so that the shells are swimming in the sauce. Grate more cheese over the top and finish with olive oil and pepper.

BROKEN NOODLE BOLOGNESE

SERVES 6 TO 8

GOES WITH: TRIPLE THREAT GARLIC BREAD (PAGE 99), SALTY COFFEE & PEANUT SLICE CREAM (PAGE 275)

PRODUCE

- 2 celery stalks
- 1 large yellow onion
- 1 medium fennel bulb
- 2 large rosemary sprigs

DAIRY

- 3 tablespoons mascarpone cheese, plus more for serving
- 2 ounces grated Parmigiano Reggiano (about ½ cup), plus more for serving

PROTEIN

- 1 pound 80% lean ground beef and/or veal
- 1 pound spicy Italian sausage, casings removed

PANTRY

- Kosher salt and freshly ground black pepper
- Extra-virgin olive oil
- 3 tablespoons white miso paste
- 3 tablespoons tomato paste
- ¾ cup dry red wine
- ¾ cup dry white wine
- 1 pound lasagna noodles (not no-cook)

This recipe has been percolating inside me for about ten years. Welcome to the inside of my brain. I've always wanted to develop a Bolognese recipe, but one that feels like it was prepared by Molly, not your nonna. It wasn't until I sat down to write this book that I felt I was ready. So please welcome the Broken Noodle Bolognese, my very Molly, very "more is more," OTT take on the classic. This version uses not one but two types of wine (why choose???), a bigggg dollop of miso paste in addition to the usual tomato paste, and rich mascarpone as it braises. Call me cray, but then tell me it doesn't taste GREAT.

1 DO SOME PREP:

- Finely chop **2 celery stalks**, **1 large yellow onion**, and **1 medium fennel bulb**, stalks and all.

- Finely chop the leaves of **2 large rosemary sprigs**.

- In a large bowl, mix together **1 pound ground beef** and **1 pound spicy Italian sausage**. Divvy up into 4 large, shaggy balls.[1] Season lightly with **salt and freshly ground black pepper**.

2 MAKE THE RAGÙ:

- In a large Dutch oven, heat **a few big glugs of olive oil** over medium-high heat until it starts to smoke. Cook the meatballs, flipping every few minutes, until a nice thick seared crust forms all over, 10 to 12 minutes total. Transfer to a plate.

- Add the chopped celery, onion, fennel, and rosemary, and cook until the veg are very cooked down and soft and begin to stick to the bottom of the pan, 10 to 13 minutes.

- Stir in **3 tablespoons miso paste** and **3 tablespoons tomato paste**. Cook until they begin to sizzle and fry in the fat and stick to the bottom, 3 to 4 minutes.

- Add **¾ cup each of dry red and white wines**, scraping to release anything from the bottom of the pot, then reduce the heat to medium.

- Crumble the meat into smaller pieces as you add it back into the pot. Cook, mashing and stirring occasionally, until most of the liquid has cooked off and the pot is mostly dry, 9 to 11 minutes.

- Stir in **2½ cups water**. Bring to a simmer, cover the pot, and reduce the heat to very low. Simmer, stirring once every 15 to 20 minutes or so, for 1½ hours.

- Stir in **a couple big spoonfuls of mascarpone cheese**. Leave the pot uncovered and cook at a very low simmer until the sauce has thickened, most of the water has cooked off, and the sauce is deeply flavorful, 1 hour or longer. Add a splash or two of water if you think it's getting too dry—the sauce should be thick and rich but not dry. Remove from the heat and cover to keep warm.

3 COOK THE PASTA AND SERVE:

- Bring a large pot of **heavily salted water** to a boil.

- Break **1 pound lasagna noodles** into irregular 2-inch shapes. Stir the broken noodles into the boiling water and cook until al dente, about 10 minutes. Just before draining, scoop out and reserve a big measuring cup full of pasta water.

- If the ragù has cooled, reheat it gently. Stir the noodles into the ragù over medium heat. While stirring, add another **fat spoonful of mascarpone** and **big handfuls of grated Parm**. Keep stirring until the noodles are super saucy, adding **splashes of the reserved pasta water** if the ragù needs to loosen and tasting as you add the cheese until you're happy. LOOSEN UP (PG 20)

- Divide the noodles among serving bowls. Top each with another dollop of mascarpone and a drizzle of olive oil. Serve with more grated Parm on the side.

[1] This makes searing the meat easier, as it helps us maximize the surface area of our skillet and avoid steaming.

RIGATONI WITH CREAMED LEEKS & CHIVE-Y BREAD CRUMBS

GOES WITH: TRIPLE THREAT GARLIC BREAD (PAGE 99), STUFFED FOCACCIA WITH SPICY GREENS & CHEESE (PAGE 134), LAMB CHOPS SCOTTADITO WITH MINTY BEANS & ARTICHOKES (PAGE 157)

SERVES 4

PRODUCE

- 4 pounds leeks (about 6 medium)
- 8 garlic cloves
- 1 bunch of chives
- 1 lemon

DAIRY

- 3 tablespoons unsalted butter
- 1 cup heavy cream
- 2 ounces grated Parmigiano Reggiano (about ½ cup), plus more for serving

PANTRY

- Kosher salt and freshly ground black pepper
- ½ cup panko bread crumbs
- 2 tablespoons extra-virgin olive oil
- 1 pound rigatoni or paccheri

Most people think the dark green parts of leeks should be discarded or reserved for stocks only. I disagree! The green parts are tougher, yes, but full of leek-y flavor, and with time they become meltingly tender. This recipe is making a case for using ALL parts of the leek. Just give them the time they need to soften before you add the cream for the most flavorful, luxurious results. Any shape pasta will work well here, but I like how the bread crumbs cling to rigatoni and paccheri. Do you!

1. DO SOME PREP:

- Bring a large pot of **heavily salted water** to a boil.

- Trim the hairy ends of **4 pounds leeks**. Cut the leeks lengthwise into quarters and then thinly slice crosswise (dark green parts as well!). If dirty, rinse the sliced leeks in a mesh strainer to remove the grit, and pat dry.

- Thinly slice **8 garlic cloves**.

- Thinly slice **1 bunch of chives**.

2. CREAM THE LEEKS:

- In a large Dutch oven, heat **3 tablespoons unsalted butter** over medium heat until the foaming subsides.

- Add the leeks, garlic, and **a big pinch of salt** and cook until bright and fragrant but not yet softened, 3 minutes. Add **1½ cups water** and simmer over medium heat, stirring often, until all the water has evaporated and the leeks are tender, 15 to 25 minutes.

- Stir in **1 cup heavy cream**. Bring the cream to a simmer and cook until slightly thickened, 2 to 3 minutes. Season the creamed leeks with salt and **lots of freshly ground black pepper** (the pepper is crucial here to cut through all of that fat). Remove from the heat and cover to keep warm.

3. MAKE THE CHIVE-Y BREAD CRUMBS:

- In a small nonstick skillet, combine **½ cup panko bread crumbs** and **a few glugs of olive oil** over medium heat. Cook, stirring frequently, until deeply golden brown, 4 to 7 minutes. Transfer to a small bowl and let cool.

4. COOK THE PASTA:

- Add **1 pound rigatoni** to the boiling water and stir well. Cook until al dente according to the package directions. Before draining, scoop out and reserve a big measuring cup full of pasta water.

- Add the pasta to the creamed leeks, along with **a big splash of pasta water**, and cook over medium heat, stirring constantly and adding **a few handfuls of grated Parmesan**, one at a time.[1]

- Once all of the cheese has been added, grate the **zest of ½ lemon** into the pasta and stir in the **juice of the whole lemon**. Taste and adjust the seasoning as needed.

- Stir the sliced chives into the cooled toasted bread crumbs and season them with salt. Divide the pasta among bowls and top with the chive-y bread crumbs and more pepper and Parm.

---

[1] You may need to add more pasta water to help thin out the sauce (it should cling nicely to the noodles), but err on the side of a looser sauce than you ultimately want because the cream will seize up some as it cools.

COOK ALONG!

AUDIO

CRISPY ORECCHIETTE WITH SPICY SAUSAGE & COLLARD RAGÙ

GOES WITH: CHILE-BASTED HALF CHICKEN WITH CAPER CHIMICHURRI (PAGE 182), RAW & ROASTED CAULI SALAD WITH CREAMY, DREAMY VEGAN RANCH (PAGE 82), PURPLE SALAD (PAGE 71)

SERVES 4

QUICK AS HECK!

The reason this pasta dish is over-the-top fantastic is because you go a tiny final step to crisp up the cooked orecchiette before it goes swimming in its spicy sausage ragù. A few minutes, one measly extra skillet—that's all it takes. I repeat, YOUR PASTA WILL BE CRISPY. You'll use only a half pound of pasta for this dish because it's loaded with greens and sausage and burrata, but I promise it will be enough to fill four bellies.

PRODUCE

- 3 large shallots (about 6 ounces)
- 1 bunch of collard greens (about 8 ounces)
- 1 lemon

DAIRY

- 2 ounces grated Parmigiano Reggiano (about ½ cup), plus more for serving
- 5 ounces burrata cheese (optional)

PROTEIN

- 1 pound sweet Italian sausage, casings removed

PANTRY

- Kosher salt
- 8 ounces orecchiette
- 6 tablespoons extra-virgin olive oil, plus more for drizzling
- ¼ cup tomato paste
- 3 to 4 tablespoons chopped jarred Calabrian chiles

1 DO SOME PREP:

- Bring a large pot of **heavily salted water** to a boil. (Big handful of salt in there, please!)
- Thinly slice **3 large shallots**.
- Strip the leaves off **1 bunch of collard greens** and slice crosswise into 1-inch-wide strips. Discard the stems.

2 COOK THE PASTA:

- Drop **8 ounces orecchiette** into the boiling water, give it a stir, and cook until al dente according to the package directions. Scoop out a few cups of pasta water before draining it (you'll need quite a bit to help cook down the greens). Drizzle the drained pasta lightly with **olive oil** so it doesn't clump together as it sits.

3 MEANWHILE, START THE RAGÙ:

- In a large Dutch oven, heat **several tablespoons olive oil** over medium-high heat. Once the oil is very hot, add **1 pound sweet Italian sausage**, breaking it into large, golf ball–size chunks as you add it. Cook, undisturbed, until well browned, 3 to 4 minutes. Using tongs, flip the sausage pieces and brown on the second side, 1 to 2 minutes.[1] Transfer to a plate.
- Reduce the heat to medium-low and add the shallots and a big pinch of salt. Cook, stirring often, until jammy and cooked down, 4 minutes.
- Stir in **¼ cup tomato paste** and **4 tablespoons chopped Calabrian chiles** (hold some back if you're spice averse) and

stir to evenly coat the aromatics. Continue to cook, stirring, until the tomato paste begins to stick to the pot, 4 to 5 minutes.

- Add the collard greens and **a few big splashes of the reserved pasta water** (this will help to steam and wilt the greens). Stir well, cover the pot, and cook until the greens are cooked down and tender (taste one, you'll know!), 4 to 5 minutes. Add more **pasta water** as needed if the pot gets dry. The ragù should be nice and saucy at the end. Remove from the heat and keep covered.

4 CRISP THE PASTA:

- In a large nonstick skillet, heat **2 tablespoons olive oil** over medium-high heat. Add about half of the cooked pasta to the skillet and cook, undisturbed, until the bottom is golden brown and crisp at the edges, 3 to 4 minutes. Add to the pot of ragù and repeat with the remaining pasta. WHEN IN DOUBT, REFRY (PG 22)

5 FINISH:

- Return the pot to medium heat. Add the sausage back in, breaking it into smaller pieces as you do, along with **a big splash of the reserved pasta water** and **a few big handfuls of grated Parm**. Cook, stirring vigorously, until a thick sauce coats the pasta, 30 seconds.
- Squeeze the **juice of 1 lemon** into the pasta and stir to combine.
- Divide the pasta among serving bowls. Tear **5 ounces burrata** (if using) into small pieces and top each bowl with a few. Drizzle with more olive oil, sprinkle with more Parm, and serve.

COOK ALONG!

AUDIO

[1] The sausage will still be slightly undercooked, which is okay, because it will finish cooking later.

KEDGEREE WITH JAMMY EGGS & SMOKED FISH

GOES WITH: FENNEL ON FENNEL ON FENNEL TORTILLA
(PAGE 212), SIZZLED SEEDY TOMATO SALAD (PAGE 75)

SERVES 4

QUICK AS HECK!

When I lived in Brooklyn, nothing could keep me away from Chez Ma Tante, a French-ish Canadian-ish restaurant in Greenpoint, where I never had a mediocre meal. One of their most popular dishes was a Frenchy interpretation of kedgeree, which traditionally consists of rice and smoked fish and whose British colonial origins are linked to the Indian rice-and-lentil dish khichari. At Chez Ma Tante, they served it over a fat *swoosh* of aioli. This is my replica version, with smoked whitefish and jammy eggs over curry-spiced rice, swimming in a pool of tangy buttermilk and topped with a celery-onion salad. ME-OW.

PRODUCE

- 2 white onions
- 3 celery stalks and their leaves
- 1 lemon

DAIRY

- 3 tablespoons unsalted butter
- 1½ cups buttermilk

PROTEIN

- 2 large eggs
- 8 ounces smoked whitefish, trout, or salmon

PANTRY

- 2 cups long-grain white rice
- Kosher salt and freshly ground black pepper
- 1 tablespoon curry powder
- Extra-virgin olive oil

MAKE THE RICE:

- Finely chop **1½ white onions**. Thinly slice the remaining **½ onion** and set it aside—this will go into the salad.

- Rinse **2 cups long-grain white rice** in a fine-mesh strainer, swirling with your hands until the water running through it is clear. Drain.

- In a medium pot with a tight-fitting lid, heat **3 tablespoons unsalted butter** over medium heat. Add the chopped onions and **a big pinch of salt** and cook, stirring occasionally, until the onions are translucent and softened, 6 to 8 minutes.

- Stir in **1 tablespoon curry powder** and cook until fragrant, 30 seconds.

- Add the drained rice, **2¾ cups cold water**, and **1 teaspoon salt**. Bring to a simmer, cover the pot, and reduce the heat to low. Set a timer for 18 minutes.

- When the timer goes off, turn off the heat, then keep the lid on the pot and allow the rice to steam for at least 10 minutes longer.

BOIL THE EGGS AND SEASON THE BUTTERMILK:

- While the rice cooks, bring a small pot of water to a boil.

- Gently lower **2 large eggs** into the water. Set a timer for 7 minutes.

- Fill a small bowl with ice and water. When the timer goes off, using a slotted spoon, plunge the eggs immediately into the ice bath to halt the cooking.

- While the eggs cook, in a glass measuring cup, season **1½ cups buttermilk** with salt and **lots of freshly ground black pepper**—this will be the saucy base of your rice bowl.

MAKE THE CELERY-ONION SALAD:

- Thinly slice **3 celery stalks** on the bias. Place in a medium bowl and combine with the reserved sliced white onion and any **celery leaves**.

- Finely grate the **zest of 1 lemon** into the celery and squeeze the **juice of the lemon** in. Drizzle the salad with **olive oil**—enough to get things nice and glossy, but make sure you taste and maintain a bright, balanced dressing. Season with **salt** and **black pepper**.

SERVE:

- Divide the seasoned buttermilk among serving bowls.

- Pile some of the curried rice into each bowl.

- Peel and halve the boiled eggs and arrange half an egg in each bowl.

- Top each bowl with **2 ounces smoked whitefish**, breaking it into large pieces. Finish with a big handful of the celery-onion salad.

COLD NOODLES WITH GRATED TOMATO SAUCE & CHILI OIL

GOES WITH: PARTY CHIX (PAGE 185), SPICY COCONUT-SMOTHERED GREEN BEANS (PAGE 225)

SERVES 4

QUICK AS HECK!

The glory of this super-simps, no-cook grated tomato sauce is the tomatoes themselves, so be sure to get nice plump, deeply hued ones and let them ripen until they give a little when pressed lightly with your fingers. Anything less than a ripe tomato will yield a blander sauce. Grating tomatoes (yes, on your box grater) turns their flesh into sauce lickety-split. You'll amp it up with soy sauce, garlic, lemon juice, and olive oil and then slurp it all up with a bowl of bouncy chilled noods. This is peak, peak, peak summertime stuff.

PRODUCE

- 1¾ pounds ripe, juicy tomatoes (preferably heirloom)
- 2 garlic cloves
- 2 or 3 lemons
- 1 small bunch of basil
- 4 scallions

PROTEIN

- 4 large eggs

PANTRY

- 3 tablespoons extra-virgin olive oil
- 2 tablespoons low-sodium soy sauce, plus more
- Kosher salt
- 20 ounces fresh noodles (ramen or pasta)
- Toasted sesame seeds
- Chili oil, for serving

1 BOIL THE EGGS:

- Bring a large pot of water to a boil.

- Gently lower **4 large eggs** into the boiling water. Set a timer for 6 minutes.

- While the eggs boil, fill a medium bowl with ice and water. When the timer goes off, using a slotted spoon, transfer the eggs to the ice bath to chill—don't discard the boiling water because we'll use it for the noodles.

2 MEANWHILE, MAKE THE SAUCE:

- Set a box grater in a large bowl. Grate **1¾ pounds ripe, juicy tomatoes** (be careful, they may squirt!) on the large holes of the box grater (skins and all) until all that's left are the skins and eye of the tomato, and all the flesh has been grated.

- Finely grate **2 garlic cloves** into the tomato pulp. Juice **2 or 3 lemons** until you have ½ cup, then add it to the bowl.

- Whisk in **3 tablespoons olive oil** and **2 tablespoons low-sodium soy sauce**. Season with **salt** to taste—the sauce should be very flavorful; keep adding salt until you get there.

- Firmly whack **a big handful of basil sprigs** (reserve the rest of the bunch for later on) on

the countertop to bruise them and then add them to the tomato sauce, burying them in it to allow them to perfume the sauce. Keep the sauce chilled until ready to serve.

3 COOK THE NOODS:

- Add **a big handful of salt** to the reserved pot of boiling water. Add **20 ounces fresh noodles** and cook until al dente according to the package directions. Drain the noodles in a colander and rinse under cold water until chilled. Add the noodles to the bowl of sauce, along with **lots of sesame seeds**, and toss well to coat. (This can be chilled at this point for up to 8 hours before serving.)

4 SERVE:

- Thinly slice **4 scallions** on the bias.

- Divide the chilled tomato sauce and noodles among 4 serving bowls, discarding the whacked basil.

- Drizzle each bowl with **chili oil** and top with the sliced scallions, **some basil leaves**, and even more toasted sesame seeds.

- Cut the eggs in half, divide them among the bowls, and season the egg yolks with soy sauce.

UMAM LASAGN!

GOES WITH: TRIPLE THREAT GARLIC BREAD (PAGE 99), MOLLZ BALLZ (PAGE 142), SALTY COFFEE & PEANUT SLICE CREAM (PAGE 275)

PRODUCE

- 10 garlic cloves
- 3 pounds cremini mushrooms
- 4 to 7 large rosemary sprigs

DAIRY

- 8 tablespoons (1 stick) unsalted butter, at room temperature
- 7 cups whole milk
- 8 ounces fresh whole-milk mozzarella cheese
- 3 ounces Piave or Parmigiano Reggiano cheese, plus more for serving
- 1 pound fresh whole-milk ricotta cheese

PANTRY

- Kosher salt and freshly ground black pepper
- ¼ cup plus 3 tablespoons all-purpose flour
- 3 tablespoons white or red miso paste
- ½ cup extra-virgin olive oil, plus more for the pan
- 8 oil-packed anchovy fillets
- 1 (9-ounce package) oven-ready lasagna noodles
- 1 cup walnuts
- Nonstick cooking spray

Homemade lasagna has always been and will always be a project. I'm not gonna sugarcoat it. And if we're going to commit a lot of time to one dish, it better be memorable. We're building layers on layers of flavor and we're not holding back. It's called Umam Lasagn for a reason: miso paste, anchovies, mushrooms, walnuts, and nutty Piave cheese—all extremely high umami factor ingredients—together do the work of a long-simmered meaty ragù, with not a lick of meat in sight!

1 MAKE THE BÉCHAMEL SAUCE:

- In a large pot, melt **7 tablespoons unsalted butter** over medium heat. When the foaming subsides, grate **2 garlic cloves** into the pot, season with **salt and freshly ground black pepper**, and stir until fragrant but not browned, 1 minute.

- Add **¼ cup plus 3 tablespoons all-purpose flour** and whisk to combine with the butter. Cook, whisking occasionally (the mixture will be very thick), until light brown, 2 to 3 minutes. Very gradually, a big splash at a time, begin to add **7 cups whole milk**, whisking to incorporate each addition before adding the next. Once a few cups of the milk have been added, you can add the milk more swiftly.

- Raise the heat to maintain a low rolling boil, and cook until reduced to about 5½ cups, 18 to 22 minutes, stirring often. Season generously with salt and pepper. Let cool. Bear in mind that because we aren't cooking the lasagna noodles in salted water, you'll need to over-season the béchamel to account for the salt the noodles would have otherwise absorbed.

2 DO SOME PREP:

- Clean **3 pounds cremini mushrooms** by wiping off any stray dirt with a paper towel. Trim only the very tips of the stems. Tear the mushrooms into large, chunky pieces, dropping them into a large bowl as you go.

- Finely chop the remaining **8 garlic cloves**.

- Remove the leaves from as many **rosemary sprigs** as necessary to measure 2 tablespoons when they are finely chopped. Discard the stems.

- In a small bowl, combine **1 tablespoon unsalted butter** and **3 tablespoons miso paste**. Mix with a small spatula or spoon until smooth.

- Thinly slice **8 ounces mozzarella cheese** and finely grate **3 ounces Piave cheese** (you'll have about ¾ cup).

3 COOK THE MUSHROOMS:

- In a large heavy-bottomed pot, heat **a generous ⅓ cup olive oil** over high heat until very hot and smoking. (Not medium-high heat! High! Mushrooms contain lots of moisture, and we want to caramelize them, so high heat is in order here!) TURN YA BURNERS UP (PG 21)

- Add the mushrooms. Season generously with salt and pepper. Cook, stirring only once the mushrooms have lost all of their liquid (it will cook off—trust!) and are turning golden, 25 to 30 minutes.

- Reduce the heat to medium. Make a well in the center and add **8 oil-packed anchovy fillets**. Cook until they begin to sizzle and disintegrate, about 1 minute.

- Add another **glug of olive oil** to the pot, along with the garlic and half of the rosemary. Stir to combine and cook until fragrant but not browned, about 2 minutes.

- Add the miso butter and cook, stirring, for 1 minute, to let the flavors marry. If the miso sticks to the pot, just add **a splash of water** and scrape and stir to deglaze all of the yummy bits from the bottom of the pan. Taste and adjust the seasoning with salt and pepper.

(CONT. ON PAGE 118)

ASSEMBLE AND BAKE:

● Position a rack in the center of the oven. Preheat the oven to 375°F.

● Grease a 12-inch cast-iron skillet with **olive oil**.

● Spread a generous 1 cup béchamel on the bottom of the prepared skillet. Top with **a single layer of lasagna sheets**, breaking pieces to fit and form an even layer.

● Now start building the layers: Spread another generous 1 cup béchamel on the pasta, being sure to cover each and every inch of the sheets. Any parts that don't get covered may become brittle and dry during baking. Next, scatter one-third of the mushroom mixture on top, followed by one-fourth of each of the cheeses (mozzarella, Piave, and **ricotta**), dolloping it on top until the sauce is covered.

● Repeat this layering two more times. End with a final layer of lasagna sheets, followed by the remaining 1 cup béchamel and the remaining one-fourth of the cheeses.

● Finely chop **1 cup walnuts** and scatter them over the top, along with the remaining chopped rosemary.

● Spray a large piece of aluminum foil with **nonstick cooking spray** and cover the pan. Place the skillet on a large rimmed baking sheet to catch any potential drips. Transfer to the oven and bake until the cheeses are melted and the noodles pierce easily with the tip of a knife, 35 to 40 minutes. Raise the oven temperature to 450°F and carefully uncover the pan. Continue to bake until the top is golden, the nuts are toasted, and the edges are browned, 12 to 18 minutes.

● Let rest for at least 10 minutes before slicing the lasagna into pieces and serving, with more grated Piave over the top.

TANGLED LEEK 'ZA

(SERVES 4)

GOES WITH: CRISPY, CRUNCHY BROCC & GRAINS WITH SO. MUCH. MINT. (PAGE 78), MONOCHROMATIC MELON SALAD (PAGE 85), MOLLZ BALLZ (PAGE 142)

PRODUCE

- 1 large leek (9 to 12 ounces)
- 3 garlic cloves
- 9 thyme sprigs
- 1 lemon

DAIRY

- 4 ounces fresh whole-milk mozzarella cheese
- 4 ounces fontina cheese
- ¾ cup heavy cream
- Parmigiano Reggiano, for grating

PANTRY

- 1 (1-pound) ball store-bought pizza dough
- Extra-virgin olive oil
- Kosher salt and freshly ground black pepper
- Semolina or fine cornmeal, for dusting
- All-purpose flour, for stretching

This pizza is for onion lovers and onion lovers only, so make sure that describes you. Garlic and leeks are cooked in heavy cream to become the aromatic allium-y base for this fontina- and mozz-topped pie. Big piles of (more) fresh tangled leeks finish it off—some of them will char in the oven, and others become tender and jammy as they cook beneath. It's a showstopper, so make sure to have people around to congratulate you when you serve it.

- Pull a **1-pound ball of pizza dough** from the refrigerator and let it come to room temperature on the counter while you prep.

- Position a rack in the lower third of the oven.

- Preheat the oven to 500°F. Place a pizza stone or an overturned rimmed baking sheet on the rack.

DO SOME PREP:

- Thinly slice 4 inches of the dark greens of **1 large leek**. If the slices are dirty, wash and pat dry.

- Cut the white and light green parts of the leek crosswise into 4-inch pieces, discarding the hairy root end. Now slice the 4-inch pieces in half lengthwise, and thinly slice or julienne them, creating lots of very thin strands. If the leeks are dirty, wash and pat dry.

- Thinly slice **4 ounces mozzarella cheese**. Cube **4 ounces fontina cheese**.

- Smash and peel **3 garlic cloves**.

- Strip the leaves from **5 thyme sprigs**—you'll sprinkle these on at the end.

MAKE THE WHITE SAUCE:

- In a small skillet, heat **a few big glugs of olive oil** over medium heat. Add the leek greens and the smashed garlic. Season with **salt and freshly ground black pepper** and sauté until softened and translucent (do not brown), 3 to 4 minutes. Add **¾ cup heavy cream** and the remaining **4 thyme sprigs** and bring to a boil. Reduce the heat as needed to maintain a brisk simmer and cook, stirring, until the cream has reduced and slightly thickened, 4 to 5 minutes. Remove from the heat and zest **1 lemon** directly into the pan. (Halve the lemon and reserve for serving.) Stir to combine and season with salt and pepper. Lightly smash the now-softened garlic cloves into the sauce and transfer the sauce to the refrigerator until cool, about 10 minutes.

BUILD THE PIZZA:

- In a small bowl, toss the julienned leeks with **a few big glugs of olive oil**—they should be well coated. Season with salt and pepper.

- Generously dust the back of an overturned large rimmed baking sheet or a pizza peel with **semolina or fine cornmeal**. With **floured** hands, stretch the dough to a 9 × 15-inch rectangle and place it on the prepared baking sheet.[1] Give the sheet a shake to make sure the dough is mobile and not sticking. If it doesn't shake freely, it'll be impossible to slide it onto the pizza stone in the oven! Continue to shake the dough from time to time as you build the pizza to ensure it's loosey-goosey.

(CONT. ON PAGE 123)

[1] If using a pizza peel and a pizza stone, stretch the dough into a round or whatever shape will fit your stone and peel.

COOK ALONG!

VIDEO

● Remove and discard the thyme sprigs from the cream sauce. Spread the sauce onto the dough in an even layer, leaving a 1-inch border for the crust. Rip the slices of mozzarella into ragged pieces and scatter them across the top, along with the cubes of fontina. Finely grate **a dusting of Parmigiano Reggiano** over the top. Give the dough a shake and make sure it's movin'!

● Pile the tangle of leeks on top of the cheese layer. Drizzle the whole pie, including the crust, with some olive oil and sprinkle with more Parmigiano (careful not to get olive oil on the peel or baking sheet, or the dough may stick).

● Open the oven door. Starting from the back of the pizza stone or baking sheet, slide and shake the pizza off whatever you built it on in one swift movement so that the dough releases onto the stone or sheet in the oven.

● Bake until the crust is blistered and the leeks are frizzled and browned on the edges, 16 to 20 minutes. If the crust is browning more on one side than the other, rotate halfway through.

● Remove from the oven and top with a final drizzle of olive oil, a grating of Parm, and lots of black pepper. Sprinkle with the reserved thyme leaves. Let the pizza cool for a couple of minutes, and then cut it into pieces and serve with the lemon halves for squeezing on top!

RAREBIT MAC 'N' GREENS

GOES WITH: PUT THE LIME IN THE COCONUT CORN BREAD WITH SALTY COCONUT JAM (PAGE 132), PARTY CHIX (PAGE 185)

SERVES 8

PRODUCE

- 10 garlic cloves

- 14 ounces leafy greens, such as kale, spinach, collards, and/or mustard greens (about 2 bunches)

DAIRY

- 6 tablespoons (¾ stick) unsalted butter, plus more for the pan

- 1½ pounds mixed cheeses, such as extra-sharp cheddar, Gruyère, Emmenthaler, and/or fontina

- 1½ cups heavy cream

- 2 cups whole milk

- 2 ounces grated Parmigiano Reggiano (about ½ cup)

PANTRY

- Kosher salt and freshly ground black pepper

- 12 ounces curly pasta, such as cavatappi or rotini

- 1 (12-ounce) bottle of dark beer or stout, such as Guinness

- ⅓ cup all-purpose flour

- 3 tablespoons Dijon mustard

- 3 tablespoons Worcestershire sauce

- 1 cup panko bread crumbs

COOK ALONG!

VIDEO

You may be wondering what the heck Welsh rarebit (a British beer-and-cheese spread served on toast) and mac 'n' cheese (no explanation needed) have to do with each other. Allow me to explain: we're transforming that beer-and-cheese spread into a creamy béchamel sauce, tossing it with pasta, topping it with bread crumbs, and baking it until golden brown and bubbling, for the best of both worlds. Worcestershire sauce, dark stout, and Dijon mustard make up the backbone of this British pub–inspired mac 'n' cheese, and two whole bunches of greens baked right into it cover your vegetable quota for dinner.

1 DO SOME PREP:

- Position a rack in the center of the oven. Preheat the oven to 400°F.

- **Butter** a 9 × 13-inch baking dish.

- Bring a large pot of **salted** water to a boil.

- Lightly smash and peel **10 garlic cloves**. Thinly slice the cloves. IF YOU'RE GONNA USE IT, USE IT (PG 20)

- Grate **1½ pounds mixed cheeses** on the large holes of a box grater.

- Strip the leaves of **14 ounces leafy greens** from the stems. Tear the leaves into bite-size pieces.

- When the water boils, stir in **12 ounces curly pasta** and cook just short of al dente, 2 minutes shy of the package directions. Drain the pasta. Reserve the pot.

2 BUILD THE CHEESE SAUCE:

- Crack open **1 (12-ounce) bottle of dark beer.**

- In the same pot you cooked the pasta in, melt **4 tablespoons unsalted butter** over medium-high heat. Add the garlic and cook, stirring constantly, until softened and fragrant, 1 minute.

- Sprinkle **⅓ cup all-purpose flour** over the garlic and cook, whisking, for 1 minute.

- Gradually whisk in the beer until smooth.

- Whisking continuously, slowly add **1½ cups heavy cream**. Once incorporated, gradually add **2 cups whole milk**. Bring to a simmer and cook, whisking, until slightly thickened, 2 minutes.

- Reduce the heat to low and add the grated cheeses, including **2 ounces grated Parm**. Stir until nearly completely melted. Add **a few big spoonfuls each of Dijon mustard** and **Worcestershire sauce** (about 3 tablespoons each, but taste and add them as you see fit!).

- Season the sauce with **1½ teaspoons salt** and **lots and lots of freshly ground black pepper**. Like, so much pepper. It will need a lot, I promise!!!

- Stir the pasta into the cheese sauce, followed by the torn greens, stirring to distribute them evenly. They'll cook down further in the oven.

3 BAKE:

- Transfer the contents of the pot to the prepared baking dish. Bake until the top is golden and beginning to crisp, 15 to 20 minutes.

4 MEANWHILE, TOAST THE BREAD CRUMBS:

- In a medium skillet, melt the remaining **2 tablespoons unsalted butter** over medium-high heat. Add **1 cup panko bread crumbs** and toast, stirring often, until deeply golden brown, 4 to 6 minutes. Transfer the bread crumbs to a bowl and season with salt.

5 FINISH THE MAC:

- Remove the baking dish from the oven, scatter the bread crumbs evenly over the pasta, and return the dish to the oven. Continue to bake until the top is deeply golden brown and the sauce is thick and bubbling, 12 to 16 minutes. Let cool for 15 minutes before serving.

CRISPY RICE EGG-IN-A-HOLE

SERVES 2

GOES WITH: BLOODY MOLLY (PAGE 259),
MONOCHROMATIC MELON SALAD (PAGE 85)

QUICK AS HECK!

Every once in a while, Willett will drop a stroke of culinary genius on me out of nowhere and send me into a tailspin. Exhibit A: this ridiculously simple dish he pulled out of his big, beautiful brain one morning like no big deal. It starts with leftover crisped-up white rice in which a couple of sunny-side-up eggs get fried, just as you would egg-in-a-hole/-frame/whatever you grew up calling it. Creamy sliced avocado and chili crisp take it over the top. Why we aren't always frying our eggs in crispy rice, I will never know.

PRODUCE

- 1 avocado
- 1 lime
- 2 scallions

DAIRY

- 2 tablespoons (¼ stick) unsalted butter

PROTEIN

- 2 large eggs

PANTRY

- Kosher salt
- 1 tablespoon extra-virgin olive oil
- 2½ cups leftover cooled cooked white rice
- Chili oil, hot honey, or hot sauce

1 DO SOME PREP:

- Cut **1 avocado** in half, discard the pit, scoop out the flesh, and cut it into wedges. Season the avocado all over with **salt** and **a squeeze of lime juice** to keep it from oxidizing.

- Thinly slice **2 scallions** on an extreme bias.

2 CRISP THE RICE:

- Heat a large (10- or 11-inch) nonstick skillet over medium heat for 2 minutes. Add **2 tablespoons unsalted butter** and **a glug of olive oil**. Swirl to coat and melt the butter.

- Add **2½ cups cooled cooked white rice**. Season the rice with salt, toss and stir a few times to ensure all the rice is coated in fat, and then use a spatula to evenly distribute the rice in the pan. Cook, undisturbed, until deeply caramelized across the bottom and golden brown at the edges, 8 to 10 minutes. This takes some time, so don't rush it. You want that supremely crispy, nutty flavor.

- Use a spoon or spatula to break up the rice into a few large pieces and flip the pieces over in the skillet. You should now have mostly golden brown rice on top.

3 COOK THE EGGS:

- Make two 4-inch divots in the pan, scooting the rice aside to clear space for **2 large eggs**.

- Crack an egg into each divot. Season the eggs with salt and cover the pan with a lid or baking sheet. Cook until the whites are set but the yolks are still runny, 2 to 3 minutes.

4 SERVE:

- Slide the rice and eggs onto a large serving plate.

- Top with the sliced avocado and scallions, and **a generous drizzle of chili oil**. Squeeze the remaining **lime juice** over everything.

RAMEN NOODLES WITH SHROOMS & SOY BUTTER

SERVES 4

GOES WITH: TRIPLE THREAT GARLIC BREAD (PAGE 99), PURPLE SALAD (PAGE 71), CRISPY, CRUNCHY BROCC & GRAINS WITH SO. MUCH. MINT (PAGE 78); SPICED PEANUT SHORTBREAD (PAGE 284)

PRODUCE

- 1 pound mixed wild fresh mushrooms, such as shiitake, oyster, maitake, etc.[1]

- 6 garlic cloves

- 1 lemon

DAIRY

- 6 tablespoons (¾ stick) unsalted butter

- 1½ ounces grated Parmigiano Reggiano (about ⅓ cup)

PANTRY

- Kosher salt and freshly ground black pepper

- 3 tablespoons extra-virgin olive oil

- ¼ cup low-sodium soy sauce

- 18 ounces fresh ramen or udon noodles, or 12 ounces dried spaghetti

On most days, there are few things I want more than the umami trinity of crispy browned mushrooms, soy sauce, and Parmesan cheese—okay, maybe also a Martini Thrice (page 145). This dish uses fresh ramen or udon noodles, which you can find in most grocery stores—they're springy and squiggly and just more fun to eat (Sun Noodle makes fab and widely available fresh ramen). If not, there's always spaghetti. Take your time with the mushrooms. Because we're adding them all to the pot at once, it will take at least ten minutes to cook off all their water and start browning. The wait is worth it.

1 DO SOME PREP:

- Bring a large pot of **salted** water to a boil. Season it lightly—'cause there are a lot of salty ingredients coming down the pipeline later on.

- Tear or cut **1 pound mixed wild mushrooms** into 2-inch pieces. They don't have to be the same shape, just generally the same size.

- Thinly slice **6 garlic cloves**.

2 BUILD THE MUSHROOM SAUCE:

- Heat a large Dutch oven over medium-high heat. Add **3 tablespoons olive oil** and swirl to coat. Once the oil just begins to emit wisps of smoke from the surface, add all the mushrooms at once and give a good stir to coat in the oil. Season lightly with **salt**. Cook, stirring only every 2 to 3 minutes or so, until the mushrooms are golden brown and crisp all over, 10 to 14 minutes.

- Reduce the heat to medium-low and add **2 tablespoons unsalted butter** and the sliced garlic. Cook, stirring, until the garlic is very fragrant but has not yet browned, 1 minute. Transfer the mushrooms to a plate (it's okay if some of the garlic sticks behind in the pot).

- Add the remaining **4 tablespoons unsalted butter**, **¼ cup soy sauce**, and **¾ cup water** from the pot that the noodles will cook in. Bring the liquid to a simmer and then remove the pot from the heat, cover with a lid, and keep warm until the noodles are cooked.

3 COOK THE NOODLES:

- Drop **18 ounces fresh ramen noodles** into the pot of boiling water. Cook until al dente according to the package directions. Using tongs, add the noodles to the pot of soy butter (reserve the pot of noodle cooking water). Return the pot to medium-low heat and start adding **handfuls of grated Parmigiano Reggiano** to the noodles, one at a time, tossing with tongs as you go and adding more of the noodle water until all the Parm has been incorporated and the sauce is very creamy, saucy, and glossy.

- Add the mushrooms and **lots of freshly ground black pepper** and toss again, loosening with more noodle water as needed.

- Remove from the heat and finely grate the **zest of 1 lemon** into the pot. Taste and add more salt here as needed.

4 SERVE:

- Divide the noodles among serving bowls and top each serving with more pepper to finish.

[1] To extend the shelf life of fresh mushrooms, immediately remove them from their plastic containers, wrap them in a double layer of paper towels, and place in a bowl or bag that allows them to breathe, then store in the fridge. Keeping them in their original plastic will speed up their deterioration, as the plastic traps moisture, which leads to rot and slime.

COOK ALONG!

AUDIO

COZY BOWL

GOES WITH: NOTHING. THIS IS A COMPLETE MEAL, AND WHEN EATEN AT THE RIGHT MOMENT, IS PERFECT ON ITS OWN.

QUICK AS HECK!

While you might crave a greasy breakfast sandwich or burger when you're hungover, I crave a cozy bowl. This is about as gentle as a meal can be—buttered rice and fluffy pillows of gingery eggs come together in what can only be described as a bowl full of coze. This is your moment to embrace fatty on fatty and resist the temptation to add lots of acid and spice . . . though, of course, you do you. This dish will settle the stomach after a long night out and prepare you for a day of couch lazing. Sometimes you gotta go easy on yourself.

PRODUCE

- 3 Persian cucumbers
- 1 (1-inch) piece of fresh ginger

DAIRY

- 6 tablespoons (¾ stick) unsalted butter

PROTEIN

- 4 large eggs

PANTRY

- 2 cups short-grain white rice
- Kosher salt
- 1 teaspoon toasted sesame oil
- Toasted sesame seeds, for serving

1 MAKE THE BUTTERED RICE:

- In a fine-mesh strainer, rinse **2 cups short-grain white rice** thoroughly under cold running water until the water is no longer cloudy, 1 minute.

- In a medium saucepan with a tight-fitting lid, combine the rice, **2½ cups water**, and **¾ teaspoon salt**. Bring to a simmer over medium-high heat, and as soon as it reaches a simmer, reduce the heat to very low, cover, and set a timer for 18 minutes. When the timer goes off, remove from the heat and keep covered for at least 10 minutes (or longer if need be) to finish steaming properly.

- Cut **6 tablespoons unsalted butter** into 6 pieces. Add 4 tablespoons to the pot of rice and stir and fluff with a fork to incorporate. Season with salt to taste. The more you add, the more it will all begin to taste like buttered popcorn, and you'll be a very happy person.

2 SEASON THE CUKES:

- Cut **3 Persian cucumbers** in half lengthwise, then crosswise into ½-inch-thick half-moons. Season the cukes with salt.

3 SCRAMBLE THE EGGS:

- In a medium bowl, vigorously whisk **4 large eggs** and **1 teaspoon toasted sesame oil** until no streaks remain. Finely grate **1 (1-inch) knob of ginger** into the eggs. Season with salt.

- Heat a medium nonstick skillet over medium heat for 2 minutes. Add the remaining 2 tablespoons butter and swirl to melt. As soon as the butter melts, add the eggs, and working quickly with a spatula, make large, sweeping figure-eight motions, dragging the outer eggs into the center until the eggs are just set and still slightly wet on top, 30 seconds (if your pan was properly preheated).

4 SERVE:

- Put a heaping mound of buttered rice in each of 2 bowls. Top with the scrambled eggs and a pile of cukes. Garnish with **lotssss of toasted sesame seeds**. IF YOU'RE GONNA USE IT, USE IT (PG 20)

PUT THE LIME IN THE
COCONUT CORN BREAD

WITH SALTY COCONUT JAM

[SERVES 6 TO 8] [GOES WITH: RAREBIT MAC 'N' GREENS (PAGE 124), CRISPY ORECCHIETTE WITH SPICY SAUSAGE & COLLARD RAGÙ (PAGE 111)]

PRODUCE

- 4 limes

DAIRY

- 12 tablespoons (1½ sticks) unsalted butter, plus more for the pan and serving

PROTEIN

- 6 large eggs

PANTRY

- 1½ cups (297g) sugar
- 2 (13.7-ounce) cans coconut cream
- 1½ cups (180g) all-purpose flour
- ⅔ cup (110g) fine cornmeal
- 1 teaspoon baking powder
- ¾ teaspoon baking soda
- 2 teaspoons kosher salt
- ¼ cup unsweetened finely shredded coconut

This recipe started as a dream about a coconut custard–filled corn bread—something that would sit happily on the table next to a pot of meaty braised short ribs or the like. I tried, and I tried, but the custard sank to the bottom every time. Twelve corn breads later, I had to change strategies. Now we have an unfathomably moist, tender, coconut-and-lime-scented corn bread and a salty coconut jam inspired by Malaysian kaya—a thick, spreadable condiment made (in this case) of coconut cream, sugar, and lime. It might not be the mic-drop corn bread moment I was looking for, but lemme tell you, it's damnnnn delicious.

1 **DO SOME PREP:**

- Position a rack in the center of the oven. Preheat the oven to 350°F.

- **Butter** a 10- or 11-inch ovenproof skillet.

- Melt **12 tablespoons unsalted butter**.

2 **MAKE THE BATTER:**

- In a large bowl, combine **1 cup (198g) sugar** and the **zest of 3 limes**. Rub with your fingers to incorporate the zest and expel its oils into the sugar.

- Whisk in the melted butter, followed by **2 large eggs**, the **juice of 3 limes**, and **1 (13.7-ounce) well-shaken can coconut cream**.

- In a medium bowl, whisk together **1½ cups (180g) all-purpose flour**, **⅔ cup (110g) fine cornmeal**, **1 teaspoon baking powder**, **¾ teaspoon baking soda**, and **1 teaspoon salt**.

- Add the dry ingredients to the wet ones. Stir together until no visible bits of flour remain.

3 **BAKE:**

- Scrape the batter into the prepared skillet. Evenly scatter **¼ cup finely shredded coconut** over the top. Bake until deeply golden on the edges and a toothpick inserted into the center comes out dry, 48 to 52 minutes. Let cool.

4 **MAKE THE SALTY COCONUT JAM:**

- Separate the remaining **4 eggs**, placing the yolks in a large bowl and making sure to remove as much of the white as possible. We don't want any of the whites in the jam. They'll coagulate, and it will get all weird. Whisk the yolks (reserve the whites for another use).

- In a medium saucepan, combine the remaining **1 (13.7-ounce) can coconut cream**, the remaining **½ cup (99g) sugar**, the **zest of the remaining lime**, and the **juice of ½ lime**. Cook over medium heat, stirring until the mixture is hot but not yet boiling and the sugar has dissolved.

- While whisking constantly, slowly pour the coconut mixture into the bowl with the egg yolks and continue whisking until it has all been added. Scrape the contents of the bowl back into the medium saucepan and set it over medium-low heat.

- Cook, stirring and scraping constantly with a heatproof rubber spatula, until the mixture reaches a very low simmer and thickens and the spatula leaves a trail of visible pan behind in its wake. Be patient. This could take up to 25 minutes, depending on how hot your pot is. You don't want to boil or rapidly simmer this mixture, or it will not turn out smooth. If it feels like it's cooking too quickly or simmering rapidly, reduce the heat.

- Once the jam is thick, remove it from the heat. Stir in the remaining **1 teaspoon salt** and transfer to a small bowl. Place plastic wrap on the top to keep it from developing a skin as it cools.

5 **SERVE:**

- Cut the corn bread into wedges and serve warm with salty coconut jam and more butter, OR level it up and crisp each slice in a butter-sliced skillet. WHEN IN DOUBT, REFRY (PG 22)

STUFFED FOCACCIA

WITH SPICY GREENS & CHEESE

SERVES 6 TO 8

GOES WITH: MOLLZ BALLZ (PAGE 142), DRUNKEN CACIO E PEPE (PAGE 96), GREEN CHICKEN SOUP WITH CHICKPEAS & SIZZLED CORIANDER (PAGE 197)

PRODUCE

- 1 large white or yellow onion
- 7 garlic cloves
- 1 lemon

DAIRY

- 1½ ounces grated Parmigiano Reggiano (about ⅓ cup)
- 8 ounces fresh whole-milk mozzarella cheese
- 8 ounces fresh whole-milk ricotta cheese

FROZEN

- 1 (16-ounce) package frozen chopped spinach or kale, thawed

PANTRY

- 3½ cups (420g) all-purpose flour
- ¾ teaspoon active dry yeast
- Kosher salt and freshly ground black pepper
- Extra-virgin olive oil
- 4 large oil-packed anchovy fillets
- Red pepper flakes
- ¼ cup sesame seeds
- Flaky sea salt

The vision was clear: to fuse two of the greatest pizza dough spin-offs, calzone and focaccia, into one epic creation. The journey was long and windy, with lots of flops along the way, but we finally did it. World, please meet Stuffed Focaccia. This one is loaded with spicy sautéed greens and not one, not two, but three cheeses, and then absolutely smothered in sesame seeds, because the only thing I've ever loved more than crusty, tender, springy fresh focaccia is crusty, tender, springy fresh sesame focaccia. This recipe requires a little forethought, so make sure to plan to make it twenty-four hours in advance. Most of those hours are inactive ones, but you'll have to plan for them nonetheless.

1 THE DAY BEFORE YOU'D LIKE TO EAT THE FOCACCIA, START THE DOUGH:

- In a large bowl, whisk together 3½ cups (420g) all-purpose flour, ¾ teaspoon active dry yeast, and 1 tablespoon plus 1 teaspoon kosher salt. Fill a measuring cup with 2 cups warm water and add 2 tablespoons olive oil. Gradually add the water mixture to the dry ingredients, stirring with a wooden spoon until a shaggy and very wet dough forms. Scrape down the sides of the bowl with a rubber spatula, cover with plastic wrap, and transfer to the refrigerator for at least 12 hours and up to overnight.

2 PROOF THE DOUGH:

- The next day, about 5 hours before you want to eat, remove the dough from the fridge. Set the oven to 350°F and let it heat up for 1 to 2 minutes, until just warm. No longer! Don't walk away! We aren't cooking anything, just warming the oven to encourage faster dough rising. Turn off the oven and place the dough in the bowl (still covered) inside to rise until puffy, bubbling, and doubled in size, about 3 hours.

3 AS THE DOUGH RISES, DO SOME PREP:

- Chop 1 large onion.

- Peel 7 garlic cloves. Thinly slice 5 of them. Reserve the other 2 for grating later.

- Drain 1 (16-ounce) package frozen chopped spinach in a colander. Squeeze and squeeze with all your might to expel as much water as possible.

4 MAKE THE FILLING:

- In a large skillet, heat 3 tablespoons olive oil over medium-high heat. Add the chopped onion and 4 large oil-packed anchovy fillets, season with kosher salt and freshly ground black pepper, and cook, stirring occasionally, until the onion is softened and just beginning to turn golden brown, about 8 minutes.

- Add the sliced garlic and a big pinch of red pepper flakes. Continue to cook, stirring, until the garlic is softened, about 2 minutes.

- Add the spinach and cook, stirring, to marry the flavors and cook off any remaining water, 2 to 3 minutes. Remove from the heat.

- Stir in 1½ ounces grated Parm, then grate in the remaining 2 garlic cloves and the zest of 1 lemon. Mix to combine and taste and adjust the seasoning with kosher salt, black pepper, and red pepper flakes. Let cool.

5 STUFF THE FOCACCIA:

- When the dough has finished rising, lightly coat a 9 × 13-inch baking dish with olive oil. Line the baking dish with parchment paper and then generously oil the parchment with a few glugs of olive oil.

(CONT. ON PAGE 136)

COOK ALONG!

VIDEO

● Smear a large rubber spatula with olive oil and, in one confident movement, scrape around the bowl, tipping it over the baking dish to release the dough into the pan. Try not to disturb any bubbles that have formed in the dough.

● Dip your fingers in the oil that has accumulated in the baking dish and carefully dimple and stretch the dough to meet the outer edges. The dough will naturally relax and spread into the corners on its own, so don't worry if it doesn't reach the edges at this point.

● Using your fingers, gently pile and scatter the spinach filling over the dough, all the way to the edges.

● Slice **8 ounces mozzarella cheese** as thinly as possible. Distribute the mozzarella over the filling.

● With the oiled fingers of both hands, and working from the short end of the baking dish, confidently creep your fingers under one-half of the dough, taking hold of the underside. Lift the dough, folding it over into the center. Re-oil your fingers and repeat on the other short side, being sure to bring this second half to the middle of the dish to meet the other half of the dough, edge to edge. The dough will be sticky enough to hold together, but feel free to pinch, seal, and poke any rogue filling back into the center or into the openings on the sides.

● Cover the baking dish with plastic wrap and let rise on your countertop for 30 minutes, until the dough is a bit more puffed and the indentation from an oiled fingertip springs back ever so slightly.[1]

● In the meantime, preheat the oven to 450°F.

6 TOP AND BAKE:

● Drizzle the top of the dough generously with **olive oil**, sprinkle with **¼ cup sesame seeds**, dollop with **8 ounces ricotta cheese**, and season with **flaky sea salt**.

● Transfer to the oven and bake, rotating it halfway through, until the focaccia is deeply golden on the top and bottom (if your baking dish is glass, you'll be able to check this easily), 50 to 60 minutes.

● Let cool for 10 minutes. Run a metal spatula around the edges and under the focaccia to free it from the dish. Transfer to a wire rack, slide the parchment paper out from under it, and let the focaccia sit until just cool enough to handle. Slice into wedges, squares, or strips, and eat!

---

[1] This indicates that when the dough hits the hot oven, she'll still have it in her to rise and puff a bit more. This is called oven spring, and it's a good thing! If the indentation of your finger seems to deflate the dough, the dough has over-proofed. Use this as a learning moment and don't stress—it happens. Just remember to decrease your rising time a bit the next time you make this recipe.

SURF

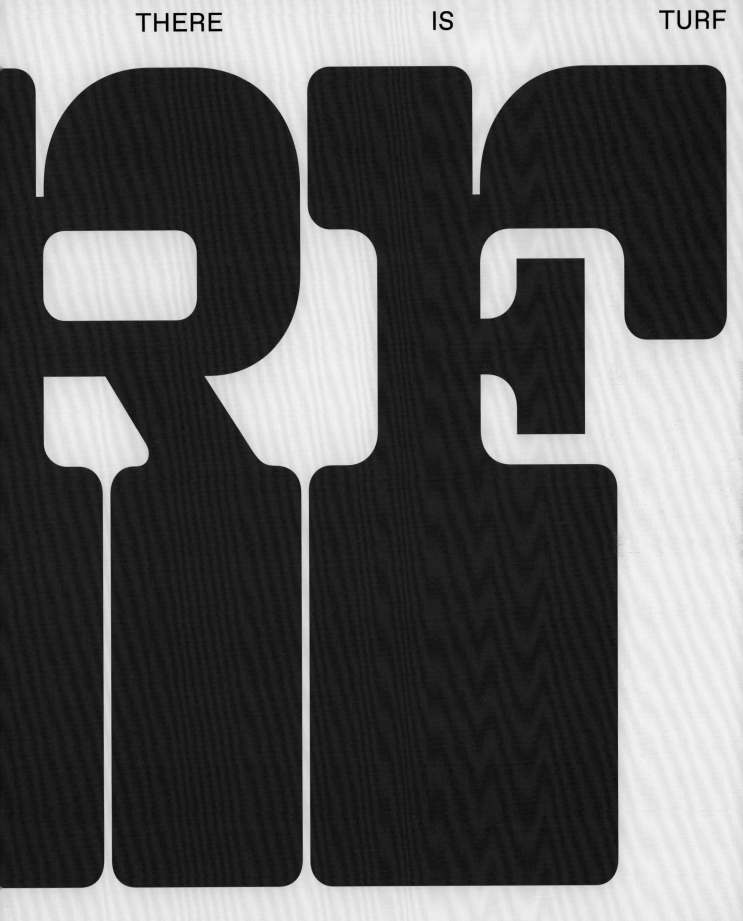

SKIRT STEAK WITH JUICY TOMATOES & SALSA MACHA

GOES WITH: CRISPY POTATO SKINS WITH FRIED HERB AIOLI (PAGE 226), CRISPY, CRUNCHY BROCC & GRAINS WITH SO. MUCH. MINT. (PAGE 78), PURPLE SALAD (PAGE 71)

SERVES 4

QUICK AS HECK!

This recipe features a very loose interpretation of salsa macha, a Mexican peanut-and-chile salsa that I could eat like soup. Traditionally, it's made with whole dried chiles that are toasted and blended together to form a homogeneous sauce. This quickie version comes together in a single small pot and uses ground chiles and spices instead. Turn this into tacos for a crowd by adding tortillas and cilantro, or try this salsa on roasted sweet potatoes (as seen in *Cook This Book*).

PRODUCE

- 3 garlic cloves
- 12 ounces ripe tomatoes (any kind)

PROTEIN

- 1½ pounds quick-cooking steak, such as skirt or flank

PANTRY

- ½ cup roasted, salted peanuts
- ⅓ cup plus 1 tablespoon extra-virgin olive oil, plus more for the pan
- 3 tablespoons toasted sesame seeds
- 1½ teaspoons red pepper flakes
- 1½ teaspoons chipotle chile powder or smoked paprika
- Kosher salt and freshly ground black pepper
- 4 tablespoons apple cider vinegar, plus more to taste
- Flaky sea salt

1 MAKE THE SALSA MACHA:

- Crush **½ cup roasted, salted peanuts** with the bottom of a saucepan.

- In a small saucepan, combine the peanuts, **⅓ cup olive oil**, and **3 tablespoons toasted sesame seeds** and cook over medium-low heat, swirling the pan often, until the peanuts are deeply golden brown and toasted, 4 to 6 minutes.

- Remove the saucepan from the heat and stir in **1½ teaspoons red pepper flakes**, **1½ teaspoons chipotle chile powder**, and **2 teaspoons kosher salt**.

- Finely grate **3 garlic cloves** into the salsa macha (while still hot! The residual heat will cook off the raw garlic flavor). It will sizzle and sputter. Stir well and set aside. IT'S ALL IN THE SAUCE (PG 21)

2 PREP THE TOMATOES:

- Cut **12 ounces ripe tomatoes** into irregular 1- to 2-inch shapes. Transfer to a bowl and season with **a splash of apple cider vinegar** and some **kosher salt**.

3 SEASON AND COOK THE STEAKS:

- Cut **1½ pounds steak** crosswise into 5-inch pieces. Season the steaks all over with kosher salt and **freshly ground black pepper**. Coat the steaks in a bit of **olive oil**.

- Heat a large cast-iron skillet over high heat (!) for several minutes until RIPPING hot. Add **a big glug of olive oil** to the skillet, and swirl to coat, making sure there's a thin layer of oil in the pan. Once the oil is visibly showing signs of smoke, arrange some of the steaks in the skillet in a single layer, without overcrowding the pan. Cook, undisturbed, until well browned underneath, 2 to 3 minutes. (Don't touch! This is your moment to trust the process and know that high heat equals good browning and deep flavor.) Flip and cook for 30 seconds to 1 minute longer (if the steaks are thick, 1 minute; if they're quite thin, 30 seconds will suffice). Transfer to a cutting board to rest and repeat with the remaining steaks. TURN YA BURNERS UP (PG 21)

- Once all the steaks have been cooked and the skillet is no longer on the burner, pour the salsa macha into the skillet and stir to scrape up any of the yummy bits on the bottom of the pan. Stir in **a few more tablespoons of apple cider vinegar**, to taste (it should be very vibrant).

4 SERVE:

- Slice the steaks crosswise and transfer to a serving platter.

- Spoon the tomatoes and their juices over the steaks. Drizzle the salsa macha all over and season with **flaky sea salt**.

MOLLZ BALLZ

GOES WITH: UMAM LASAGN! (PAGE 116), TRIPLE THREAT GARLIC BREAD (PAGE 99), DRUNKEN CACIO E PEPE (PAGE 96)

PRODUCE

- 12 garlic cloves
- 1 bunch of mint
- 1 large yellow onion

DAIRY

- ½ cup fresh whole-milk ricotta cheese
- 2 ounces grated Parmigiano Reggiano (½ cup), plus more for serving
- 3 tablespoons unsalted butter

PROTEIN

- 2 large eggs
- ½ pound spicy Italian sausage, casings removed
- ¾ pound 80% lean ground beef

PANTRY

- 4 tablespoons extra-virgin olive oil, plus more for drizzling
- Kosher salt and freshly ground black pepper
- 6 oil-packed anchovy fillets, plus 1½ teaspoons of their oil
- 1¼ cups panko bread crumbs
- Red pepper flakes
- 1 (28-ounce) can tomato puree
- Garlic-rubbed toast, for serving (optional)

I've never been much of a spag and balls girl, but I do LOVE a side of meatballs. From my perspective, meatballs belong on garlic-rubbed toast, or at least alongside it. Spaghetti isn't sturdy enough to handle my balls. These are BIG meatballs—the size of tennis balls—because that's how I like them. And while they might look classic at a glance, they've got a lot going on inside. Umami anchovies for depth of flavor, creamy ricotta for moistness, and a butt-load of fresh mint take them to a very delicious, extra-special place.

1 MAKE THE MEATBALLS:

- In a medium bowl, whisk together **2 large eggs, 6 grated garlic cloves, ½ cup ricotta cheese, 2 ounces grated Parmigiano Reggiano, 2 tablespoons olive oil, 2½ teaspoons salt, 1½ teaspoons anchovy oil** from the tin, and **lots of freshly ground black pepper.**

- Add **1¼ cups panko bread crumbs,** whisking until well hydrated by the egg mixture.

- Finely chop the leaves of **about half of 1 bunch of mint.** Add the mint and **½ pound spicy Italian sausage** to the panko mixture, and work with your hands until the meat is evenly distributed. Add **¾ pound ground beef** and work together gently until well mixed.

- Divide the meat into 8 equal portions and roll them into balls—they'll be about the size of tennis balls. Transfer to a rimmed baking sheet or large plate.

2 MAKE THE SAUCE:

- Finely chop **1 large yellow onion.**

- Thinly slice the remaining **6 garlic cloves.**

- In a large Dutch oven, heat **a few more glugs of olive oil** over high heat. Add the meatballs in a single layer and cook, turning every minute or so, until browned in most areas, 6 to 7 minutes total. Transfer to a plate—the meatballs will still be raw in the center but will finish cooking in the sauce later on. Pour off all but 2 tablespoons of fat from the skillet.

- Reduce the heat to medium, add the chopped onions, sliced garlic, **6 oil-packed anchovy fillets,** and **a pinch or two of red pepper flakes,** and cook, stirring often, until the onions are translucent and just barely beginning to brown at the edges, 6 to 8 minutes.

- Stir in **1 (28-ounce) can tomato puree, 3 tablespoons unsalted butter,** and **a few more mint sprigs** (reserving some for garnish). Season the sauce with salt—it'll need quite a bit. Bring the sauce to a simmer, then reduce the heat as needed to maintain a very gentle simmer and cook until slightly thickened, 4 to 6 minutes.

- Nestle the meatballs back into the sauce, cover the pot, and cook over medium heat, turning the meatballs occasionally, for 8 minutes. Uncover the pot and continue to cook, reducing the heat as necessary if the sauce is boiling too rapidly, until the meatballs are springy/bouncy when pressed with your fingers and cooked through and the sauce has reduced, 8 to 10 minutes.

3 SERVE:

- Pick the leaves of the remaining **mint,** scatter the leaves over the balls with more Parm, and drizzle generously with olive oil. Serve with garlic-rubbed toast alongside, if desired.

COOK ALONG!
AUDIO

COOK ALONG!
VIDEO

DRINK

BREAK

MARTINI THRICE

MAKES 1 STIFF DRINK

- Ice
- 2½ ounces gin
- ½ ounce dry vermouth
- Splash of olive brine
- Splash of pickled onion or cornichon brine
- Green olive, choice of pickle, and lemon twist, for garnish

This is what happens when you take a classic martini and you "MORE IS MORE" that shit. We're leaning into the dirty martini and adding ALL the possible garnishes because they each bring something that complements that cold, savory brine: bright lemon zest, vinegary pickles, and meaty olives. Introducing the Martini Thrice, made with gin, served up, cold as hell, extremely dirty, with not one, not two, but three garnishes. Please put your martini glasses in the freezer NOW.

● In an **ice**-filled cocktail shaker, combine **2½ ounces gin, ½ ounce dry vermouth, a big splash of olive brine,** and **a slightly smaller splash of pickled onion brine.** Stir vigorously until the cocktail shaker is really freakin' cold.

● Strain into a chilled martini glass and garnish with **an olive, a pickle of your choice,** and **a twist of lemon zest.**

CRISPY SALMON WITH COCONUT RICE & CRACKLE SAUCE

GOES WITH: SPICY COCONUT-SMOTHERED GREEN BEANS (PAGE 225), BRUSSELS SPROUTS WITH SHALLOTS & STICKY FISH SAUCE (PAGE 72)

SERVES 4

QUICK AS HECK!

The key to crispy-skinned salmon (or any piece of skin-on fish) is patting it dry and starting it skin-side down in a cold nonstick skillet. As the skillet heats up, the skin begins to expel some of its fat, and after ten-ish minutes, you're left with evenly golden brown, shattery skin that's been fried in its own fat. With regard to the garlic-peanut crackle sauce, bear in mind that it should be spicier and saltier than you're comfortable spooning straight to the face because it's ultimately going to be served with a fatty piece of fish and a pile of coconut rice. Don't hold back.

PRODUCE

- 1 English (hothouse) cucumber
- 2 garlic cloves
- 1 (½-inch) piece of fresh ginger

PROTEIN

- 4 (6-ounce) skin-on salmon fillets

PANTRY

- 2 cups long-grain white rice
- 1 (13.5-ounce) can full-fat coconut milk
- Kosher salt
- ½ cup roasted, salted peanuts
- ¼ cup extra-virgin olive oil
- 3 tablespoons sesame seeds
- 1½ teaspoons red pepper flakes
- 1 teaspoon ground turmeric
- 1 teaspoon honey

1 START THE COCONUT RICE:

- In a fine-mesh strainer, rinse **2 cups long-grain white rice** until the water runs clear. Drain well and add to a medium saucepan with a tight-fitting lid.

- Crack open **1 (13.5-ounce) can full-fat coconut milk**. Set aside a few tablespoons of the coconut milk in a small bowl. Stir the remaining coconut milk into the saucepan with the rice, **¾ cup water**, and **a big pinch of salt**. Bring to a simmer over medium-high heat. As soon as it simmers, reduce the heat to as low as possible, cover with the lid, and set a timer for 16 minutes. When the timer goes off, remove the pan from the heat and keep covered until ready to serve.

- While the rice cooks, thinly slice **1 English cucumber** crosswise (use a mandoline if you have one!). Toss the sliced cucumber with salt to taste in a medium bowl and keep chilled until ready to serve.

2 MAKE THE CRACKLE SAUCE:

- Chop or coarsely crush **½ cup roasted, salted peanuts**. In a large nonstick skillet, combine the chopped peanuts, **¼ cup olive oil,** and **3 tablespoons sesame seeds**. Set the skillet over medium heat and cook, stirring often, until the peanuts are several shades darker and the sesame seeds are toasted, 6 to 8 minutes.

- Transfer to a small bowl. While the mixture is still hot, immediately finely grate **2 garlic cloves** and **1 (½-inch) piece of fresh ginger** right into the oil. Stir in **1½ teaspoons red pepper flakes**, **1 teaspoon ground turmeric**, **1 teaspoon honey**, and the reserved coconut milk and season the sauce with salt. YOU'RE PROBS NOT USING ENOUGH ... SALT (PG 20)

3 COOK THE SALMON:

- Wipe out the nonstick skillet with a paper towel. Season **4 (6-ounce) skin-on salmon fillets** all over with salt. Working in batches if needed, arrange the salmon fillets, skin-side down, in the skillet and set over medium heat. Cook, pressing down on the top of the salmon occasionally to encourage it to make contact with the pan, until the skin is golden and very crisp, 7 to 9 minutes. If the skin's not looking crispy enough, keep cooking! Don't settle for anything less than crisp.

- Flip the fillets and cook until the salmon is mostly opaque on the sides, with a slight hint of translucence, 1 to 2 minutes longer.[1]

4 SERVE:

- Fluff the coconut rice with a fork and divide it among shallow bowls. Top each bowl with a salmon fillet and a pile of salted cucumbers. Drizzle the crackle sauce over the top.

[1] This timing will yield salmon that is cooked to medium; adjust according to your doneness preference and the thickness of your fillets.

COOK ALONG!

AUDIO

HOT SAUCE– **SHORT RIBS** WITH WINTER
BRAISED SQUASH

GOES WITH: PUT THE LIME IN THE COCONUT CORN BREAD WITH
SALTY COCONUT JAM (PAGE 132), PICKLE-MARINATED FETA (PAGE 65),
SPICY COCONUT-SMOTHERED GREEN BEANS (PAGE 225)

SERVES 6

PRODUCE

- 1 large or 2 medium red onions
- 1 (5-inch) piece of fresh ginger
- 1 garlic head
- 2 delicata or other winter squash (about 1½ pounds)
- 1 bunch of collard greens

PROTEIN

- 4½ pounds bone-in short ribs

PANTRY

- 3 cups apple cider vinegar
- ¾ cup Frank's RedHot cayenne pepper sauce
- ½ cup low-sodium soy sauce
- ½ cup packed brown sugar
- Kosher salt
- 3 dried bay leaves
- 3 cinnamon sticks
- Cooked white rice, for serving

Rich and fatty short ribs really shine when cooked low and slow in a spicy, acidic mixture of hot sauce and apple cider vinegar. Though this recipe takes a couple of hours, most of that is hands-off time—you're literally dumping a bunch of stuff into a pot and letting it ride. No searing is necessary, thanks to a jump-start in a hot oven that helps caramelize the ribs before they stew. A side of corn bread is a must.

1 DO SOME PREP:

- Position a rack in the lower third of the oven. Preheat the oven to 450°F.

- Cut **1 large red onion** into 1-inch-thick wedges.

- Thinly slice **1 (5-inch) piece of fresh ginger.** (No need to peel.)

- Peel and smash all the cloves from **1 garlic head.**

2 START THE BRAISE:

- In a large Dutch oven with a tight-fitting lid, combine **3 cups apple cider vinegar, 1 cup water, ¾ cup Frank's RedHot sauce, ½ cup low-sodium soy sauce, ½ cup packed brown sugar,** and **1 tablespoon plus 2 teaspoons salt.** Bring to a boil over high heat, whisking to dissolve the sugar and salt.

- Add **3 bay leaves, 3 cinnamon sticks,** the ginger, half of the red onion wedges, and the garlic cloves. Nestle **4½ pounds bone-in short ribs** into the pot, in as even a layer as possible. Cover the pot and transfer to the oven. Immediately reduce the oven temperature to 350°F.

- Braise, basting the top of the meat every hour, until the meat is tender, 3 hours.

3 ADD THE SQUASH AND FINISH:

- While the meat braises, halve **2 delicata squash.** Scoop out and discard the seeds and cut each half crosswise into ¾-inch-thick half-moons.

- When the meat is tender, remove the Dutch oven from the oven and discard any bones that the meat has fallen away from. Add the squash half-moons and the remaining red onion wedges to the pot, nuzzling them beneath the braising liquid.

- Return the pot to the oven, uncovered, and braise the squash until just barely tender, 15 to 20 minutes.

- Remove and discard the thick stems from **1 bunch of collard greens.** Tear the leaves into irregular pieces, remove the pot from the oven, and add the collards to the stew. Stir to combine and return the pot to the oven. Braise until the collards are wilted and softened and the squash is tender, about 15 more minutes.

- Taste the cooking liquid and season with salt to taste.

- If desired, skim any fat from the surface of the braise. Divide the braise among rice-filled serving dishes.

CRISPY CORNMEAL CALAMARI WITH FRIED BASIL & OTHER YUMMY STUFF

GOES WITH: CUCUMBER BAG SALAD WITH MISO-POPPY DRESSING (PAGE 93), PUT THE LIME IN THE COCONUT CORN BREAD WITH SALTY COCONUT JAM (PAGE 132)

SERVES 4

QUICK AS HECK!

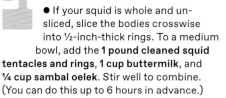

PRODUCE

- 2 large shallots
- 3 limes
- 1 small bunch of basil

DAIRY

- 1 cup buttermilk

PROTEIN

- 1 pound cleaned squid tentacles and tubes

PANTRY

- ½ cup sambal oelek (Indonesian chili sauce)
- Kosher salt
- ½ cup mayonnaise
- 1½ cups all-purpose flour
- ¾ cup cornmeal
- 4 cups vegetable oil or canola oil, for frying

God, I love calamari. In fact, it's the dish that inspired this book (did you read the intro??), and I firmly believe we should all be making it more frequently at home. Lots of people shy away from cooking squid, but it's one of the quickest (and cheapest) protein options out there. This is a highly rewarding recipe to get you past your hesitation. It's not only simple, it's fried, so it's basically guaranteed to be delicious. More calamari, 2024!

1 SOAK THAT SQUID:

- If your squid is whole and un-sliced, slice the bodies crosswise into ½-inch-thick rings. To a medium bowl, add the **1 pound cleaned squid tentacles and rings**, **1 cup buttermilk**, and **¼ cup sambal oelek**. Stir well to combine. (You can do this up to 6 hours in advance.)

- Slice **2 large shallots** into rings the same width as the calamari. Add to the buttermilk mixture and season with **a few pinches of salt**.

2 MAKE THE SAMBAL-LIME MAYO:

- In a small bowl, stir together **½ cup mayonnaise** and the remaining **¼ cup sambal oelek**. Zest **1 lime** into the sauce and squeeze in the **juice of 2 limes**. Season with **salt**. CONDIMENTS ARE YOUR BFFL (PG 22)

3 DREDGE AND FRY:

- In a large bowl, whisk together **1½ cups all-purpose flour**, **¾ cup cornmeal**, and **1½ teaspoons salt**.

- To a large Dutch oven or heavy-bottomed pot, add enough **vegetable oil** to come 1½ inches up the sides. Heat over medium heat until it reaches 375°F. (If you don't have a thermometer, proceed with breading the calamari and add one small piece to the pot—if the oil is hot enough, it should sputter and sizzle immediately.)

- Line a rimmed baking sheet with a double layer of paper towels.

- Using a slotted spoon and working in 2 batches, add the squid and shallots to the cornmeal mixture and toss well to coat.

- Carefully lower the squid and shallots into the oil (add only as much as can easily fit in each batch). Fry, moving the squid around with a slotted spoon or spatula, until light golden brown and crisp, 2 to 3 minutes per batch. Transfer to the lined baking sheet and season the calamari with salt. Repeat the breading and frying until all of the calamari and shallots have been fried.

- Lastly, pick **a large handful of basil leaves** from their stems and add to the oil (be careful; they may sputter, so stand back while they fry!). Fry for 30 seconds, until the leaves stop bubbling and turn bright green (it'll happen fast), then quickly fish them out with a slotted spoon. Add to the calamari on the baking sheet.

4 SERVE:

- Pile the fried calamari, shallots, and basil on a serving platter. Grate the **zest of another lime** over the top, then cut the lime into wedges for serving along with the sambal-lime mayo.

THE ONLY MEAT LOAF THAT MATTERS

SERVES 6 TO 8

GOES WITH: DRUNKEN CACIO E PEPE (PAGE 96), MARINATED ZUCCH & MOZZ WITH FRIED SUNFLOWER SEEDS (PAGE 90)

PRODUCE

- 5 garlic cloves
- 3 big handfuls of arugula
- 1 small bunch of basil
- 2 lemons

DAIRY

- 4 ounces Parmigiano Reggiano (in wedge form)
- 3 ounces fresh whole-milk mozzarella cheese (not shredded)

PROTEIN

- 2 large eggs
- 2 pounds spicy Italian sausages

PANTRY

- Kosher salt and freshly ground black pepper
- 6 ounces French bread or ciabatta (about one 6-inch piece)
- 4 tablespoons extra-virgin olive oil

Sorry to all the classic ketchup-slicked meat loaves of yore. There's a new hot loaf in town. It's still a bread-bound, rich loaf of meat, but we're skipping the ketchup and onion and building flavor with Italian sausage as the base and grated garlic, Parmesan, and mozzarella as the flavoring agents. This loaf is allll about the interplay of crisp and tender. Cheese oozes out of every slice, and to take it OTT, we fry each slice in a skillet until crispy and browned. You can understand why the bright arugula-herb salad on the side is simply not optional.

1 MAKE THE MEAT LOAF:

- Preheat the oven to 300°F.

- In a large bowl, beat **2 large eggs** and **1 teaspoon salt**.

- Tear **6 ounces French bread** into 3-inch pieces (crusts as well!), place them in a fine-mesh strainer, and run them under cold water to moisten and soften them.[1] Wring out as much water as possible and add them to the bowl of beaten eggs. Whisk to incorporate.

- Remove the casings from **2 pounds spicy Italian sausage** and add the meat to the bowl.

- Grate **3 ounces Parmesan** (about ¾ cup) into the bowl, reserving the remaining ounce for shaving later. Finely grate in **5 garlic cloves** into the bowl. Using your hands, squeeze, knead, and work the mixture together until it's homogeneous and pasty. You don't want big chunks of bread floating around. It should all be pretty uniform.

- Tear **3 ounces mozzarella cheese** (about ½ ball) into bite-size pieces and gently work them into the meat loaf mixture.

- Pat the meat loaf mixture into a 9 × 5-inch (or similar size) loaf pan, pressing firmly to evenly pack it in. Cover tightly with aluminum foil and bake until an instant-read thermometer inserted into the center registers 150°F, 70 to 90 minutes. Let cool, uncovered, for at least 20 minutes.[2]

2 CRISP UP THE MEAT LOAF: WHEN IN DOUBT, REFRY (PG 22)

- Remove the meat loaf from the loaf pan and slice it into 1½-inch-thick slices.

- In a large nonstick skillet, heat **a big glug of olive oil** over medium heat. Working in batches, add the meat loaf slices and cook, undisturbed, until deeply golden brown and crisp on the bottom, about 3 minutes, then flip and repeat on the other side. Transfer to a large plate and repeat with the remaining slices.

3 ASSEMBLE THE SALAD AND SERVE:

- In a medium bowl, combine **3 big handfuls of arugula** and the leaves of **1 small bunch of basil** with **lots of big shards of Parm**. Dress the arugula salad with the **juice of 2 lemons, a couple glugs of olive oil**, salt, and **freshly ground black pepper**—it should be bright and lemony!!

[1] This is called a *panade*. It's a paste made of soaked fresh bread that functions to replace fresh bread crumbs in meatballs, meat loaf, etc.

[2] You can also chill the cooked meat loaf overnight. To serve the next day, preheat the oven to 350°F. After crisping up the meat loaf slices, transfer them to the oven for a few minutes to finish warming them through.

COOK ALONG!

AUDIO

CRISPY CUTLETS WITH GIARDINIERA SLAW

GOES WITH: RAW & ROASTED CAULI SALAD WITH CREAMY, DREAMY VEGAN RANCH (PAGE 82), OLIVE OIL–DROWNED POTATOES WITH LEMONY ONIONS & HERBS (PAGE 222)

SERVES 4

There's a reason you often see a crispy breaded cutlet served with something cold, crunchy, or refreshing alongside, and that's because it's exactly what the doctor ordered. In this case, that cold, crunchy element is a slaw. This one features savoy cabbage, jarred pickled giardiniera (a current obsession), and lots of crunchy almonds and Parmesan cheese. Frankly, I think the slaw steals the show, but the pork cutlets ain't half bad either! If you're more of a chicken lover yourself, use chicken breast cutlets instead of the pork.

PRODUCE

- ½ large savoy cabbage
- 1 small red onion
- 2 garlic cloves
- 1 bunch of mint and/or basil
- 1 lemon

DAIRY

- 3 ounces grated Parmigiano Reggiano (¾ cup), plus more as needed

PROTEIN

- 4 (6-ounce) slices pork shoulder steaks, cut ½ inch thick
- 2 large eggs

PANTRY

- 2 (16-ounce) jars giardiniera pickles in brine
- ¼ cup extra-virgin olive oil, plus more as needed
- 3 tablespoons red wine vinegar, plus more as needed
- ½ teaspoon red pepper flakes
- Kosher salt and freshly ground black pepper
- 2 big handfuls of roasted almonds (about 5 ounces)
- Vegetable oil, for frying
- 2 tablespoons mayonnaise
- 2 cups panko bread crumbs
- Flaky sea salt

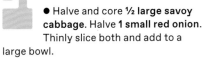

1 START THE SLAW:

- Halve and core **½ large savoy cabbage**. Halve **1 small red onion**. Thinly slice both and add to a large bowl.

- Drain **2 (16-ounce) jars giardiniera**, reserving about ¼ cup of the brine. Roughly chop the giardiniera and add it to the bowl, along with **¼ cup olive oil, 3 tablespoons red wine vinegar, 3 tablespoons of the giardiniera brine**, and **½ teaspoon red pepper flakes** (or more if you like it spicier!). Season with **kosher salt**.

- Chop **2 big handfuls of roasted almonds**.

2 PREP THE MEAT:

- Spread out a 14-inch piece of plastic wrap on a cutting board. Place a second piece slightly overlapping the first to make a double-wide work surface.

- Place a **6-ounce slice of pork shoulder** on top of the plastic wrap. Cover with another 2 pieces of plastic wrap and, using a meat mallet or heavy skillet, pound the pork into a thin ¼-inch-thick cutlet. Repeat with the remaining pieces of pork.

- Season the cutlets with kosher salt and pepper.

3 DREDGE AND FRY THE MEAT:

- Preheat the oven to 300°F. Set a wire rack inside a rimmed baking sheet.

- Fill a wide, deep saucepan with enough **vegetable oil** to reach a depth of ½ inch and heat over medium heat.

- In a pie plate or shallow bowl, whisk together **2 eggs, 2 finely grated garlic cloves**, and **a couple big tablespoons of mayonnaise**.

Season with **kosher salt** and **freshly ground black pepper**.

- In another pie plate or shallow dish, place **2 cups panko bread crumbs**.

- Dunk one pork cutlet into the egg mixture and turn to coat. Transfer to the panko and flip, pressing to adhere the bread crumbs, until thoroughly coated. Transfer to a plate and repeat with the remaining cutlets.

- Raise the heat under the skillet to medium-high. Drop a pinch of panko into the oil. If it begins to sizzle with gusto, the oil is ready. If not, wait until it does.

- Carefully slide a cutlet into the oil. Fry until deeply golden and crisp on the underside, 3 to 4 minutes. Flip and continue to fry, basting the top with oil if there are any areas that didn't get as much color, until golden, 3 to 4 minutes. Transfer to the rack. Repeat with the remaining cutlets.

4 FINISH THE SLAW AND PLATE IT UP:

- Add **3 ounces grated Parm** and the chopped almonds to the slaw. Tear the leaves from **1 bunch of mint and/or basil** and add them to the bowl. Toss to combine.

- Season to taste with vinegar, remaining giardiniera brine, olive oil, and/or grated cheese. Every giardiniera mix is different! The slaw should be super bright and punchy, balanced with a nice roundness from the olive oil and cheese.

- Cut **1 lemon** into wedges. Top the cutlets with **flaky sea salt** and serve with the lemon wedges and slaw.

COOK ALONG!

AUDIO

LAMB CHOPS SCOTTADITO WITH MINTY BEANS & ARTICHOKES

GOES WITH: BLISTERED PEPPS WITH TORN HALLOUMI & WARM SHALLOT DRESSING (PAGE 211), BAKLAVA RUFFLE PIE (PAGE 288)

SERVES 4

There are a few things that make this recipe a total banger: (1) the garlicky rosemary marinade that the chops get smothered in before going in the oven; (2) the jarred artichokes that get seared until crisp and caramelized (the ultimate artichoke level-up); (3) the anchovy/caper/red wine vinegar sitch that soaks into the beans and becomes a sauce for fatty lamb chops. As someone who has historically not been the biggest fan of lamb, I can assure you this recipe is a really freakin' good time.

PRODUCE

- 3 large rosemary sprigs
- 4 garlic cloves
- 1 bunch of mint

PROTEIN

- 2 (8-rib) racks of lamb (2 pounds)

PANTRY

- ⅓ cup plus 3 tablespoons extra-virgin olive oil, plus more as needed
- Kosher salt and freshly ground black pepper
- 1 (12-ounce) jar marinated artichokes
- 1 (15.5-ounce) can butter or cannellini beans
- 3 tablespoons capers in brine, drained
- 6 oil-packed anchovy fillets
- ¼ cup red wine vinegar, plus more as needed

1 DO SOME PREP:

- Position a rack in the center of the oven. Preheat the oven to 375°F.

- Finely chop the leaves of **3 large rosemary sprigs** (about 1 heaping tablespoon). Transfer to a small bowl and stir in **4 finely grated garlic cloves** and **a couple tablespoons olive oil**.

- Cut **2 (8-rib) racks of lamb** in half, leaving you with 4 (4-rib) sections. Season all over with **salt and freshly ground black pepper**.

- Drain **1 (12-ounce) jar marinated artichokes** and **1 (15.5-ounce) can butter beans**, separately.

- Finely chop **3 tablespoons drained capers**.

2 SEAR AND ROAST THE RIBS:

- In a large cast-iron skillet, heat **a glug of olive oil** over high heat until you see signs of smoke. Add the lamb and sear, turning every 2 minutes or so, until golden brown all over, including the sides, 6 to 8 minutes total. Remove from the heat, scoot the racks to the side, and add the artichokes to the skillet. Lamb chops cook fairly quickly, so we wanna make sure that skillet is reallllll hot in order to get great caramelization! TURN YA BURNERS UP (PG 21)

- Arrange the lamb racks on top of the artichokes and, using a pastry brush, brush all over with the garlic-rosemary oil (including the undersides!). Nestle the racks back on top of the artichokes, fat-side up. Transfer to the oven to roast until an instant-read thermometer registers 130°F at the chops' thickest points, 13 to 17 minutes.

- Transfer the lamb racks to a cutting board to rest. Return the skillet (artichokes and all) to the stovetop and set over medium-high heat. Add the chopped capers and **6 oil-packed anchovy fillets**. Cook, stirring occasionally, until the capers are crisp and the anchovies have disintegrated, 3 to 4 minutes. Remove from the heat and stir the butter beans along with the remaining **⅓ cup olive oil** and **¼ cup red wine vinegar**. Taste and add more oil or vinegar as you see fit.

- Pick the leaves of **1 bunch of mint** and finely chop. Stir into the chokes and beans. Taste and add more salt or vinegar if needed.

3 SERVE:

- Slice the racks into individual chops, cutting between each bone. Spoon the bean mixture and its juices onto a serving platter and arrange the chops on top. Drizzle generously with more olive oil.

COOK ALONG!

VIDEO

THE **FLAKIEST FISH** WITH SHINGLED POTATOES & WALNUT GREMOLATA

GOES WITH: BRING BACK BRUSCHETTA (PAGE 57), MARINATED ZUCCH & MOZZ WITH FRIED SUNFLOWER SEEDS (PAGE 90), HALLOUMI, CUKE & WALNUT SPOON SALAD (PAGE 81)

SERVES 4

PRODUCE

- 8 garlic cloves
- 8 oregano or thyme sprigs
- 1½ pounds Yukon Gold potatoes (4 medium)
- 2 lemons
- 1 bunch of flat-leaf parsley

DAIRY

- 6 tablespoons (¾ stick) unsalted butter

PROTEIN

- 1 (1½-pound) large boneless, skinless fillet of flaky white fish, such as halibut, cod, sea bass, or snapper

PANTRY

- Kosher salt and freshly ground black pepper
- ⅔ cup walnuts
- Flaky sea salt

Roasting a big piece of fish on a bed of garlic-butter potatoes is one of my favorite dinner formulas. The potatoes get a jump-start in the oven because they take longer to cook, and just as they begin to turn golden at the edges, the fish gets tossed on top. The potatoes underneath the fish stay juicy and tender while the ones at the edges turn into potato chips, and everybody's happy. A nutty, bright walnut gremolata (an Italian condiment typically made of herbs, raw garlic, and lemon zest) livens everything up and will have you licking the baking sheet. Speaking from experience.

 PREP THE POTATOES:

- Position a rack in the center of the oven. Preheat the oven to 400°F.

- Finely chop **6 garlic cloves**.

- To a small saucepan set over medium heat, add **6 tablespoons unsalted butter**. As the butter begins to melt, add the chopped garlic and **3 oregano sprigs**. Cook, swirling, until the garlic is fragrant but not browned and the butter has fully melted, 2 minutes. Remove from the heat.

- Using a mandoline or sharp knife, thinly slice **1½ pounds Yukon Gold potatoes** into ⅛-inch-thick rounds.

 ROAST THE POTATOES AND TOAST THE WALNUTS:

- Using a pastry brush, lightly brush a large rimmed baking sheet with one-third of the garlic butter.

- Arrange the sliced potatoes in an overlapping shingled manner on the baking sheet until the entire surface is covered. Brush generously with another third of the garlic butter and season well with **kosher salt and freshly ground black pepper**.

- Roast until the potatoes around the edges have begun to turn golden brown, 13 to 18 minutes. (This will vary based on how thick your potatoes are sliced. As long as the potatoes at the center of the baking sheet are barely tender at this point, you'll be in good shape.)

- Meanwhile, place **⅔ cup walnuts** on a small rimmed baking sheet and toast in the oven alongside the potatoes until golden brown, 8 to 10 minutes.

 MEANWHILE, PREP THE FISH:

- Pat dry **1½ pounds boneless, skinless flaky white fish** with a paper towel. Season all over with kosher salt.

- Using a veg peeler, peel 6 large strips of zest from **1 lemon**. Set the zest aside.

- Cut the zested lemon crosswise into thin wheels.

- When the potatoes are browned at the edges, remove from the oven and arrange the fish in the center of the potatoes. Brush the fish with the remaining garlic butter. Scatter the lemon slices and the remaining **5 oregano sprigs** over the fish. Roast until the flesh of the fish turns opaque and easily flakes away and the potatoes around the edges of the pan are crisp and those at the center are tender, 15 to 20 minutes.

MAKE THE WALNUT GREMOLATA:

- While the fish roasts, pick the leaves of **1 bunch of flat-leaf parsley** and finely chop.

- Thinly slice the lemon zest and then chop it finely.

- Finely chop the toasted walnuts.

- In a small bowl, combine the chopped parsley, lemon zest, and walnuts. Grate the remaining **2 garlic cloves** into the bowl, season with kosher salt, and toss well with your fingers to combine.

 SERVE:

- Scatter the gremolata over the fish and potatoes. Squeeze the **juice of the remaining lemon** over everything and finish with **flaky sea salt**.

SURF & TURF WITH GOCHUJANG BLACK PEPPER BUTTER

GOES WITH: LE GRAND GREEN GRILLED AIOLI (PAGE 221), SIZZLED SEEDY TOMATO SALAD (PAGE 75)

PRODUCE

- 4 garlic cloves
- 1 lemon
- 2 white onions, or 2 bunches of scallions

DAIRY

- 8 tablespoons (1 stick) unsalted butter, at room temperature

PROTEIN

- 1 pound shell-on (size U10 or U15) shrimp and/or lobster tails[1]
- 1 (1½-pound) New York strip, hanger, or rib-eye steak

PANTRY

- ½ cup gochujang (Korean red chili paste)
- Kosher salt and freshly ground black pepper

SPECIAL EQUIPMENT

- Food processor
- Grill or grill pan

Surf and turf isn't just for 1950s steak houses, people, and it doesn't have to break the bank either. And while this looks like a lot of work, in reality, all you've got to do is mash together some butter, gochujang, and lemon zest and slather it over whatever steak and shellfish you can get your hands on.

1 MAKE THE GOCHUJANG BUTTER:

- In a **food processor**, combine **4 grated garlic cloves, 8 tablespoons unsalted butter** (it must be at room temperature!), **½ cup gochujang**, the finely grated **zest of 1 lemon**, and **lots of freshly ground black pepper**. Pulse in long pulses until bright orange and homogeneous, 30 seconds. Instead of using a food processor, you can combine all ingredients in a medium bowl and paddle together with a spatula until well combined—this will take a couple of minutes.

- Set about half of the butter aside for serving and place the rest in a bowl to use while grilling.

2 PREP AND SEASON:

- Prepare a **grill** for medium-high heat or heat a **grill pan** over medium-high heat.

- Season **1 pound shell-on shrimp and/or lobster tails** and **1 (1½-pound) steak** all over with **salt** and pepper. (If using lobster tails, cut them in half lengthwise.)

- Cut **2 white onions** into 1½-inch wedges through the root end. (If using **scallions**, keep them whole.)

- Just before they go on the grill, brush the prepped fish, meat, and vegetables all over with gochujang butter, reserving some for

brushing later on. (They'll be cold, so the butter won't spread evenly. But we're going to keep brushing as we grill, so no worries if it's a little uneven at first.)

3 GRILL EVERYTHING:

- Grill the steak and onions first, brushing with gochujang butter every 2 to 3 minutes and flipping once or twice, until an instant-read thermometer inserted into the thickest part of the steak registers 135°F (for medium-rare) and the onions are charred all over and softened. Transfer to a cutting board and tent with aluminum foil to keep warm.

- Next, grill the seafood, again brushing several times with more gochujang butter and flipping once halfway through, until charred and just cooked through, 4 to 5 minutes. The lobster tails will turn from translucent to opaque when cooked, and the shrimp will turn bright pink with grill marks all over. Don't overcook them!

4 SERVE:

- Slice the steak across the grain. Arrange on a platter with the shrimp, lobster tails, and onions.

- Shower the **juice of the zested lemon** over everything. Serve the reserved gochujang butter alongside for slathering.

[1] If you don't have access to fresh seafood, it's often better to buy frozen. It sounds as if it should be the reverse, but most of the seafood at your grocery store was previously frozen and then thawed a few days before it was displayed at the fish counter. Seafood gets frozen immediately after being caught, preserving its freshness at the optimal moment.

KIELBASA & CABBAGE PITAS WITH CURRY MUSTARD

GOES WITH: OLIVE OIL–DROWNED POTATOES WITH LEMONY ONIONS & HERBS (PAGE 222), DILLY BEANS & BURRATA WITH FRIZZLED SHALLOTS (PAGE 218), HALLOUMI, CUKE & WALNUT SPOON SALAD (PAGE 81)

SERVE 4

PRODUCE

- 1 large green cabbage (2¼ pounds)
- 1 bunch of dill

PROTEIN

- 1 (14-ounce) kielbasa

PANTRY

- 5 tablespoons extra-virgin olive oil
- Kosher salt and freshly ground black pepper
- ¾ cup apple cider vinegar
- 1 tablespoon sugar
- 3 tablespoons whole-grain mustard
- ⅓ cup Dijon mustard
- 1 tablespoon mild curry powder
- 4 pitas or flatbreads

SPECIAL EQUIPMENT

- Grill or grill pan

I will not be surprised if my tombstone reads "Took any excuse to eat kielbasa," because that will be a real and truthful statement. Here, that iconic Polish sausage gets paired with a quick curry mustard and cabbage that has been grilled and pickled, creating a somewhat similar effect to sauerkraut but with more goin' on. If you don't have a grill, a large cast-iron skillet or grill pan will work, too. Set everything out on a big board and let your guests stuff their own pitas according to their personal preference.

1 GRILL AND PICKLE THE CABBAGE:

- Preheat a **grill** to medium or heat a cast-iron skillet or **grill pan** over medium heat.

- Cut **1 large green cabbage** in half through the root end. Cut each half into 4 equal wedges, keeping the root attached. Place on a rimmed baking sheet, drizzle generously with **olive oil**, and season with **salt and freshly ground black pepper**. Place the cabbage wedges on the grill or in the skillet and cook, turning occasionally, until blackened all over, 16 to 20 minutes.

- In a large bowl, whisk together **¾ cup apple cider vinegar**, **1 tablespoon sugar**, and **1½ teaspoons salt**.

- Once the cabbage wedges are charred, add them to the bowl, turning to coat occasionally, until cool. Once cool, coarsely chop the cabbage, discard any tough cores, and return to the bowl of pickling liquid. Stir in **3 tablespoons whole-grain mustard**.

- Finely chop **1 bunch of dill** and stir it into the cabbage.

2 MAKE THE CURRY MUSTARD:

- In a small bowl, whisk together **⅓ cup Dijon mustard** and **1 tablespoon mild curry powder**.

CONDIMENTS ARE YOUR BFFL (PG 22)

3 GRILL THE KIELBASA:

- Grill **14 ounces kielbasa** over medium heat, turning occasionally, until charred all over and heated through, 8 to 10 minutes.

- Gently warm **4 pitas** on the grill or in the skillet, taking care not to leave them on too long or they will become crisp and brittle.

4 SERVE:

- Slice the kielbasa. Set out the pitas, curry mustard, and pickled cabbage for a DIY sitch.

GINGERY
CLAMS WITH CHILI CRISP & TOFU

GOES WITH: CUCUMBER BAG SALAD WITH MISO-POPPY DRESSING (PAGE 93), PUT THE LIME IN THE COCONUT CORN BREAD WITH SALTY COCONUT JAM (PAGE 132)

SERVES 4

PRODUCE

- 8 shallots
- 1 garlic head
- 1 (4-inch) piece of fresh ginger

DAIRY

- 5 tablespoons unsalted butter
- 1½ cups heavy cream

PROTEIN

- 4 pounds littleneck clams
- 1 (14-ounce) package silken tofu

PANTRY

- Kosher salt
- 1½ cups dry white vermouth or white wine
- ⅓ cup chili crisp, for serving
- Crusty bread, for serving

Clams and tofu? Oh hell yes. If you've ever had Korean sundubu-jjigae (seafood and tofu stew), you know exactly what I'm talking about. Clams are inherently briny, salty, and meaty, while silken tofu is creamy and light. Together, along with a little help from their friends heavy cream and chili crisp, magic happens. Tofu gives the broth body and heft, and an undeniable slippery texture that contrasts with the bouncy clams.

1 DO SOME PREP:

- Thinly slice **8 shallots**.

- Thinly slice the cloves from **1 garlic head**.

- Mince **1 (4-inch) piece of fresh ginger**, enough to measure 3 tablespoons. (No need to peel it.)

- Scrub **4 pounds littleneck clams** with a sponge, discarding any clams with broken shells.

2 SAUTÉ THE AROMATICS AND STEAM THE CLAMS:

- Heat a large Dutch oven over medium-high heat. Add **5 tablespoons unsalted butter**. When the foaming subsides, add the shallots, garlic, and ginger. Season with **salt** and sauté, stirring occasionally, until the aromatics are translucent, 4 to 5 minutes. Reduce the heat if necessary to prevent browning.

- Raise the heat to high and add **1½ cups vermouth**, stirring and scraping the bottom of the pot to deglaze it. Bring to a brisk simmer and let reduce slightly, 1½ to 2 minutes.

- Add **1½ cups heavy cream** and the clams. Cover, adjust the heat to maintain a low boil, and let the clams steam until they are nearly all open, 6 to 10 minutes. As you start to peek in the pot to check on the clams, use a pair of tongs to transfer any opened clams to a bowl to prevent overcooking.

- When all the clams have opened, return any of the early openers back to the pot. (Discard any that haven't opened.) Stir to coat the clams with their cooking broth. Season with salt to taste.

- Drain **1 (14-ounce) package silken tofu** and carefully add it to the pot in large spoonfuls, submerging it in the broth as you go.

- Ladle the clams, tofu, and broth into 4 serving bowls. Top each portion with **a couple big spoonfuls of chili crisp**, swirl to distribute, and serve with **crusty bread**! CONDIMENTS ARE YOUR BFFL (PG 22)

TABLESIDE TARTARE

SERVES 4

GOES WITH: LAST-MEAL SCALLOPS (PAGE 174), OLIVE OIL–DROWNED POTATOES WITH LEMONY ONIONS & HERBS (PAGE 222), CRISPY POTATO SKINS WITH FRIED HERB AIOLI (PAGE 226)

Flavor-wise, there are a lot of directions you can take this iconic raw meat preparation (I wish there were a more appealing way to describe it), so instead of a recipe, I've given you a formula. Use this as a guide, then go raid your fridge for mix-ins. I love to serve tartare at dinner parties because you can prep it in advance and make a scene by standing tableside and preparing it to order for your guests. It's always best to start small and go big—a teaspoon of an ingredient from every category will get you going, then build from there, tasting as you go. You can mix the egg yolk directly into the tartare or top the tartare with the egg yolk. Do start with high-quality, organic, responsibly raised meat whenever possible, and talk to your butcher about what cuts they recommend for tartare.

THE STAPLES
- 1 pound lean, high-quality beef, such as hanger, top round, filet, or bavette
- 1 large egg yolk
- Extra-virgin olive oil
- Kosher salt and freshly ground black pepper

THE MIX-INS:

BRINY THINGS
- Capers
- Pitted olives
- Worcestershire sauce
- Fish sauce

PICKLY THINGS
- Cornichons
- Baby dill pickles
- Dill pickle relish
- Pickled green beans
- Pickled onions

SPICY THINGS
- Hot sauce
- Sriracha
- Sambal oelek
- Chili crisp
- Salsa verde

ACIDIC THINGS
- Mustard
- Vinegar
- Citrus juice

ALLIUM-Y THINGS
- Shallots
- Scallions
- Garlic chives
- Chives
- White onions
- Ramps

SERVING THINGS
- Toast
- Crostini
- Potato chips
- French fries
- Shoestring potato chips

Coarsely chop the beef into about ¼-inch dice. Finely chop your pickly things and alliums. Add an egg yolk and some olive oil to the beef, stir vigorously, and then start adding the rest to taste, choosing something from every category. Serve with your choice of "serving things"!

A LAST
MEAL
FOR THE
LIVING

My last meal is a morbid, delicious fantasy that I can't stop thinking about. Why I obsess over what I'll consume in my last moments on earth I can't say, but I can tell you exactly what's on the menu. When I sit down to a plateful of perfectly seared, butter-drenched scallops and swipe each bite through the juices left on the plate, a little voice in my head whispers, *This one's gonna make the cut.* Over time, that (very hypothetical and, knock on wood, not for a very long time) last meal has evolved into a list of dishes that each represents a point in my life, a meal that left its mark on me like a kitchen burn. Ten years ago, the menu would probably have included a never-ending bowl of fresh-cut tagliatelle with butter and truffles. Right now, I'm leaning toward a 1950s New York steak house meal. In my dreams, the meal commences with an over-the-top, multitiered seafood platter, and the air is filled with Lucky Strike smoke. There's something about that time that's been given an opulent, hazy glow from the movies, where meals go on late into the night, the table is constantly filled with more, more, more dishes. You're dining in the company of all your favorite people. The lights are dim, there's a pianist in the corner, the conversation is raucous, and you better believe the martinis are overflowing. If that's how I have my last bite, I know I'll die happy.

Here's my last-meal menu as it stands now. The beauty of the last-meal fantasy is that it's envisioned for the living. Occasionally I decide to pull out all the stops to make this meal a reality so I can savor every bite. The truth is, you never know what your last meal will be, so why not make it as often as you can?

TO START
- Martini Thrice (page 145) with Sidecar
- Tableside, All-You-Can-Eat Cae Sal
- Sesame Sourdough
- Towers of Cultured Butter with Flaky Sea Salt on the side
- Piles of Morty-d
- Pickle Platters

FROM THE RAW BAR
- Seafood Plateau: raw oysters, pickled mussels, shrimp cocktail, crudo, lobster tails & accompaniments

FROM THE GRILL
- Broiled Scallops with Parsley-Garlic Butter (see Last-Meal Scallops, page 174)

FROM THE ROTISSERIE
- Slow-Cooked Rotisserie Chicken with Toum and Hot Sauce

TO ACCOMPANY
- Schmaltzy Chicken Fat Potatoes with Dill
- French Fries
- Aioli

DESSERT:
- Brioche with Pralines

LAST-MEAL SCALLOPS

GOES WITH: TABLESIDE TARTARE (PAGE 166), MARTINI THRICE (PAGE 145), FAUX FRENCH ONION SOUP (PAGE 207)

SERVES 4

QUICK AS HECK!

PRODUCE

- 1 bunch of flat-leaf parsley
- 8 garlic cloves
- 1 lemon

DAIRY

- 10 tablespoons (1¼ sticks) unsalted butter, at room temperature

PROTEIN

- 1½ pounds dry-packed sea scallops (size U10 or U15)[1]

PANTRY

- Kosher salt
- Extra-virgin olive oil
- Crusty bread, for serving

SPECIAL EQUIPMENT

- Food processor

I first tasted a version of these scallops at a big, vibe-y, bustling French restaurant called Les Vapeurs on the coast of Normandy. It was as fancy as it sounds. And when I tell you I nearly died and went to heaven . . . I knew it was my responsibility to come up with a recipe that would come close. The key is a garlicky, lemony herb butter that melts into each scallop after you've given them a caramelized crust. You may have more garlic-parsley butter than you need—rub the leftovers on a whole chicken before roasting, or toss it with hot boiled potatoes and tell me that's not your idea of a good time.

1 MAKE THE GARLIC-PARSLEY BUTTER:

- If it's not already quite soft and malleable, cut **10 tablespoons unsalted butter** into small pieces and set out at room temperature or pulse in the microwave in 10-second increments until soft but not melted.

- Pick the leaves of **1 bunch of flat-leaf parsley** and either very finely chop them by hand or add them to a **food processor**. If mixing by hand, add the parsley to a medium bowl.

- Finely grate **8 garlic cloves** and the **zest of 1 lemon** into the bowl or food processor and mix or pulse to combine.

- When the butter is soft, add it to the bowl or food processor, along with **a big pinch of salt**, and mix or pulse well to combine, scraping the sides of the bowl as necessary to be sure it's all incorporated.

2 COOK THE SCALLOPS:

- Position a rack in the top of the oven. Preheat the broiler.

- Pat dry **1½ pounds dry-packed sea scallops** with a paper towel. Season all over with salt.

- Heat a large cast-iron skillet over high heat. Add enough **olive oil** to coat the skillet. Once you see smoke emanating from the surface of the pan, add the scallops in a single layer and cook, undisturbed, moving them only if they seem to be burning in some areas, until a deep, golden brown crust forms, about 3 minutes. Don't rush this process! It's crucial to the flavor development of the scallops—they cook VERY quickly, so high heat, and no touching, are musts to establish that golden crust. TURN YA BURNERS UP (PG 21)

- Momentarily transfer the scallops to a plate, seared-side up. Tip out and discard the oil that remains in the skillet.

- Schmear a generous dollop of garlic-parsley butter on top of each scallop (½ tablespoon or so each) and then return them to the skillet, butter-side up. Place the skillet under the broiler and broil until the butter melts and the scallops have firmed up but still have considerable bounce (they shouldn't be tough), 1 to 2 minutes.

3 SERVE:

- Squeeze the **juice of the zested lemon** over the scallops and serve right out of the skillet, with **lots of crusty bread** for soaking up all the buttery juices.

---

[1] Scallops are sold by their quantity per pound, so, for example, U10 scallops means there will be 10 scallops to the pound. The lower the number, the bigger the scallops. Always look for dry-packed scallops because they are not treated with preservatives. The wet ones will never caramelize properly.

CHIC

MISO-BRAISED CHICKEN & LEEKS

GOES WITH: DILLY BEANS & BURRATA WITH FRIZZLED SHALLOTS (PAGE 218), PURPLE SALAD (PAGE 71)

SERVES 4 TO 6

PRODUCE

- 3 medium leeks (about 1¾ pounds)
- 1 bunch of tarragon or mint

DAIRY

- 3 tablespoons unsalted butter, cold

PROTEIN

- 4 large bone-in, skin-on chicken legs, or 6 bone-in, skin-on thighs (about 2 pounds)

PANTRY

- 1 heaping tablespoon fennel seeds
- Kosher salt and freshly ground black pepper
- 1 teaspoon red pepper flakes
- Extra-virgin olive oil
- 5 tablespoons white miso paste
- 1 cup sake, dry vermouth, or white wine

I know leeks are a pain to clean when they're super dirty, but stay with me, because they're so much more interesting texturally than straight-up onions. Leeks quickly turn from raw and biting to mellow, sweet, tender, and toothsome. They caramelize beautifully and become downright creamy in this miso-butter braise. For how few ingredients this recipe requires, the flavors are mind-blowingly complex. We've got a punchy combo of miso paste, tarragon, and sake to thank for that.

1 DO SOME PREP:

- Position racks in the lower and upper thirds of the oven. Preheat the oven to 375°F.

- In a mortar and pestle or spice grinder, place **1 heaping tablespoon fennel seeds**. Grind until finely ground. (You can finely chop the fennel seeds instead!) Add to a small bowl, along with **1 tablespoon salt, 1 teaspoon freshly ground black pepper**, and **1 teaspoon red pepper flakes**. Mix to combine.

- Place **4 large bone-in, skin-on chicken legs** on a small rimmed baking sheet or plate and season with the fennel spice blend, being sure to sprinkle thoroughly underneath the skin (between the skin and the flesh) as well. Reserve a teaspoon or two of the spice blend for seasoning later. Ideally, season your chicken at least 1 hour and up to a day in advance.

- Trim the hairy ends of **3 medium leeks**, halve the leeks lengthwise, and then cut the halves into 3-inch pieces. If they are super dirty, submerge them in cold water and rinse, taking care to leave the layers intact if possible. Drain well.

2 BROWN THE CHICKEN:

- In a large Dutch oven, position the chicken legs in an even layer, skin-side down, over medium heat. Let the chicken skin render its fat, rotating the pot 180 degrees halfway through to encourage even cooking, until the chicken pieces release easily and the skin is deeply golden and super crisp, 16 to 20 minutes.[1]

- Using tongs, transfer the chicken pieces to a small rimmed baking sheet.

3 CARAMELIZE THE LEEKS:

- You should have a good amount of fat left over in the pot, but every chicken is different, so if the pot seems dry, add **a glug or two of olive oil**.

- Raise the heat to medium-high and add the leeks, cut-side down. Season with the reserved spice blend. Cook until the leeks are deeply caramelized, 5 to 7 minutes.

4 BRAISE THE CHICKEN AND LEEKS:

- While the leeks caramelize, place **5 tablespoons miso paste** in a medium bowl. Slowly whisk in **1 cup sake** until smooth and homogeneous. Then whisk in **1 cup water**.

- Once the leeks are caramelized, add the sake-miso mixture to the pot, along with **a couple tarragon sprigs**. Bring the liquid to a simmer over medium heat.

- Dot the leeks with **3 tablespoons cold unsalted butter**.

- Nestle the chicken back in. Transfer the pot to the oven, uncovered. Braise until the chicken and leeks are tender, and the sauce has reduced but is still brothy, 40 to 50 minutes. Discard the tarragon sprigs.

5 SERVE:

- Spoon the leeks and their broth into serving bowls. Top each one with a chicken leg. Tear **some fresh tarragon** over each bowl and finish with a few grinds of pepper.

---

[1] You don't want to rush this process, so make sure your heat isn't too high! The trick is to render the fat slowly. And trust: The chicken WILL release from the pot.

COOK ALONG!

AUDIO

CHICKEN PICCATA
WITH SWEET CORN, CHILES & BUTTERMILK

GOES WITH: SPICY GREEN FREGOLA WITH SALTY YOG (PAGE 204), BRING BACK BRUSCHETTA (PAGE 57), TRIPLE THREAT GARLIC BREAD (PAGE 99)

SERVES 4

QUICK AS HECK!

Chicken piccata is not only a beloved Italian American classic, it's also easy enough to be a weeknight dinner on the reg. Dredging boneless, skinless chicken thighs in flour helps both with browning and thickening the pan sauce. Chicken piccata pan sauce is typically made of butter, lemon juice, and capers—briny, bright, and fatty all at once. My take leans on buttermilk for tang and anchovies, chiles, and shallots for brininess and spice. It's got a deeper, more profound flavor than the classic, and we fuck with profound flavor in this house.

PRODUCE

- 3 large shallots
- 6 garlic cloves
- 1 red Fresno chile, or ¾ teaspoon red pepper flakes
- 2 ears of corn[1]
- 1 small bunch of mint or basil
- 2 lemons

DAIRY

- 6 tablespoons (¾ stick) unsalted butter
- 1½ cups buttermilk

PROTEIN

- 2 pounds boneless, skinless chicken thighs (about 6)

PANTRY

- Kosher salt and freshly ground black pepper
- ¾ cup all-purpose flour
- Extra-virgin olive oil
- 6 oil-packed anchovy fillets

1 DO SOME PREP:

- Thinly slice **3 large shallots**, **6 garlic cloves**, and **1 Fresno chile**.

- Shuck and remove the kernels from **2 ears of corn**.

2 POUND AND DREDGE THE CHICKEN:

- Take **2 pounds boneless, skinless chicken thighs** and, working with one at a time, place a thigh between 2 pieces of parchment paper. Use a rolling pin or heavy skillet to pound the chicken to a ½-inch thickness. Season the thighs with **salt and freshly ground black pepper**.

- In a shallow bowl, place **¾ cup all-purpose flour**. Thoroughly dredge each chicken thigh in the flour, shaking off any excess, and place on a large rimmed baking sheet.

3 COOK THE THIGHS:

- Heat a large cast-iron skillet over high heat until hot. Add **a few big glugs of olive oil (about 2 tablespoons)** and heat until you see wisps of smoke. Gently place 2 thighs in the skillet. Cook the chicken until deeply golden on the bottom, 4 to 5 minutes. Flip and cook for 2 minutes longer. Transfer to a plate, browned-side up, and repeat with the remaining thighs, adding more oil when needed.

4 MAKE THE PAN SAUCE

- Reduce the heat to low and add **2 tablespoons unsalted butter, 6 oil-packed anchovy fillets**, the shallots, garlic, chile, and **6 mint sprigs**. Season with salt and pepper and sauté, stirring, until the aromatics are softened, about 3 minutes. Add the corn and continue cooking for 2 minutes, until just softened.

- Add **1½ cups buttermilk** and adjust the heat as needed to maintain a brisk simmer. Cook, shaking the pan and stirring occasionally, until slightly reduced but still quite saucy, 3 to 4 minutes. The buttermilk will split, and you'll see small curds throughout the pan. That's okay and good!

- Cube the remaining **4 tablespoons butter**, add to the pan, and continue cooking, vigorously shaking the pan as you stir, until the butter is incorporated, about 2 minutes. The agitation of the pan will help create a thick emulsion.

- Cut **2 lemons** in half. Divide the chicken among plates, top with the pan sauce, and serve with plenty of fresh mint and the lemon halves alongside for squeezing.

[1] If you don't wanna be that person who's shucking corn at the grocery store in search of the perfect cob, there are other ways to tell if an ear is on point. Look for bright green husks that are tightly wrapped around the cob and silks that are pale and pearly looking—the brown ones indicate an old ear of corn.

COOK ALONG!

AUDIO

CHILE-BASED HALF CHICKEN WITH CAPER CHIMICHURRI

SERVES 2

GOES WITH: SPICY GREEN FREGOLA WITH SALTY YOG (PAGE 204), PICKLE-MARINATED FETA (PAGE 65), RAW & ROASTED CAULI SALAD WITH CREAMY, DREAMY VEGAN RANCH (PAGE 82)

PRODUCE

- 1 large Yukon Gold potato (8 ounces)
- 3 garlic cloves
- 1 small shallot
- 1 bunch of cilantro
- 1 serrano chile or jalapeño

PANTRY

- 1 tablespoon Aleppo pepper, or ¾ teaspoon red pepper flakes
- 2 teaspoons smoked paprika
- Extra-virgin olive oil
- Kosher salt
- 1 tablespoon capers in brine, drained
- 2 tablespoons sherry vinegar

PROTEIN

- ½ chicken (leg and breast attached), or any combination of 2 bone-in, skin-on chicken breasts or legs (about 2 pounds total)

SPECIAL EQUIPMENT

- Food processor or blender

When you're cooking for one or two, a half-chicken is the perfect size, plus the flattened shape ensures maximal crispy skin—the reason we're all here in the first place. If you can't find a halved chicken at the market, you can use either 2 bone-in, skin-on chicken breasts or 2 chicken legs (or a combo of both). You've got options! The most important takeaway is that tucking shingled potatoes underneath a chicken is one of the greatest ways to consume a tuber.

1 DO SOME PREP:

- Preheat the oven to 450°F.

- Thinly slice **1 large Yukon Gold potato** into ¼-inch-thick rounds.

- In a small bowl, stir together **2 finely grated garlic cloves**, **1 tablespoon Aleppo pepper**, **2 teaspoons smoked paprika**, and **a few glugs of olive oil**—enough to turn it into a wet-sand-like paste.

- Pat dry **½ chicken** with a paper towel and season all over with **salt**.

2 COOK THE CHICKEN AND POTATOES:

- In a large cast-iron skillet, heat **a glug of olive oil** over medium-high heat until you see wisps of smoke. Arrange the chicken in the skillet, skin-side down, and reduce the heat to medium. Place a second heavy skillet on top of the chicken to encourage the skin to make contact with the oil. Cook until the skin is deeply golden brown and crisp, 8 to 10 minutes. (This timing will depend greatly on the pan you are using and how hot your burners are, so keep an eye on things.) Turn off the heat.

- Transfer the chicken to a plate, skin-side up (it will still be raw underneath; this is only temporary). Carefully arrange the potato slices in the skillet in concentric circles, overlapping some. Brush with some of the chile-garlic oil and season with salt.

- Place the chicken on top of the potatoes, skin-side up. Brush the chicken all over with more of the chile-garlic oil. Transfer to the oven and roast, brushing the chicken or spooning it with some of the schmaltz once or twice as it roasts, until an instant-read thermometer placed in the thickest part of the breast registers 150°F, about 30 minutes. Transfer the chicken to a cutting board to rest. If the potatoes are not yet crisp around the edges, return them to the oven until the outside rings are brown and crisp and the interior potatoes are tender and schmaltzy. This is a best-of-both kind of situation—you're not looking for full-blown potato chips.

3 WHILE THE CHICKEN ROASTS, MAKE THE CAPER CHIMICHURRI:

- Coarsely chop **1 small shallot**, **1 bunch of cilantro** (leaves and stems!), and **1 serrano chile** (remove the seeds if you are spice averse).

- In a **food processor or blender**, combine the shallot, cilantro, serrano, remaining **garlic clove**, and **1 tablespoon capers** and pulse to finely chop.[1] Add **¼ cup olive oil** and **2 tablespoons sherry vinegar** and blend again until combined but not totally smooth. Season with salt.

4 SERVE:

- Let the chicken rest for 10 minutes before carving. Serve the chicken and potatoes with chimichurri alongside.

---

[1] You can also do this whole thing by hand by finely chopping all of the herbs and vegetables and stirring in the oil and vinegar.

PARTY CHIX

SERVES 4

GOES WITH: SPICY COCONUT-SMOTHERED GREEN BEANS (PAGE 225),
CUCUMBER BAG SALAD WITH MISO-POPPY DRESSING (PAGE 93)

PRODUCE

- 6 garlic cloves
- 1 orange

PROTEIN

- 3 pounds bone-in, skin-on chicken parts (breast, thigh, wings, and/or drumstick)

PANTRY

- 1 cup dill pickle brine
- ¼ cup low-sodium soy sauce
- 1 tablespoon toasted sesame oil
- 3½ teaspoons sugar
- Kosher salt
- 3 tablespoons nutritional yeast
- 1 teaspoon red pepper flakes
- 2¾ teaspoons smoked paprika
- 1 large sheet of nori
- Neutral oil, such as canola or vegetable, for frying
- 1 cup all-purpose flour
- 1 cup cornstarch

This recipe takes cues from Japanese karaage and American Southern fried chicken and pickles, two exceptional ways to eat a bird. You'll marinate the chicken in soy sauce and dill pickle brine for a one-two punch of salt and tang. Once it comes out of the oil all crispy and craggy, you'll toss the chicken in an absolute party of a spice blend—nutritional yeast, crushed nori, smoked paprika, salt, sugar, and orange zest—you'll be licking your fingers by the end, and that's a promise.

1 BRINE THE CHICKEN:

- Firmly smash and peel **6 garlic cloves**. Remove 2 long strips of **zest from 1 orange**.

- In a large bowl or resealable bag, whisk together **1 cup dill pickle brine**, **¼ cup soy sauce**, **1 tablespoon toasted sesame oil**, **2 teaspoons sugar**, the garlic, orange zest, and **2 teaspoons salt**.

- Add **3 pounds bone-in, skin-on chicken parts** and turn to coat. (If using bone-in chicken breasts, you may want to cut them in half crosswise first to create more manageably sized pieces.) Cover and chill for at least 2 hours and up to overnight. Remove from the fridge 30 minutes before you are ready to fry.

2 MAKE THE PARTY DUST:

- In a small bowl, whisk together **3 tablespoons nutritional yeast**, the remaining **1½ teaspoons sugar**, **1 teaspoon red pepper flakes**, **1 teaspoon salt**, **¾ teaspoon smoked paprika**, and the finely grated **zest of the rest of the orange**.

- Using a spice grinder, blitz **1 large sheet of nori**[1] into very small pieces (you can crumble it first with your hands and then finely chop it instead). Add to the bowl and mix.

3 FRY THE CHICKEN:

- Preheat the oven to 200°F.

- In a large Dutch oven, add enough **neutral oil** to reach 2 inches up the sides and heat over medium heat until the oil registers 350°F.

- In a large bowl, whisk together **1 cup all-purpose flour**, **1 cup cornstarch**, the remaining **2 teaspoons smoked paprika**, and **1 teaspoon salt**.

- Transfer ¾ cup of the flour mixture to another medium bowl and slowly whisk in some of the chicken brine until it turns into a thick pancake batter–like consistency.

- Working with one or two pieces at a time, using tongs, remove the chicken from its brine, dunk the pieces first in the wet flour mixture and then into the dry flour mixture, using your hands to pinch and pat the chicken until it is very well coated and there are some straggly bits. Transfer to a plate.

- Working in batches, fry 2 or 3 pieces of chicken at a time until deeply golden brown and crisp and an instant-read thermometer inserted into the center of the largest pieces (right by the bone) registers 155°F, 10 to 14 minutes per batch. Transfer the chicken pieces to a wire rack as they finish and immediately dust them generously all over with the party dust. Keep the finished pieces warm in the oven while you cook those that remain.

[1] Nori is a great seasoning sprinkle—if you've got a bunch leftover, play around with crumbling it into salads, over rice bowls, and on top of eggs for a little moment of oceanic bliss.

COOK ALONG!

VIDEO

YUMMY JUICE

MAKES 2

GOES WITH: PUT THE LIME IN THE COCONUT CORN BREAD WITH SALTY COCONUT JAM (PAGE 132), PARTY CHIX (PAGE 185)

- 2 lemons
- Ice
- 2 ounces Aperol or Cappelletti
- 4 ounces mezcal
- ¾ ounce agave syrup
- Kosher salt

This cocktail has become so integral to our lives that my husband now refers to it as a YJ. It typically goes something like this: "Babes, can I get a YJ?" (Ahem.) With any luck, YJ will enter your household lexicon, too. This recipe makes two cocktails because what, pray tell, is the point of making just one???

● Juice **1½ lemons** and slice the remaining half for garnish.

● In an **ice**-filled cocktail shaker, combine **2 ounces lemon juice, 2 ounces Aperol, 4 ounces mezcal, ¾ ounce agave syrup**, and a nice **big pinch of salt**. Shake the shit out of it until the shaker is so cold, you can't hold it a second longer.

● Place some **salt** on a plate. Rub a juiced lemon half around the rims of 2 collins glasses, then roll the rims in the salt to coat. Fill the glasses with ice, pour the Yummy Juice in, garnish with a **lemon slice**, and sluuuuurp.

CHICKY CHICKY BREAD BREAD

SERVES 4

GOES WITH: PURPLE SALAD (PAGE 71), FAUX FRENCH ONION SOUP (PAGE 207)

PRODUCE

- 2 garlic heads
- 8 small shallots
- 2 large bunches of kale, collard greens, Swiss chard, or spinach
- 1 lemon

DAIRY

- 1 cup plain whole-milk yogurt (not Greek)

PROTEIN

- 4 bone-in, skin-on chicken legs, or 6 bone-in, skin-on thighs (about 2½ pounds)

PANTRY

- 2 tablespoons mild chile flakes, such as Aleppo pepper or gochugaru, or 2 teaspoons red pepper flakes
- 1 tablespoon fennel seeds
- ¾ teaspoon ground cinnamon
- 5 tablespoons extra-virgin olive oil
- Kosher salt and freshly ground black pepper
- 4 (1-inch-thick) slices stale sturdy sourdough bread (the staler, the better)[1]

SPECIAL EQUIPMENT

- Blender

[1] If you have only fresh bread, slice it up and leave it out at room temperature to dry for a few hours, if possible. If you don't have time for that, embrace your crispy-gone-soggy bread (which I happen to think is pretty special in its own right).

If you've ever made Samin Nosrat's famous buttermilk-marinated roast chicken, you're familiar with the incredible tenderizing effect that cultured dairy has on meat. The enzymes in dairy products like buttermilk and yogurt help to break down the proteins in the chicken, resulting in supremely juicy meat with an undeniable tang. I like to nestle some stale bread beneath the chicken as it roasts; it soaks up the fat without getting soggy, and you end up with custardy schmaltz-soaked bread with crispy! fried! edges!

1 MARINATE THE CHICKEN:

- In a **blender**, combine **2 tablespoons mild chile flakes, 1 tablespoon fennel seeds**, and **¾ teaspoon ground cinnamon**. Blend on high until the spices are finely ground. Add **1 cup plain whole-milk yogurt, 2 tablespoons olive oil, 8 garlic cloves**, and **1½ teaspoons salt**, and blend again until smooth. Alternatively, crush the spices, finely grate the garlic, and then whisk together with the yogurt, olive oil, and salt.

- Pat dry **4 bone-in, skin-on chicken legs** with a paper towel and generously season with salt. Place the chicken in a large baking dish or large resealable plastic bag. Pour the chile yogurt all over the chicken and let sit at room temp, turning occasionally, for 1 hour or up to overnight in the fridge.

2 MEANWHILE, PREP YOUR VEG AND BREAD:

- When you're ready to cook, position a rack in the center of the oven. Preheat the oven to 450°F.

- Peel **8 small shallots** and cut them in half through the root end. If they're large, cut them into quarters.

- Cut the remaining **whole garlic head** in half crosswise.

- Cut or tear **2 bunches of kale** into 3-inch pieces (discard the tough center stems).

3 ROAST THE CHICKEN:

- Place the shallots, halved garlic head, and **4 (1-inch-thick) slices stale sourdough bread** in a clean 9 × 13-inch baking dish.

- Generously drizzle everything with olive oil and season with salt and **freshly ground black pepper**, turning to coat the bread and nestling the aromatics around the bread.

- Arrange the chicken legs on top of the bread and aromatics. Roast until the bread is golden brown and very crisp underneath, 25 to 30 minutes. (The chicken will not yet be browned and crisp.) Using tongs, move the chicken legs to a plate momentarily while you flip the bread slices over and stir the shallots and garlic. Return the chicken legs to the bread and continue to roast until the chicken skin is crisp and deeply burnished, 12 to 16 minutes. Transfer the chicken and bread to a plate or cutting board, leaving the shallots and garlic behind.

4 ADD THE GREENS AND FINISH:

- Stir the greens into the baking dish, drizzle with some more olive oil, and season with salt and pepper. Return the dish to the oven to cook, stirring once halfway through, until the greens are wilted and tender, 5 to 10 minutes (depending on what greens you're using). If it looks like the drippings at the bottom of the pan are burning, you can add **a couple of tablespoons of water** to loosen them up.

- Squeeze the **juice of 1 lemon** all over the greens, chicken, and bread. Divide the bread, shallots, and greens among serving bowls. Top each bowlful with a chicken leg. Serve the roasted garlic alongside for schmearing on the schmaltzy bread.

RED CURRY
HOT WINGS ROLLED IN PEANUTS

SERVES 4 TO 6

GOES WITH: SPICY COCONUT-SMOTHERED GREEN BEANS (PAGE 225), BRUSSELS SPROUTS WITH SHALLOTS & STICKY FISH SAUCE (PAGE 72), PUT THE LIME IN THE COCONUT CORN BREAD WITH SALTY COCONUT JAM (PAGE 132)

PRODUCE

- 1½ cups packed cilantro leaves and tender stems
- 2 limes

PROTEIN

- 3 pounds chicken wings (25 to 30), drumettes and flats separated

PANTRY

- 1 tablespoon kosher salt
- 3 tablespoons vegetable oil
- 1 (4-ounce) jar or can red curry paste
- 1 (13.5-ounce) can full-fat coconut milk
- 1½ teaspoons honey or sugar
- Red pepper flakes (optional)
- ½ cup roasted, salted peanuts

¹ This will allow the wings to properly absorb the seasoning, leaving them both tastier and more tender. You can also do this up to a day in advance and keep the wings, uncovered, in the fridge. Let them hang out at room temperature for at least 30 minutes before baking.

² They'll be pretty pale still, but this low temperature helps render out some of the fat from the skin, resulting in crispier wings once you crank the heat.

There's no reason to bust out a large pot of oil and a deep-fry thermometer for chicken wings when you can achieve the same effect by oven roasting. (Bust it out for the Shoestring Onion Rings with Peperoncini & Yummy Dust on page 217 and the Maple Ricotta Munchkins on page 280 instead.) These wings take an hour in the oven, but in that time, they render all of their fat, leaving the skin as crispy-crunchy as ever. The Thai-inspired sauce that glazes them is a mix of fatty coconut milk, aromatic red curry paste, and honey. As for the boatloads of chopped peanuts you'll generously coat the wings in . . . I think those speak for themselves.

1 SEASON THE WINGS:

- Line a rimmed baking sheet with parchment paper. Pat dry **3 pounds chicken wings** with a paper towel. Toss the chicken wings with **1 tablespoon salt** on the baking sheet until well coated. Leave at room temperature for at least 30 minutes and up to 1½ hours.¹

2 ROAST THE WINGS:

- Preheat the oven to 300°F.

- Drizzle the wings generously with **vegetable oil** and toss to evenly coat.

- Bake for 25 minutes.²

- Raise the oven temperature to 450°F and continue to cook the wings, flipping them with tongs halfway through, until the skin is very crisp and golden brown, 30 to 35 minutes.

3 WHILE THE WINGS COOK, MAKE THE COCONUT GLAZE:

- In a medium saucepan with a lid, heat **another glug of vegetable oil** over medium heat. Add **1 (4-ounce) jar red curry paste** and immediately cover the pan. Cook, shaking the (still covered) pan often, until you hear the violent sputtering die down, about 2 minutes, then remove the lid. Continue to cook until the paste is slightly darker and begins to stick to the pan, 2 minutes.

- Whisk in **1 (13.5-ounce) can full-fat coconut milk** and **1½ teaspoons honey**. Bring the mixture to a boil. Lower the heat as needed to maintain a simmer and cook, whisking often, until the liquid has reduced substantially and thickened—it should coat the back of a spoon without totally dripping off, 10 to 12 minutes.

- Determine your heat factor: At this point, the sauce is mild to medium in spice level depending on what brand of curry paste you used. If you like your wings HOT, start stirring in **red pepper flakes**, to taste.

- Cover the pot until the wings are ready. (You may need to briefly rewarm the sauce over medium heat before tossing them.)

4 PREP YOUR GARNISHES:

- Finely chop **½ cup roasted, salted peanuts** so all the pieces are around the size of a lentil.

- Coarsely chop **1½ cups packed cilantro leaves and tender stems**.

- Cut **2 limes** in half.

5 TOSS THE WINGS:

- Transfer the cooked wings to a large bowl. Pour the hot coconut glaze over them and toss to coat. Add the peanuts and cilantro and toss again. Squeeze the juice of 1 lime over everything and toss once more.

- Transfer to serving platter with the remaining lime halves and lots of napkins 'cause these guys are not NOT messy.

COOK ALONG!

VIDEO

ONE-POT CHICKEN MUJADARA

SERVES 6

GOES WITH: SIZZLED SEEDY TOMATO SALAD (PAGE 75),
HALLOUMI, CUKE & WALNUT SPOON SALAD (PAGE 81)

PRODUCE

- 6 large shallots
- 2 medium yellow onions
- 3 lemons

DAIRY

- 2½ cups plain whole-milk yogurt (not Greek), plus more for serving

PROTEIN

- 1 (4½- to 5-pound) whole chicken

PANTRY

- 6 tablespoons extra-virgin olive oil, plus more for drizzling
- Kosher salt and freshly ground black pepper
- 1 tablespoon ground cinnamon
- 1 tablespoon ground cumin
- 1 tablespoon ground turmeric
- 1 cup long-grain white rice, such as jasmine or basmati
- 1 cup dried brown or black lentils (not quick-cooking)

Heaps of shallots, lentils, and rice cook along with a whole chicken for a Middle Eastern mujadara–inspired one-pot meal that defies everything I thought I knew about roasting a chicken. Somehow, despite the fact that you will roast a whole chicken in a Dutch oven with the lid on (!!!), what emerges is a deeply burnished, perfectly cooked bird. The moisture from the rice and lentils in the pot yields the most evenly cooked, juicy chicken meat I've ever had in a whole-bird format. This may be my favorite recipe in the book—please don't tell the others.

1 MARINATE THE BIRD:

- "Collar" a large zip-top bag by folding the top few inches of the bag down over itself. Doing so will help the bag stand more easily on its own and will make the process of marinating much neater. Place 1 (4½- to 5-pound) chicken inside the bag.

- In a large bowl, combine 2½ cups yogurt with a few big glugs of olive oil (about 3 tablespoons), 2 tablespoons salt, 1 tablespoon ground cinnamon, 1 tablespoon ground cumin, 1 tablespoon ground turmeric, and 2 teaspoons freshly ground black pepper. Scrape the mixture into the bag with the chicken. Seal the bag and squish the marinade around to distribute, working some of the marinade into the chicken cavity as well. Transfer to the refrigerator and marinate for at least 1 hour and up to 24 hours.

2 WHILE THE BIRD MARINATES, DO SOME PREP:

- Thinly slice 6 shallots and 2 medium yellow onions crosswise into ¼-inch-thick rings.

3 COOK THE BIRD:

- Position a rack in the lower third of the oven. Preheat the oven to 475°F.

- In a large Dutch oven, place the shallot and onion slices. Drizzle with the remaining 3 tablespoons olive oil, season with salt and pepper, and toss to combine. Remove the chicken from the marinade and transfer it directly on top of the shallots and onions. No need to scrape the marinade off the chicken; it should still be coated. Reserve the bag of remaining marinade.

- Cut 1 lemon in half and stuff it into the cavity of the chicken. Drizzle the top of the chicken with some olive oil, cover the pot with the lid, and transfer to the oven. Roast for 35 minutes.

4 ADD THE RICE AND LENTILS:

- Add 3 cups water to a large measuring cup or bowl. Pour and scrape the marinade from the bag into the measuring cup with the water. Add 1½ teaspoons salt and stir to combine.

- In a fine-mesh strainer, combine and rinse 1 cup long-grain white rice and 1 cup dried lentils.

- Remove the pot from the oven. With a large wooden spoon, tilt the chicken to one side and pour the rice and lentils into the pot, along with the water-marinade mixture. Stir the rice and lentils around the bird to distribute evenly. Cover the pot and return it to the oven.

- Braise until the rice and lentils are tender and the chicken is burnished in some spots, 45 to 55 minutes. Remove from the oven and let rest (still covered) for 10 minutes.

5 SERVE:

- Cut the remaining 2 lemons in half.

- Transfer the chicken to a carving board and carve it up. Season the lentils to taste and serve with more yogurt and the lemon halves for squeezing.

COOK ALONG!

AUDIO

GREEN CHICKEN SOUP WITH CHICKPEAS & SIZZLED CORIANDER

GOES WITH: SIZZLED SEEDY TOMATO SALAD (PAGE 75), RAW & ROASTED CAULI SALAD WITH CREAMY, DREAMY VEGAN RANCH (PAGE 82)

SERVES 6

This hearty chicken, barley, and chickpea soup gets its bright green color from being pureed with spinach and herbs. You can totally skip the blending if you're not feeling up for it, but that's the "more is more" moment here. I love the creaminess it lends to the soup in contrast to the tender poached chicken and spicy sizzled coriander, and it also looks a lot cooler that way. How often do you eat bright green chicken soup?? This makes a lot of soup, but you can always freeze any leftovers.

PRODUCE

- 1 large leek
- 1 white or yellow onion
- 1 large or 2 small celery stalks
- 6 garlic cloves
- 8 ounces baby spinach
- 1 large bunch of cilantro
- 1 large bunch of dill
- 3 lemons

DAIRY

- Yogurt, labne, or sour cream, for serving

PROTEIN

- 1½ pounds boneless, skinless chicken thighs (about 5)

PANTRY

- Extra-virgin olive oil
- Kosher salt and freshly ground black pepper
- Red pepper flakes
- 1 (15.5-ounce) can chickpeas, drained but unrinsed[1]
- 1 cup pearled barley, brown rice, white rice, or quick-cooking farro
- 1 heaping tablespoon coriander seeds
- Flaky sea salt

SPECIAL EQUIPMENT

- Blender

1 DO SOME PREP:

- Trim the hairy end of **1 large leek** and discard. Slice the entire leek (including the dark green portion) in half and rinse well under cold water to remove any dirt and grit from all the layers. Thinly slice crosswise.

- Roughly chop **1 white onion**, **1 large celery stalk**, and **6 garlic cloves**.

2 START THE SOUP:

- In a large Dutch oven, heat **a few generous glugs of olive oil** over medium-high heat. Add the leek, onion, and celery and season with **2 teaspoons kosher salt** and **½ teaspoon freshly ground black pepper**. Sauté, stirring occasionally, until the vegetables are softened and translucent, 8 to 10 minutes. Reduce the heat if necessary to prevent browning.

- Add the chopped garlic and **a few pinches of red pepper flakes** and continue to cook, stirring, until the garlic is softened and aromatic, 2 to 3 minutes.

- Add **10 cups water**, **1 (15.5-ounce) can drained (but unrinsed!) chickpeas**, **1 cup pearled barley**, **1½ pounds boneless, skinless chicken thighs**, and **1 teaspoon kosher salt**.

- Bring to a boil over high heat. As foam collects on the surface, skim it with a spoon and discard. Reduce the heat as needed to maintain a simmer and cook until the chicken and barley are tender and the soup has reduced and thickened, 35 to 45 minutes.

3 WHILE THE SOUP SIMMERS, SIZZLE THE CORIANDER:

- Chop **1 heaping tablespoon coriander seeds** with a chef's knife or crush with the bottom of a heavy skillet or a mortar and pestle.

- In a small skillet, warm **several tablespoons olive oil** over medium heat. Add the crushed coriander seeds, along with **½ teaspoon coarsely ground black pepper**. Sauté until aromatic and sizzling. Transfer to a small bowl and season with **flaky sea salt**.

4 FINISH THE SOUP:

- Remove the chicken from the soup. Transfer to a cutting board and shred the meat into large pieces.

- Add **8 ounces baby spinach** to the pot. Stir until just wilted, about 1 minute.

- Roughly chop **1 large bunch of cilantro** and **1 large bunch of dill**.

- Transfer 2 cups of the soup to a **blender**, along with half of the cilantro and dill. Puree until very smooth and green. Add the puree back into the soup, along with the shredded chicken, the **juice of 2 lemons**, and the remaining chopped dill and cilantro. Taste and decide for yourself if you want it brighter before adding the **juice of the third lemon**—it should be vibrant and lemony—don't be shy! YOU'RE PROBS NOT USING ENOUGH ... LEMON (PG 20)

- Taste and adjust the seasoning with kosher salt and black pepper. Divide the soup among serving bowls and serve topped with **a hefty dollop of yogurt** and a drizzle of sizzled coriander oil.

[1] In this case, we aren't rinsing, because canned chickpeas are surrounded by a thick liquid called aquafaba that will help give our soup more body, which is a good thing!

BENNY'S TENDER TENDERS

SERVES 4

GOES WITH: SALTED CITRUS SHANDY (PAGE 229),
RAREBIT MAC 'N' GREENS (PAGE 124)

PRODUCE

- 2 celery stalks
- 2 Persian cucumbers
- 2 medium carrots
- 1 garlic clove
- 4 heads Little Gem lettuce or 3 romaine hearts (about 1½ pounds total)

DAIRY

- ½ cup sour cream
- ½ cup crumbled blue cheese

PROTEIN

- 2 large boneless, skinless chicken breasts (about 1½ pounds)
- 2 large eggs

PANTRY

- ⅔ cup plus 2 tablespoons unseasoned rice vinegar
- 1 tablespoon sugar
- Kosher salt and freshly ground black pepper
- ¼ cup tahini
- ¾ cup all-purpose flour
- ¾ cup Frank's RedHot cayenne pepper sauce
- 1½ cups panko bread crumbs
- ⅔ cup sesame seeds (toasted or raw—both are fine), plus more for serving
- Vegetable oil, for frying

It is my pleasure to introduce to you the first and only recipe that my husband has ever developed. Let's be clear, there was quite a bit of assistance on my part. Regardless, this recipe, a take on Buffalo wings with blue cheese, has become a staple in our household. So without further ado, a word from Willett:

Here it is, people . . . the moment you have all been waiting for (or at least the moment Molly has): my supremely crispy, tender Buffalo chix salad. I threw in a couple sneaky moves to keep things interesting, in case you, too, are trying to impress your overly dubious spouse.

1 QUICKLY PICKLE SOME VEG:

- Thinly slice **2 celery stalks**, **2 Persian cucumbers**, and **2 medium carrots** on the bias. In a medium bowl, combine the sliced veg with **⅔ cup rice vinegar**, **1 tablespoon sugar**, and **1½ teaspoons salt**. Stir the veg and brine together and keep chilled until serving.

2 MAKE THE TAHINI–BLUE CHEESE DRESSING:

- In a medium bowl, whisk together **½ cup sour cream**, **¼ cup tahini**, and the remaining **2 tablespoons rice vinegar**. Whisk in some **cold water** (you'll need about ½ cup) until the dressing is pourable and creamy. Grate **1 garlic clove** into the dressing and stir in **½ cup crumbled blue cheese**. Season with salt and **lots of freshly ground black pepper**.

3 PREP THE CHICKEN BREASTS AND SALAD:

- Cut **2 large boneless, skinless chicken breasts** in half horizontally to create 4 thin cutlets total (so, making a cut parallel to the cutting board, with the breast lying flat). Season all over with **salt**.

- Cut **4 heads Little Gem lettuce** crosswise into 2-inch pieces. Wash and thoroughly dry the lettuce. Transfer to a large bowl.

4 DREDGE AND FRY:

- In one medium bowl, place **¾ cup all-purpose flour**. In a second medium bowl, whisk together **2 large**

eggs and **¼ cup Frank's RedHot sauce**. In a third medium bowl, combine **1½ cups panko bread crumbs** and **⅔ cup sesame seeds**. Grab a large plate (this will be your landing pad).

- Working with one at a time, using tongs, dip each cutlet first into the flour, then into the egg mixture, allowing any excess to drip off. Transfer to the panko mixture and use your hand to cover the cutlet in the crumbs, firmly pressing and packing them on to encourage as many as possible to adhere. Transfer to your chicken landing pad and repeat with the remaining cutlets.

- In a large skillet, heat about **¾ inch of vegetable oil** until it reaches 375°F.[1] Line a large plate with paper towels.

- Add 2 chicken cutlets and cook until deeply golden brown on both sides, about 3 minutes per side. Transfer to the paper-towel-lined plate and season all over with salt. Repeat, adding more oil to the skillet as necessary.

5 TOSS THE SALAD AND FINISH:

- Drizzle about ⅔ cup of the tahini dressing over the lettuce, toss well to coat, and season with salt and pepper. Divide among serving bowls and top each with a handful of the pickled vegetables.

- Place the remaining **½ cup Frank's RedHot sauce** on a small rimmed plate. Dip each cutlet into the hot sauce to coat both sides and transfer to a cutting board. Slice crosswise into ½-inch-wide pieces and arrange one cutlet on top of each salad. Sprinkle with extra sesame seeds. Serve the remaining dressing alongside for cutlet dunking.

[1] If you don't have a thermometer, you can check by throwing a piece of panko into the oil. If it sizzles violently, you are ready!

COOK ALONG!

AUDIO

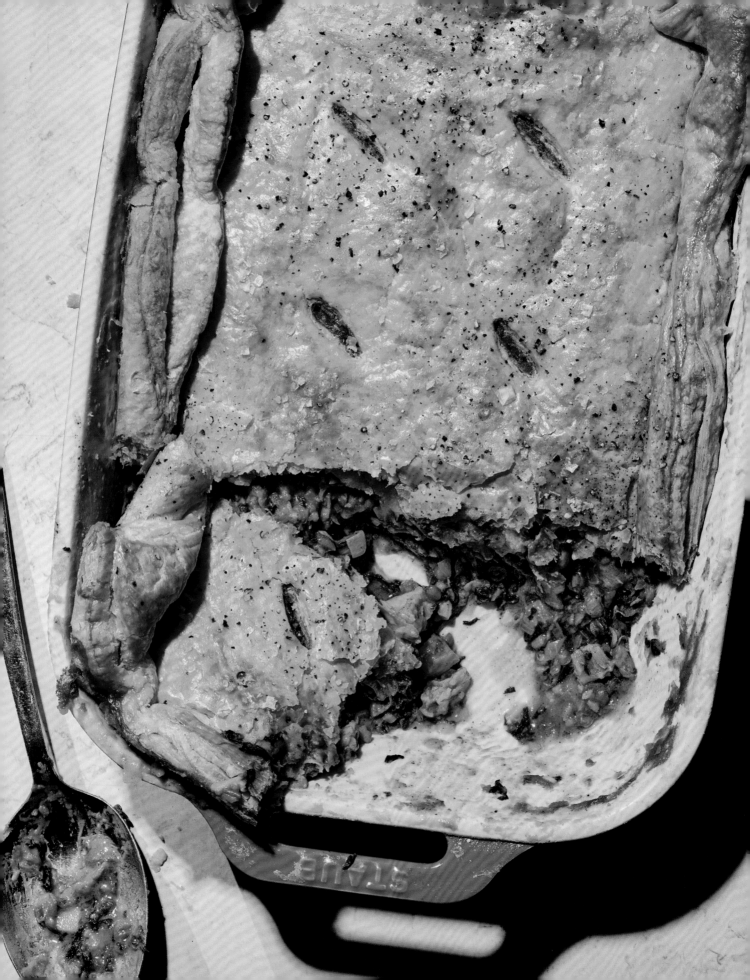

CURRIED LENTIL & SWEET POTATO POTPIE

SERVES 6 TO 8

GOES WITH: PICKLE-MARINATED FETA (PAGE 65), SPICED PEANUT SHORTBREAD (PAGE 284)

This easy-as-hell, rich-and-soul-nourishing vegetarian potpie leans on canned lentils, frozen spinach, and puff pastry for an effortless buttery crust. But let's be clear: these are shortcuts on time and effort, not on flavor. Warm spices like curry powder and cinnamon do the heavy lifting in the dal-adjacent stewed lentil filling.

PRODUCE

- 2 medium white or yellow onions
- 1 (5-inch) piece of fresh ginger
- 6 garlic cloves
- 2 medium sweet potatoes (1½ pounds)

DAIRY

- Melted butter, for brushing (optional)
- 1 large egg

PANTRY

- 1 (15.5-ounce) can lentils
- ¼ cup extra-virgin olive oil
- Kosher salt and freshly ground black pepper
- 1 tablespoon plus 1 teaspoon curry powder
- 1½ teaspoons ground turmeric
- 1 teaspoon ground cinnamon
- ¼ teaspoon red pepper flakes, plus more to taste
- 2 (13.5-ounce) cans full-fat coconut milk
- All-purpose flour, for dusting
- Flaky sea salt

FROZEN

- 2 (10-ounce) packages frozen chopped spinach, thawed
- 1 (14- to 17-ounce) package puff pastry, thawed overnight in the refrigerator

[1] To thaw the spinach, place the frozen spinach in a large sieve and run warm water over it until room temp, then wring out as much water as possible.

1 DO SOME PREP:

- Preheat the oven to 400°F.
- Chop **2 medium onions**.
- Finely chop enough of a **5-inch piece of fresh ginger** to measure ¼ cup (no need to peel).
- Finely chop **6 garlic cloves**.
- Peel **2 medium sweet potatoes** and cut them into ½-inch cubes (about 4 heaping cups).
- Drain and rinse **1 (15.5-ounce) can lentils**.

2 START THE AROMATICS:

- Heat a large Dutch oven over medium-high heat. Add **several generous glugs of olive oil** and the chopped onions and ginger and season generously with **kosher salt and freshly ground black pepper**. Sauté, stirring occasionally, until softened and lightly golden, 8 to 10 minutes.
- Add the garlic. Stir until fragrant and softened but not browned, about 1 minute.

3 TOAST THE SPICES:

- Push the aromatics to one side and add **another glug of olive oil** to the empty spot. To the oil, add **1 tablespoon plus 1 teaspoon curry powder, 1½ teaspoons ground turmeric, 1 teaspoon ground cinnamon**, and **¼ teaspoon red pepper flakes**. Cook in the oil until fragrant, 1 minute. Stir the spices into the aromatics and continue cooking for another minute.
- Stir in ⅔ **cup cold water**. Add the lentils, sweet potatoes, and **2 (13.5-ounce) cans full-fat coconut milk**.
- Bring to a boil, then reduce the heat as needed to maintain a brisk simmer. Cook, stirring occasionally to prevent scorching, until the sweet potatoes are just barely tender, 7 to 9 minutes (they'll continue cooking in the oven).
- Place **2 (10-ounce) packages thawed chopped spinach** in a kitchen towel and squeeze firmly to expel as much water as possible.[1]
- Add the spinach and stir to distribute and warm through. Adjust the seasoning with kosher salt, black pepper, and/or red pepper flakes. This will need a lot of salt! Don't be shy. YOU'RE PROBS NOT USING ENOUGH ... SALT (PG 20)
- Transfer the filling to a 9 × 13-inch baking dish.

TOP WITH PUFF AND BAKE:

4

- If your **puff pastry** comes in 2 sheets, on a **lightly floured** surface, unfurl one sheet, brush it lightly with **melted butter**, and place the second right on top, stacking them. Roll the sheets to about 10 × 14 inches, or slightly larger than the size of your baking dish. Lay the puff pastry on top of the filling. The pastry should come just over the sides of the baking dish. Press down on the pastry to allow it to slump into the dish and adhere to the inside edges, then gently fold the corners to crease and make a seal. If using one sheet, simply roll the puff pastry to a 10 × 14-inch rectangle and proceed as stated above.
- In a small dish, beat **1 egg**. Using a pastry brush, lightly coat the top of the pastry with the egg wash. Sprinkle with **flaky sea salt** and black pepper.
- With a knife, cut a series of vent slits, about 2 inches in length and 2 inches apart, in the top of the pastry. Bake for 15 minutes, then reduce the oven temp to 350°F and continue baking until the pastry is puffed and deeply golden brown, 25 to 30 minutes. Let rest for 15 minutes before serving.

SPICY GREEN FREGOLA WITH SALTY YOG

SERVES 4 TO 6

GOES WITH: MORTADELLA-WRAPPED GRISSINI (PAGE 52), KIELBASA & CABBAGE PITAS WITH CURRY MUSTARD (PAGE 162)

QUICK AS HECK!

When I know I need to get vegetables into my body, an entire clamshell of fresh spinach is the easiest way to do it. Mixing bouncy fregola (a Sardinian couscous-like pasta) with a blender full of spicy green sauce is a surefire way to meet your daily quota. You can serve this cold or at room temp, making it a nice little meal-prep dish if you're into that, and perf for taking to potlucks, camping, on an airplane, etc.

PRODUCE

- 1 large bunch of dill
- 2 serrano chiles, or 1 jalapeño
- 5 ounces baby spinach
- 1 garlic clove
- 1 lemon

DAIRY

- ⅔ cup plain whole-milk yogurt (not Greek)

PANTRY

- Kosher salt and freshly ground black pepper
- 2½ cups fregola or pearl couscous
- ⅔ cup extra-virgin olive oil
- Sesame seeds, for sprinkling

SPECIAL EQUIPMENT

- Blender or food processor

1 COOK THE FREGOLA:

● Bring a large pot of **salted** water to a boil. Stir in **2½ cups fregola** and cook until al dente according to the package directions, tasting as you go.

● Drain in a fine-mesh strainer and rinse under cold water until cool. Transfer to a large bowl.

2 MAKE THE SPICY GREEN SAUCE:

● Coarsely chop **1 large bunch of dill**. Coarsely chop **2 serrano chiles**.

● To a **blender** or **food processor** add the dill, chiles, **5 ounces baby spinach**, **1 garlic clove**, and **a big pinch of salt**. Pour in **⅔ cup olive oil**, then blend on high until smooth, 1 minute. Taste and add more salt if it needs it.

3 MAKE THE SALTY YOG AND ASSEMBLE:

● In a small bowl, season **⅔ cup plain whole-milk yogurt** with salt and stir to combine. It should taste salted, but not overly salty! You decide!

● Pour the spicy green sauce over the fregola. Add the **juice of 1 lemon** and stir well to coat. Taste and adjust the seasoning— does it need more salt? More lemon? LOOSEN UP (PG 20)

● Make a well in the center of the fregola and spoon the salty yog into the well. Sprinkle the whole platter with **sesame seeds** and a crack or two of **black pepper** and serve!!

FAUX FRENCH ONION SOUP

GOES WITH: CRICK-CRACKS! (PAGE 58), CRISPY POTATO SKINS WITH FRIED HERB AIOLI (PAGE 226), TABLESIDE TARTARE (PAGE 166)

SERVES 4 TO 6

If you ask me, French onion soup is one of the greatest soups of all time, and I don't think it's fair that vegetarians get left out of the conversation. This version is meatless and you can even make it vegan by skipping the Gruyère and using olive oil in place of butter. It might not be very French at all, but it *is* very oniony, and it's got the depth of flavor and stick-to-your-bones-ness that a classic FOS does. Kombu, miso paste, and shiitake mushrooms stand in for beef stock, and although I'd never claim this tastes like it was made with beef, I will say it is a mother-effing delicious alternative.

PRODUCE

- 8 medium yellow or Vidalia onions
- 2 garlic heads
- 1 (5-inch) hand of fresh ginger

DAIRY

- 3 tablespoons unsalted butter
- 6 ounces grated Gruyère cheese (about 1 cup)

PANTRY

- 3 tablespoons extra-virgin olive oil
- 2 (4 × 6-inch) sheets of kombu
- 2 star anise pods
- 6 dried shiitake mushrooms
- Kosher salt and freshly ground black pepper
- 2 tablespoons white miso paste
- ¾ cup sake or white wine
- 4 (1-inch-thick) slices sourdough bread

1 DO SOME PREP:

- Quarter **2 medium yellow onions** (leave the skins on). Remove and reserve **6 garlic cloves** from 1 garlic head, then halve what remains of the 2 whole heads.

- Thinly slice **1 (5-inch) hand of fresh ginger** lengthwise into planks (no need to peel first).

2 START THE BROTH:

- In a large pot, heat **a couple glugs of olive oil** over medium-high heat. When the oil is smoking, add the onions, halved garlic heads, and ginger and cook, turning occasionally, until charred in spots, 8 to 10 minutes.

- Add **2 sheets of kombu, 2 star anise pods**, and **6 dried shiitake mushrooms**, breaking the shrooms in half as you add them. Cover with **10 cups water**. Bring to a boil over medium-high heat, then reduce the heat to low and simmer for 1 hour, or until you've completed step 3.

3 CARAMELIZE THE ONIONS:

- Thinly slice the remaining **6 onions**.

- Heat a large Dutch oven over medium-high heat. Add another **glug of olive oil** and **3 tablespoons unsalted butter** and swirl to melt. Add the sliced onions and **2 big pinches of salt**. Using tongs, vigorously stir the onions to coat them, then cover the pot and cook for 5 minutes to encourage them to steam and collapse. This will help jump-start the caramelization process.

- Uncover and cook, stirring often, until the liquid has mostly been driven off and the onions begin to stick to the bottom of the pot, about 10 minutes. Reduce the heat to medium and cook, stirring occasionally, every 7 minutes or so, until the onions are deeply golden and jammy, 35 to 40 minutes.[1]

- Thinly slice the reserved **6 garlic cloves** and stir into the onions, along with **2 tablespoons miso paste**. Cook until the mixture starts to stick to the bottom of the pot, 2 minutes.

- Taste the onions and add more salt if needed. They should be sweet and salty, not JUST sweet. Season with **lots of freshly ground black pepper**.

- Stir in **¾ cup sake** and cook for 2 minutes.

4 COMBINE:

- Set a strainer over the caramelized onions and pour the broth right into the pot, pressing on the solids with the back of a spoon to extract all their liquid. Discard the solids—they've given us their all, and we thank them for that.

- Bring the soup to a simmer over medium heat and simmer for 10 to 15 minutes to allow all the flavors to meld. Taste and adjust the seasoning.

5 BROIL AND SERVE:

- Position a rack in the top third of the oven. Preheat the broiler.

- Cut **4 (1-inch-thick) slices sourdough bread** as wide as the bowls you will be serving the soup in. Place on a rimmed baking sheet and broil until toasted on both sides, flipping once, 2 to 3 minutes total.

- Divide the soup among bowls, place a slice of toast in each, and top with **a generous handful of grated Gruyère**. Place the bowls on a rimmed baking sheet and broil until the cheese is melted and spotted brown, 2 minutes-ish. Serve hottttt.

[1] Do not rush this process! If the onions look like they are burning and not turning golden, you can add a splash of water or reduce the heat slightly.

COOK ALONG!

VIDEO

SAUCY, GLOSSY SPANISH EGGS

GOES WITH: MASHED POTATO ARANCINI (PAGE 63), SIZZLED DOLMAS WITH YOGURT & BROWN-BUTTERED PINE NUTS (PAGE 54), FENNEL ON FENNEL ON FENNEL TORTILLA (PAGE 212)

SERVES 4

QUICK AS HECK!

This smoky, spicy Spanish chorizo, pepper, tomato, and egg stew falls under the "if you're gonna use it, use it" philosophy of *More Is More* and will (I hope) teach you about being resourceful in your pantry. You'll use jarred roasted red peppers and pickled peperoncini plus the leftover brine in both jars (instead of dumping it down the drain), imparting even more pepper flavor. Groceries are very expensive—waste nothing!!

PRODUCE

- 1 large red onion
- 6 garlic cloves
- 1 pound cherry tomatoes

PROTEIN

- 4 ounces Spanish-style cured chorizo
- 4 large eggs

PANTRY

- 1 (16-ounce) jar roasted red peppers, plus their brine
- 3 tablespoons extra-virgin olive oil
- Kosher salt and freshly ground black pepper
- 1½ teaspoons smoked paprika
- 1 teaspoon red pepper flakes
- 3 tablespoons tomato paste
- 2 tablespoons sherry vinegar
- ½ cup sliced jarred peperoncini, plus ¼ cup of their brine
- Warmed tortillas, grilled bread, or charred pita, for serving

1 DO SOME PREP:

- Thinly slice **1 large red onion** and **6 garlic cloves**.

- Halve **1 pound cherry tomatoes**.

- Drain **1 (16-ounce) jar roasted red peppers**, reserving their brine. Thinly slice crosswise.

- Cut **4 ounces cured chorizo** into ¼-inch-thick slices on the bias. Stack the slices and cut them lengthwise into ¼-inch-thick matchsticks.

2 GET COOKING:

- In a large Dutch oven, warm **a couple glugs of olive oil** over medium-high heat. Add the red onion, garlic, and chorizo. Season with **salt and freshly ground black pepper** and sauté, stirring occasionally, until the onion begins to char on the edges, 7 to 9 minutes.

- Add the roasted red peppers and continue to cook, stirring, until jammy and cooked down, 4 to 5 minutes.

- Stir in **1½ teaspoons smoked paprika** and **1 teaspoon red pepper flakes** and cook until fragrant, about 1 minute.

- Make a well in the center of the pot and add another **glug of olive oil** and **3 tablespoons tomato paste**, stirring to coat the tomato paste in the oil. Cook until the paste is toasted and well combined with the oil, gradually incorporating the aromatics, 3 minutes.

- Stir in **2 tablespoons sherry vinegar**, scraping the bottom of the pot to deglaze, 1 minute. Add the cherry tomatoes and cook until they're just beginning to break down, 3 to 4 minutes.

- Add **¼ cup peperoncini brine**, along with all of the reserved roasted red pepper brine. Taste and adjust the seasoning with salt and black pepper. Reduce the heat to medium-low.

3 COOK THE EGGS AND SERVE:

- Crack **1 large egg** into a small dish. With the back of a spoon, create a little indentation in the sauce and gently tip in the egg. Repeat with the remaining **3 eggs**, spacing them evenly apart. Season the tops of the eggs with salt and black pepper, cover with a lid or baking sheet, and cook until the yolks are just set, 10 to 12 minutes.

- When ready to serve, scatter with **a big handful of sliced peperoncini**, scoop the stew into bowls, and serve with warmed tortillas or bread.

COOK ALONG!

AUDIO

BLISTERED PEPPS

WITH TORN HALLOUMI & WARM SHALLOT DRESSING

GOES WITH: CHILE-BASTED HALF CHICKEN WITH CAPER CHIMICHURRI (PAGE 182), KIELBASA & CABBAGE PITAS WITH CURRY MUSTARD (PAGE 162)

SERVES 4

QUICK AS HECK!

PRODUCE

- 2 medium shallots
- 4 garlic cloves
- 2 poblano peppers (about 8 ounces)
- 8 ounces shishito peppers

DAIRY

- 8 ounces halloumi cheese

PANTRY

- 1 cup canned chickpeas
- ⅓ cup extra-virgin olive oil, plus more for greasing and drizzling
- Kosher salt and freshly ground black pepper
- ½ cup red wine vinegar
- Sugar
- Grilled pita, lavash, or bread, for serving (optional)

SPECIAL EQUIPMENT

- Grill or grill pan

The chickpeas in this recipe were that "more is more" moment when I realized that a shallot vinaigrette is great, but chickpeas add both texture and protein—and now we have a full meal. This dressing would pair easily with any type of grilled/roasted vegetable or green salad, so don't stop at pepps! (Speaking of pepps, I like poblano peppers and shishitos for a mix of flavors and spice levels, but use any peppers you like.)

1 MAKE THE WARM SHALLOT DRESSING:

- Thinly slice **2 medium shallots** and **4 garlic cloves**.

- Drain and rinse **1 cup canned chickpeas**.

- In a large skillet, combine **⅓ cup olive oil**, the shallots, and the garlic and cook over medium heat, stirring often, until they are softened and aromatic but not browned, about 3 minutes.

- Stir in the chickpeas, season with **salt and lots of freshly ground black pepper** and cook 1 minute longer to encourage the chickpeas to soak up all the flavor. Remove from the heat and stir in **½ cup red wine vinegar** and **a pinch of sugar**.

2 DO SOME PREP:

- Lightly grease the grates of your **grill**. Preheat the grill to medium-high.[1]

- Cut **8 ounces halloumi cheese** into ½-inch-thick slices.

- Combine **2 poblano peppers, 8 ounces shishito peppers**, and the halloumi on a large rimmed baking sheet. Drizzle with **olive oil**, using your hands to rub it all over and ensure an even coating. Season everything with salt and pepper.

3 GRILL THE PEPPS:

- Grill the poblanos first, turning every few minutes until charred all over. Return them to the baking sheet. Add the shishitos to the grill and cook, turning occasionally, until charred in spots, 4 to 5 minutes. Return them to the baking sheet.

- Before you grill the halloumi, transfer the poblanos to a cutting board. Scrape the skins off the poblanos, cut the peppers in half, discard the stems, and scrape out the seeds. Tear the poblanos into large pieces.

4 GRILL THE HALLOUMI:

- Oil the grill grates once more before adding the halloumi to ensure the cheese doesn't stick. Add the halloumi to the hottest part of the grill and cook until golden brown and crispy underneath, about 2 minutes. Flip and cook on the second side for 1 to 2 minutes. (This would also be a good time to grill your **pita, lavash**, or **bread**, if you've got it!)

5 SERVE:

- Arrange the peppers on a large serving platter. Tear the halloumi as you add it to the platter.

- Spoon the chickpeas and warm shallot dressing over everything. Season with more black pepper and serve with your grilled bread for scooping it all up.

[1] If you have access to a grill, you should absolutely use it. However, I have also made this dish indoors many times on a cast-iron grill pan. You might lose some of that smoky charred flavor, but the vinegary shallot and chickpea vinaigrette will make up for it, and then some.

FENNEL TORTILLA

SERVES 8 TO 10

GOES WITH: DILLY BEANS & BURRATA WITH FRIZZLED SHALLOTS
(PAGE 218), THE ONLY MEAT LOAF THAT MATTERS (PAGE 153),
MISO-BRAISED CHICKEN & LEEKS (PAGE 178)

ONE INGREDIENT, MANY WAYS (PG 21)

PRODUCE

- 2½ pounds fennel bulbs (about 4 medium)
- 1½ pounds Yukon Gold potatoes (about 4 large)
- 1 garlic clove
- 2 lemons

PROTEIN

- 13 large eggs plus 1 large egg yolk

PANTRY

- 1 heaping tablespoon fennel seeds
- 3 cups extra-virgin olive oil
- Kosher salt and freshly ground black pepper

SPECIAL EQUIPMENT

- Mini food processor or blender

If you don't like fennel—too licorice-y, yada yada, I've heard it all before—you can go ahead and flip to the next page. I'm not even gonna try. If, like me, you fall into the camp of fennel lovers, then BOY OH BOY, do I have something special for you. This is Spanish tortilla adjacent. It occurred to me that fennel behaves like onions (sweetening as it caramelizes), and wouldn't it be great if the whole thing tasted like sweet jammy fennel instead of onions? This is a labor of love, but a fennel lover will understand why it's allll worth it.

1 DO SOME PREP:

- Trim the tops from **2½ pounds fennel**. Slice the stalks as thin as possible to measure about two nice handfuls. Chop a big handful of fennel fronds. Transfer the fronds and sliced stalks to a medium bowl. Keep chilled until ready to serve.

- Cut the fennel bulbs in half lengthwise. Cut each half crosswise into ¼-inch-thick slices.

- Using a mortar and pestle or a spice grinder, finely grind **1 heaping tablespoon fennel seeds**.[1]

2 COOK THE FENNEL:

- Line a rimmed baking sheet with a triple layer of paper towels.

- Into a large Dutch oven, pour **3 cups olive oil** and place over medium heat. Add one small slice of the fennel bulb. When the fennel slice begins to sizzle, add the rest of the sliced fennel bulbs. (The fennel won't be fully submerged at this point, but it will shrink substantially as it cooks.) Cook, stirring occasionally, until the slices are softened, seriously shrunken in size, and just starting to turn golden, 15 to 18 minutes.

3 COOK THE POTATOES:

- While the fennel is cooking, slice **1½ pounds Yukon Gold potatoes** ¼ inch thick.

- Raise the heat under the oil to medium-high and add the potatoes to the pot, being sure to separate the slices as they go into the oil so they don't stick together. Add the ground fennel, reserving about ½ teaspoon to use in the aioli. Fry, stirring frequently, until the potatoes are golden brown in places and tender on the insides, about 12 minutes.

- Using a slotted spoon, transfer the potatoes and fennel to the paper towels, leaving the oil behind. (You're going to have a messy pile of broken-down veg. That's what you want!) Season the veg with **2 teaspoons salt** and **freshly ground black pepper**.

- Transfer ¾ cup of the fennel oil to a heatproof vessel, and chill until cool. Once cool, remove it from the refrigerator so that it doesn't solidify. Reserve the rest of the oil for cooking the eggs.

4 MAKE THE TORTILLA:

- Into a large bowl, crack **12 large eggs**. Whisk until smooth and season with **1 teaspoon salt**. Add the cooked fennel and potatoes to the bowl and fold gently to combine.

(CONT. ON PAGE 214)

[1] Alternatively, put the fennel seeds on a cutting board and crush them with the bottom of a heavy skillet or saucepan.

COOK ALONG!

AUDIO

● In a large (11- or 12-inch) nonstick skillet, heat 3 tablespoons of the remaining fennel oil over medium-high heat. To make sure the oil is hot enough, drop a bit of the egg mixture into the skillet; it should sizzle furiously.

● Scrape the egg mixture into the skillet. Let the edges bubble and set ever so slightly, 10 to 15 seconds. This step should basically feel like you're scrambling eggs and will take 2 to 3 minutes: Using a rubber spatula, begin to scrape around the sides of the skillet, then the center, too, shaking and tilting the pan as you go to encourage the uncooked egg to reach the outer edges. Continue until the top of the tortilla has no more super-runny parts but is still quite wet and uncooked.

● Reduce the heat to medium-low and let the tortilla cook until the bottom is lightly golden brown (peek with a spatula), 5 to 6 minutes. The top should still look quite uncooked.

● Run the spatula around the edge of the pan and shake to ensure the tortilla will release. REALLY shake it. You don't want it falling apart on you! Remove the skillet from the heat and invert a large rimless plate. In one swift move, flip the skillet so that the tortilla lands on the plate. Gently slide the tortilla back into the skillet so that the bottom is now the top. Tuck and nudge the edges inward so that it encloses itself and becomes puck-like in shape.

● Cook over medium heat for 2 to 3 minutes, just until the underside gets color. The goal is to keep the inside slightly undercooked and soft.

● Slide the tortilla onto a serving platter to rest as you make the aioli, if you so choose. You could skip this next step if you're not up for aioli, and just stir together some mayo and garlic and call it a day, or . . .

5 MAKE THE FENNEL SEED AIOLI:

● Finely grate ½ **garlic clove** and add it to a **mini food processor** or **blender**, along with the **juice of ½ lemon**, the ¾ cup cooled fennel oil, the remaining **1 large egg plus 1 large egg yolk**, the reserved ½ teaspoon ground fennel seed, and a very large pinch of salt. Process until smooth and thick. Add more salt and lemon juice as needed till the aioli tastes really bright and yummy.

6 FINISH IT UP AND SERVE:

● Dress the sliced fennel stalks and fennel fronds with **lemon juice** and some more of the fennel oil. Season generously with salt and pepper.

● Slice the tortilla and serve, topped with aioli and the fennel stalk salad.

SHOESTRING ONION RINGS WITH PEPERONCINI & YUMMY DUST

SERVES 2 TO 4

GOES WITH: SURF & TURF WITH GOCHUJANG BLACK PEPPER BUTTER (PAGE 161),
HOT SAUCE–BRAISED SHORT RIBS WITH WINTER SQUASH (PAGE 149)

QUICK AS HECK!

This is one of those rare occasions where I believe deep-frying at home is wholeheartedly worth the hassle. You can use ANY kind of onion for these rings, and either hand-slice them or use a mandoline to get them super thin. A note on the yummy dust: It's a super-savory mix of nutritional yeast and spices and truly is yummy AF, so scale up the recipe and keep the excess on hand to toss it on popcorn, roasted vegetables, and salads.

PRODUCE

● 1 pound onions, any kind
(1 large or 2 small)

DAIRY

● 2 cups buttermilk

PANTRY

● 3 cups all-purpose flour

● Kosher salt and freshly ground black pepper

● 2 teaspoons smoked paprika

● 2 teaspoons garlic powder

● Vegetable oil, for frying
(about 10 cups)

● 2 tablespoons nutritional yeast

● ½ cup sliced jarred peperoncini, drained

1 SET UP YOUR FRY STATION:

● In a 9 × 13-inch baking dish, whisk together **3 cups all-purpose flour**, **2 teaspoons salt**, and **1½ teaspoons freshly ground black pepper**.

● In a large bowl, whisk together **2 cups buttermilk**, **1½ teaspoons smoked paprika**, **1½ teaspoons garlic powder**, **1½ teaspoons salt**, and **1 teaspoon pepper**.

● Fill a large Dutch oven or heavy-bottomed pot with enough **vegetable oil** to reach a depth of 2 inches.

2 PREP THE ONIONS:

● Trim the ends of **1 pound onion(s)** and peel and discard the skins. Sharpen your knife! Slice your onions into ⅛-inch-thick rings.[1]

● Separate the onion slices into individual rings and place the rings in the buttermilk mixture. Let sit at room temperature, tossing occasionally, for at least 10 minutes and up to 2 hours before frying.

3 MAKE THE YUMMY DUST:

● In a small bowl, combine **2 tablespoons nutritional yeast**, the remaining **½ teaspoon smoked paprika**, remaining **½ teaspoon garlic powder**, **1 teaspoon salt**, and **1 teaspoon pepper**. Rub between your fingers to incorporate and break down the nutritional yeast.

4 DREDGE THE RINGS:

● Heat the pot of oil over medium heat until it reaches 350°F. If you don't have a thermometer, you'll know the oil is ready when a little bit of batter dropped in sputters violently. It's too hot if the bit of batter immediately burns. Line a large plate with paper towels.

● While the oil heats, using a pair of tongs or 2 forks, transfer the onion rings to the seasoned flour and toss to coat thoroughly. Get your hands involved, because coating the rings super well is key to crispiness![2]

5 FRY AND SERVE:

● Shake off any excess flour from the rings. Working in batches, use a spider or a pair of tongs to gently lower about one-third of the onions into the oil, being sure not to overcrowd the pot. Gently stir to prevent clumping and immediately raise the heat to high to maintain an oil temperature of 350°F (adjust the heat as needed to keep the temp steady). Fry until crisp and golden brown, 3 to 5 minutes.

● Transfer the rings to the paper-towel-lined plate and sprinkle liberally with the yummy dust. Repeat with the remaining onions, being sure to return the oil to 350°F before dropping in the next batch.

● Toss the onion rings with **½ cup sliced peperoncini** and serve piled high.

[1] Alternatively, use a mandoline. If your onions are wider than your mandoline, cut them in half through the root end before slicing. Set the mandoline to a thickness of about ⅛ inch.

[2] Note that the longer the rings stay in the marinade, the more they'll break down/collapse. You may need to take a bit more time when dredging them to ensure that every ring is individually coated in flour, but the payoff to longer marinating is more flavor.

DILLY BEANS & BURRATA WITH FRIZZLED SHALLOTS

GOES WITH: CRISPY ORECCHIETTE WITH SPICY SAUSAGE & COLLARD RAGÙ (PAGE 111), FENNEL ON FENNEL ON FENNEL TORTILLA (PAGE 212)

SERVES 4

QUICK AS HECK!

PRODUCE

- 4 medium shallots
- 1 bunch of scallions
- 4 garlic cloves
- 1 small red onion
- 1 bunch of dill

DAIRY

- 1 (8-ounce) ball burrata cheese

PANTRY

- ½ cup extra-virgin olive oil, plus more for drizzling
- Kosher salt and freshly ground black pepper
- 2 (15.5-ounce) cans black-eyed peas or other small canned bean
- ½ cup white balsamic or red wine vinegar

This one goes out to my dear friend Nora, who once made me a black-eyed pea salad that I will never forget for its multitude of jammy alliums and obscene amounts of dill. When I told Nora (an incredibly talented cook, recipe developer, and food stylist herself) that I was going to include an ode to her black-eyed pea salad in my book, she replied, "THAT'S what I'm going to be remembered for?!?!" Yes, Nora, yes it is.

1 FRIZZLE THE SHALLOTS:

- Line a plate with paper towels.

- Thinly slice **4 medium shallots**. In a medium pot, combine half of the shallots with **½ cup olive oil**. Place over medium heat and cook, stirring every 2 minutes or so, to encourage the shallot rings to separate and cook evenly, until golden brown and frizzled, 8 to 10 minutes. Using a slotted spoon, transfer the shallots to the paper-towel-lined plate to drain, reserving the oil in the pot.

- Season the shallots with **salt**.

2 MEANWHILE, PREP AND SAUTÉ THE REMAINING ALLIUMS:

- While the shallots frizzle, slice **1 bunch of scallions** and **4 garlic cloves**. Finely chop **1 small red onion**. Set the garlic aside.

- Drain and rinse **2 (15.5-ounce) cans black-eyed peas**.

- Return the pot to medium heat and add the sliced scallions, onions, and remaining shallots to the oil. Season with **a few BIG pinches of salt** and cook, stirring occasionally, until jammy, 8 to 10 minutes. Add the sliced garlic and cook, stirring, until fragrant, 1 to 2 minutes.

- Stir in **½ cup white balsamic vinegar**, the beans, some more salt, and **lots of freshly ground black pepper**. Cook until just warmed through, 2 to 3 minutes. Taste and adjust the seasoning (I'm going to say it one last time: these need a lot of salt, especially if your beans had no sodium to begin with). YOU'RE PROBS NOT USING ENOUGH ... SALT (PG 20) Remove from the heat and transfer the beans to a bowl to cool.

3 ADD THE HERBS AND SERVE:

- When the beans are room temp, finely chop **1 bunch of dill** and stir it into the beans.

- Transfer the beans to a serving dish and tear open an **8-ounce ball of burrata** right on top. Season the burrata with salt and black pepper.

- Top with the frizzled shallots and a drizz of olive oil!

COOK ALONG!

AUDIO

GOES WITH: SURF & TURF WITH GOCHUJANG BLACK PEPPER BUTTER (PAGE 161), SPICED LENTIL BURGER WITH A VERY SPECIAL SAUCE (PAGE 245), KIELBASA & CABBAGE PITAS WITH CURRY MUSTARD (PAGE 162)

SERVE 4 TO 6

QUICK AS HECK!

Nothing screams "PARTY!" like a grand aioli, a classic French platter of cold vegetables and protein served with a big bowl of garlicky aioli for dipping. Okay, there are probably a few things that scream "party" more (see Party Chix, page 185), but I definitely get hyped when there's a grand aioli on the table. This version is vegan (!) thanks to the hazelnuts used as the creamy base for the aioli, and a lotttt more fun because all of the veg get grilled instead of boiled! The upgrade you never knew you always needed. This aioli can stick around in the fridge all week to use as a sauce for roasted veg or (thinned with a little more vinegar) as a salad dressing.

PRODUCE

● 5 large garlic cloves

● 3 pounds grillable green vegetables, such as zucchini, leeks, romanesco cauliflower, cabbage, scallions, green beans, asparagus, Broccolini, and/or broccoli

PANTRY

● ¾ cup blanched hazelnuts or almonds

● 1 cup extra-virgin olive oil

● 3 tablespoons sherry vinegar, plus more for drizzling

● Kosher salt and freshly ground black pepper

SPECIAL EQUIPMENT

● Blender

● Grill

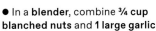

MAKE THE HAZELNUT AIOLI:

● In a **blender**, combine **¾ cup blanched nuts** and **1 large garlic clove**. Blend until pulverized.

● Add **¾ cup olive oil, ¼ cup water, 3 tablespoons sherry vinegar**, and **2 teaspoons salt**. Blend on high for 1 minute. If the aioli is still quite thick, add water, a few tablespoons at a time, until creamy and similar in consistency to mayonnaise. (You may end up needing quite a bit more water.) Taste and add more salt as needed! Transfer to a small serving bowl.

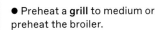

GRILL THE GREEN THINGS:

● Preheat a **grill** to medium or preheat the broiler.

● In a small bowl, whisk together the remaining **4 finely grated garlic cloves** and **¼ cup olive oil**.

● Separate **3 pounds of grillable green vegetables** into two groups: smaller/thinner veg, like green beans, scallions, and asparagus (leave these whole), and everything else (cut these into 2-inch-thick pieces; any length will do). Add all the veg to a large rimmed baking sheet. Season well with salt and **freshly ground black pepper**, add the garlic oil, and toss well until everything is evenly coated.

● Arrange the veg on the grill, starting with the longest-cooking vegetables, cover, and cook, turning occasionally, until tender and charred all over. Broccoli, cabbage, or cauliflower will need 18 to 20 minutes. Broccolini and zucchini will take 8 to 10 minutes. Shishito peppers, asparagus, and green beans will cook in 5 to 7 minutes. Throw your scallions on last—they require only 2 to 3 minutes to char and get tender. If you're broiling, set the baking sheet under the broiler and keep an eye on things; you'll need to transfer items from the baking sheet to a serving platter as they finish cooking.

SERVE:

● Arrange all the grilled veg on a serving platter with the bowl of aioli in the center for dipping. IT'S ALL IN THE SAUCE (PG 21)

● Lightly drizzle the veg with a splash or two more sherry vinegar and serve at any temperature you'd like.

OLIVE OIL–DROWNED POTATOES WITH LEMONY ONIONS & HERBS

SERVES 4

GOES WITH: CHICKEN PICCATA WITH SWEET CORN, CHILES & BUTTERMILK (PAGE 181)

PRODUCE

- 2 pounds Yukon Gold potatoes
- ½ small red onion
- 2 lemons
- 1 bunch (or a mix) of tender herbs, such as cilantro, basil, parsley, dill, and/or chives

PANTRY

- Kosher salt and freshly ground black pepper
- ⅓ cup extra-virgin olive oil, plus more for drizzling

This recipe is allll about the olive oil. You'll drench salted boiled potatoes in extra-virgin olive oil and let them luxuriate in grassy deliciousness. It sounds like a lot of olive oil, and it is. That's the point. No need to break the bank in the olive oil department, but definitely seek out something that is "extra-virgin" and "cold-pressed" for the best flavor. Lucini and California Olive Ranch are relatively affordable and two of my faves.

1 COOK THE POTATOES:

- If your potatoes are larger than the size of your palm, cut them in half crosswise. Otherwise, in a large pot, cover **2 pounds Yukon Gold potatoes** with 3 quarts water. Season with **1 cup Diamond Crystal (or ¾ cup Morton) kosher salt** and bring to a simmer over medium heat. Simmer until the potatoes are tender when pierced with a fork, but not falling apart and mushy. The timing will vary depending how big your potatoes are, so just keep checking. Drain the potatoes.

2 MAKE THE LEMONY ONIONS:

- While the potatoes cook, thinly slice **½ small red onion**. Place in a medium bowl and season with **a big pinch of salt** and the **juice of ½ lemon**, squeezing together to help them macerate in the lemon juice. Set aside.

3 ASSEMBLE:

- Once the potatoes are drained but still warm, break them apart with your hands or crush them with the bottom of a glass measuring cup to encourage them to break into a few pieces. Transfer the potatoes to a serving dish and drizzle them with **⅓ cup olive oil**. Season them with salt and **lots and lots of freshly ground black pepper**. Add more olive oil if they seem to soak it all up very quickly. YOU'RE PROBS NOT USING ENOUGH ... OLIVE OIL (PG 20)

- Cut the remaining **lemon** in half and squeeze the juice of both halves over the potatoes.

- Pick the leaves from **a bunch of mixed tender herbs**, add to the lemony onions, tossing once or twice to combine. Pile the onions and herbs on top of the potatoes. Season with more black pepper, lemon juice, and olive oil.

SPICY COCONUT-SMOTHERED GREEN BEANS

GOES WITH: COLD NOODLES WITH GRATED TOMATO SAUCE & CHILI OIL (PAGE 115), PUT THE LIME IN THE COCONUT CORN BREAD WITH SALTY COCONUT JAM (PAGE 132), RED CURRY HOT WINGS ROLLED IN PEANUTS (PAGE 191)

SERVES 4

QUICK AS HECK!

The coconut-chile mixture that absolutely smothers these green beans is an ode to one of the greatest condiments I've ever had in my life, Filipino palapa. I first tasted it when Tom Cunanan, former chef at Bad Saint restaurant in Washington, D.C., came to the Bon Appétit Test Kitchen years ago. He brought an arsenal of homemade Filipino condiments, and the coconut palapa stole my heart. It was absolutely everything and then some—sweet, sticky, spicy, salty, and crunchy—and we ate it on eggs, salads, grilled fish, and even ice cream. My take is a decidedly lazier and less-authentic version (I sadly don't have the tools to grate the flesh of a fresh coconut), but it brings me close enough to the memory of Tom's.

PRODUCE

- 1 (1½-inch) piece of fresh ginger
- 1 medium shallot
- 2 Fresno chiles or small jalapeños
- 5 garlic cloves
- 2 limes
- 1¼ pounds green beans

PANTRY

- ⅔ cup unsweetened shredded coconut
- Neutral oil, such as canola or vegetable
- Kosher salt
- ¼ cup roasted, salted peanuts

SPECIAL EQUIPMENT

- Food processor

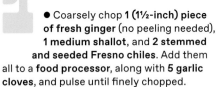

1 MAKE THE COCONUT JAZZ:

- Coarsely chop **1 (1½-inch) piece of fresh ginger** (no peeling needed), **1 medium shallot**, and **2 stemmed and seeded Fresno chiles**. Add them all to a **food processor**, along with **5 garlic cloves**, and pulse until finely chopped.

- In a large nonstick skillet, toast **⅔ cup shredded coconut** over medium heat, stirring and tossing often so it cooks evenly, until golden brown, 4 to 5 minutes.

- Scoot the coconut over to the edge of the pan to make room for the aromatics. Add **a couple big glugs of neutral oil** to the center of the skillet, along with all the finely chopped aromatics, and cook, stirring often, until their moisture has cooked off and they are jammy and beginning to turn golden at the edges, 4 to 5 minutes.

- Remove from the heat. Stir the scooted coconut back into the aromatics to combine. Finely grate the **zest of 2 limes** into the skillet. Season with **salt** and set aside.

2 BLISTER THE GREEN BEANS:

- Finely chop **¼ cup roasted, salted peanuts**.

- Trim the ends of **1¼ pounds green beans**.

- Heat a large cast-iron skillet over high heat. YES! HIGH! We want to blister these babies! TURN YA BURNERS UP (PG 21)

- Add **a few very generous glugs of neutral oil** and wait until you see wisps of smoke emanating from the pan. Add the green beans, season well with salt, and toss with tongs to coat in the oil. Cook, tossing with tongs every 2 to 3 minutes, until blistered, charred in places, and shriveled, 7 to 8 minutes.

- Remove from the heat and stir in the coconut mixture and crushed peanuts.

- Squeeze the **juice of both limes** onto the green beans and taste and add more salt if needed. Pile high and serve!

CRISPY POTATO SKINS WITH FRIED HERB AIOLI

GOES WITH: THE ONLY MEAT LOAF THAT MATTERS (PAGE 153), LAMB CHOPS SCOTTADITO WITH MINTY BEANS & ARTICHOKES (PAGE 157), SALTED CITRUS SHANDY (PAGE 229)

SERVES 4 TO 6

Potatoes and aioli—a match made in heaven. You could stop right there and have yourself a real nice time. Orrrr, you could throw a bunch of fried herbs, capers, and cornichons into the mix and have an unforgettable one. Frying woody herbs tones down their bitterness and intensity, leaving behind pure herbaceous flavor, so you can use a lot of them without overwhelming your palate. If watching sports is your thing or whatever, add these to your next gameday lineup. They'll dominate, I promise.

PRODUCE

- 4 large russet potatoes (3 pounds)
- 1 bunch of flat-leaf parsley
- 1 garlic clove
- 24 sprigs mixed hardy herbs, such as rosemary, sage, thyme, and/or marjoram

PANTRY

- 8 cornichons, plus 2 tablespoons of their brine
- ½ cup mayonnaise
- 2 tablespoons capers in brine, drained
- Kosher salt and freshly ground black pepper
- ½ cup extra-virgin olive oil
- ½ cup neutral oil, such as canola or vegetable
- Flaky sea salt

1 BAKE THE POTATOES:

- Preheat the oven to 425°F.

- Rinse and scrub **4 large russet potatoes**. Place on a rimmed baking sheet. Transfer to the oven and bake until tender when pierced with a toothpick, about 1½ hours. Let sit until they are cool enough to handle. Keep the oven on.

2 MEANWHILE, START THE AIOLI:

- Finely chop **8 cornichons** and the **leaves from 1 bunch of parsley**. Grate **1 garlic clove**. Add all to a small bowl.

- Stir in **½ cup mayonnaise**, **2 tablespoons drained capers**, and **a big splash of cornichon brine**. Season with **kosher salt and freshly ground black pepper** and set aside. IT'S ALL IN THE sAUCE (PG 21)

3 ROAST THE SKINS:

- Cut the baked potatoes in half lengthwise. Scoop the flesh into a large bowl, leaving a ¼-inch-thick layer attached to the skin. Reserve the scooped potato flesh for another use. (The Mashed Potato Arancini on page 63 would be perf!!) Rip the potato skins into ragged 2- to 3-inch pieces. Season with kosher salt and black pepper.

- In a 12-inch cast-iron skillet, heat **½ cup olive oil** and **½ cup neutral oil** over medium-high heat. Add one piece of potato skin to the skillet. When it begins to sizzle vigorously, add the remaining pieces, turning to coat, and position them flesh-side down. Remove from the heat.

- Transfer the skillet to the oven and roast the potato skins until deeply golden on the undersides, 8 to 10 minutes. Flip and roast until nearly golden all over, about 10 minutes longer.

- Using tongs or a slotted fish spatula, remove the potato skins from the skillet, leaving the oil behind, and place them on a rimmed baking sheet. Reduce the oven temperature to 300°F and transfer to the oven to keep the skins warm.

4 FRY THE HERBS:

- Line a plate with paper towels.

- Transfer the skillet with the oil back to the stovetop and place over medium-high heat.

- Working in batches to avoid crowding the skillet, add the **24 sprigs of mixed hardy herbs** (keep them on their stems) and fry until very lightly golden in spots, about 30 seconds. Transfer the herbs to the paper-towel-lined plate and season with kosher salt.

5 SERVE:

- Strip the fried herb leaves off any stalks that are thick or tough and discard the stalks. Finely chop two-thirds of the herbs and add to the mayonnaise mixture.

- Plate up the potato skins with the aioli and garnish with the remaining fried herbs and **flaky sea salt**. Serve hotttt.

DRINK
BREAK

SALTED CITRUS SHANDY

SERVES 4

GOES WITH: ARTY REUBEN (PAGE 247), CRISPY CORNMEAL CALAMARI WITH FRIED BASIL & OTHER YUMMY STUFF (PAGE 150), PARTY CHIX (PAGE 185)

- 3¼ pounds mixed citrus, such as lemons, limes, grapefruit, and/or oranges

- ¾ cup sugar

- Kosher salt

- Ice

- 4 (12-ounce) cans wheat beer or pilsner

I'm at the point in my life where I now prefer a shandy to a beer. In the winter, we'll make them with amaro as the sugar syrup, and in the summer, I make this recipe with a mixed citrus simple syrup (lemons, oranges, whatever I've got) and serve it in a glass with a salted rim. This recipe will yield more syrup than needed for four shandies, which will come in handy when, inevitably, everyone asks for another round.

- Using a peeler, remove the **zest of 3¼ pounds mixed citrus** in long strips. Place the zest and **¾ cup sugar** in a resealable container. Using your hands, work the zest into the sugar to help expel its oils, about 2 minutes.

- Add **¾ cup very hot tap water**, cover tightly, and shake vigorously until the sugar has fully dissolved. Let cool.

- Squeeze the **juice of all the citrus** into a pitcher, making one big citrus juice mix.

- Spread some **salt** on a small plate.

- Run one of the spent citrus halves around the rim of each glass and roll the rim in the salt to coat. Fill each glass with **ice** and add ¾ ounce of the citrus syrup and 1½ ounces of the mixed citrus juice, then top with **about 6 ounces beer**. Serve the remaining beer alongside for top-ups.

BIG-ASS LATKE

GOES WITH: GREEN CHICKEN SOUP WITH CHICKPEAS & SIZZLED CORIANDER (PAGE 197), SAUCY, GLOSSY SPANISH EGGS (PAGE 208)

PRODUCE

- 1 large white or yellow onion
- 2 lemons
- 3 pounds russet potatoes (4 or 5 large)
- 1 small bunch of dill

DAIRY

- ½ cup sour cream

PANTRY

- Kosher salt and freshly ground black pepper
- 2 tablespoons prepared horseradish
- 2 tablespoons capers in brine, drained
- 3 tablespoons all-purpose flour
- ½ cup canola oil

Latkes take a long time to make because you've got to fry them in batches, and by the time the last latke is done, the first is either cold or soggy. Enter the Big-Ass Latke, a "one size serves all" kind of joint, like a rösti but with raw potatoes. You'll achieve a crispy exterior and tender interior by rotating the pan over the burner, but you'll serve it up in big fat wedges. Onions, capers, dill, and the works make this dish as suitable for a random Sunday brunch as it is for Hanukkah.

1 PICKLE THE ONIONS:

- Peel **1 large white or yellow onion**. Very thinly slice about a third of it crosswise into rings. Place the rings in a small bowl, grate the **zest of 1 lemon** over them, and squeeze the **juice of ½ lemon** on top. Season with **salt** and let sit.

2 MAKE THE HORSERADISH SAUCE:

- In a small bowl, combine **½ cup sour cream** and **a nice big spoonful each of the prepared horseradish** and **capers**. Zest the remaining **1 lemon** into the bowl and season generously with salt and **freshly ground black pepper**. Taste and adjust with more salt, pepper, horseradish, or capers.

3 MAKE THE LATKE MIX:[1]

- Grate what remains of the **onion** on the large holes of a box grater. Transfer to a large, clean kitchen towel and wring out as much moisture as possible over the sink. Place in a medium bowl.

- Peel **3 pounds russet potatoes**, then coarsely grate them right onto the used kitchen towel. Try to get the longest shreds possible by making long lengthwise gratings of the potato. Wrap the grated potatoes up in the towel, then wring out the liquid over the sink. Add to the bowl of grated onions.

- Add **3 tablespoons all-purpose flour**, season with salt and pepper, and toss to combine. Taste a pinch (it's okay to eat a little bit of raw potato and flour, don't worry!)—is it seasoned enough? Prolly not; add some more!

4 GET COOKING:

- In a 9- to 11-inch nonstick skillet with sloped sides, heat **½ cup canola oil** over medium-high heat. When the oil is very hot, add the potato mixture and press lightly into an even layer, covering the surface and up the sides of the pan.

- Reduce the heat to medium. Let cook, rotating the pan 90 degrees every few minutes to encourage even browning, until the edges are deeply golden brown and crisp, 7 to 9 minutes. Remove from the heat.

- Working carefully, grab a heatproof bowl and a spatula and use the spatula to hold the latke in place in the skillet as you tip the hot oil into the bowl. Once all the oil has been removed from the skillet, slide the latke onto a large dinner plate. Invert the skillet on top of the plate and swiftly flip the latke back into the skillet so that the cooked, crispy bottom is now the top. Scoot the sides of the latke in to create a puck-like shape.

- Pour the reserved oil back into the skillet around the edges of the latke. Keep the heat on medium and cook, rotating the pan 90 degrees once or twice, until deeply golden brown and crisp on the bottom, 6 to 8 minutes.

- Pour off any remaining oil at this point (and discard it once it's cool; it's done its job) and carefully transfer the latke to a serving plate. Season with salt. Top the latke with horseradish cream, a bigggg pile of lemony onions, and **lots of torn dill**.

[1] Note: Don't let this mixture sit around or the potatoes will oxidize. Start grating only when you're ready to get cooking!

COOK ALONG!

VIDEO

COLD
FRIED CHICKEN SANDO WITH CHILI CRISP MAYO

MAKES 2

GOES WITH: CUCUMBER BAG SALAD WITH MISO-POPPY DRESSING (PAGE 93), BRUSSELS SPROUTS WITH SHALLOTS & STICKY FISH SAUCE (PAGE 72)

QUICK AS HECK!

PRODUCE

- 6 large butter lettuce leaves
- ½ small white onion

PROTEIN

- 2 pieces leftover fried chicken (see Party Chix, page 185)

PANTRY

- ½ cup mayonnaise
- 2 tablespoons chili crisp
- 2 teaspoons toasted sesame oil
- Unseasoned rice vinegar
- Kosher salt
- 4 slices brioche
- 4 baby dill pickles

I love cold leftover fried chicken, and I know I'm not the only one. (We're the same cohort of people who get down with cold pizza.) In an ideal scenario, you would have fried up some Party Chix (page 185) last night so that all you've got to do today is stir together some chili crisp mayo, throw this sandwich together, and take it to the beach, as the universe intended. But let's be honest, this will also work with a couple fried breasts from Popeyes or KFC. Live ya life.

1 MAKE THE CHILI CRISP MAYO:

- In a small bowl, stir together **½ cup mayo, 2 big spoonfuls chili crisp, 2 teaspoons toasted sesame oil,** and **a small splash of rice vinegar.** Season with **salt.** CONDIMENTS ARE YOUR BFFL (PG 22)

2 PREP THE SANDO:

- Position a rack in the top third of the oven. Preheat the broiler.

- Separate, wash, and dry **6 large butter lettuce leaves.**

- Slice **½ small white onion** crosswise into paper-thin rings.

- If your **leftover fried chicken** is still on the bone, cut off the meat and discard the bones.

- Place **4 slices brioche** on a rimmed baking sheet and toast under the broiler until golden brown on the top sides, about 90 seconds total.

- Slice **4 baby dill pickles** lengthwise into planks.

3 ASSEMBLE:

- Slather some chili crisp mayo on the toasted sides of the bread.

- Working from the bottom up, pile each sando with lettuce. Drizzle it lightly with rice vinegar to dress it and season it with salt.

- Add the pickles, leftover fried chicken, and some thinly sliced white onion. Top with the remaining slices of brioche, cut the sando in half, and eat!!

NOT SO BASIC B TURKEY SANDO

[MAKES 2]

GOES WITH: PEACH & PICKLED PEPPER PANZANELLA (PAGE 68), PISTACHIO, BROWN BUTTER & HALVA CHOCOLATE CHUNK COOKIES (PAGE 283)

QUICK AS HECK!

In this turkey sandwich rebrand, boring-ass L, T, O can GTFO and make room for crunchy potato chips, tender herbs, avocado, and chimichurri mayo! If you can swing it, roasting your own turkey (or using leftover roasted turkey, say, after a certain holiday) will yield the best results. That way, you can slice the turkey into thicker, more substantial pieces. If roasting turkey is not gonna happen, deli-style turkey will also do the trick. If you're lucky, your butcher might be able to slice it thickly for you.

PRODUCE

- 1 cup packed cilantro leaves
- 1 cup packed flat-leaf parsley leaves
- 2 jalapeños
- 3 scallions
- 1 avocado
- 1 head Little Gem lettuce, or a few romaine leaves

PROTEIN

- 8 ounces roasted turkey, thickly sliced

PANTRY

- 2 teaspoons capers in brine, drained
- ½ cup mayonnaise
- 1 tablespoon sherry vinegar, plus more for drizzling
- Kosher salt and freshly ground black pepper
- 2 (5-inch) focaccia squares
- 2 handfuls of salt 'n' vinegar potato chips

1 MAKE THE CHIMICHURRI MAYO:

- Finely chop **2 teaspoons drained capers**.

- Finely chop **1 cup packed cilantro leaves** and **1 cup packed parsley leaves**.

- Trim and discard the stems from **2 jalapeños** and finely chop (discard the seeds if you are spice averse).

- Thinly slice **3 scallions**.

- In a medium bowl, whisk together **½ cup mayonnaise**, along with the chopped capers, cilantro, parsley, jalapeños, and scallions and **1 tablespoon sherry vinegar**. Season the chimichurri mayo with **salt and freshly ground black pepper**.

2 ASSEMBLE:

- Cut **2 (5-inch) focaccia squares** in half to split them. Slather each side with chimichurri mayo. Top the 2 bottom squares with **a few thick slices of turkey**.

- Cut **1 avocado** in half. Remove the pit, slice the flesh thinly, and layer it on top of the turkey. Season the avocado with salt and pepper and a drizzle of sherry vinegar.

- Top each with **a few Little Gem leaves** and **a handful of salt 'n' vinegar potato chips**. Place the remaining squares of focaccia on top, cut the sandos in half, and serve.

THE ONE & ONLY HOAGIE

MAKES 2

QUICK AS HECK!

PRODUCE

- ½ head iceberg lettuce
- ¼ medium red onion

DAIRY

- 2 ounces grated Parmigiano Reggiano (½ cup)

PROTEIN

- ⅓ pound sliced mortadella
- ⅓ pound sliced capicola
- ⅓ pound sliced spicy soppressata or salami

PANTRY

- ¾ cup jarred hot or mild giardiniera (preferably oil-packed)
- ¼ cup red wine vinegar
- Extra-virgin olive oil
- Kosher salt and freshly ground black pepper
- 2 hoagie rolls
- Chopped jarred Calabrian chiles (optional)

GOES WITH: SALTED CITRUS SHANDY (PAGE 229), DILLY BEANS & BURRATA WITH FRIZZLED SHALLOTS (PAGE 218)

While scientists tackle climate change and NASA explores dark matter in the universe, I spend my time dreaming up the ideal version of an Italian-style hoagie. FWIW, I think I've landed in a pretty great place. You may be surprised to see that there is no provolone on this sandwich. That is correct! It wasn't bringing enough flavor, so it got the boot in favor of Parmigiano Reggiano. A well-executed hoagie is all about the balance of fat and acid. The fat, in this case, is coming from a trifecta of deli meats (mortadella, capicola, and spicy soppressata), though any cured pork-based deli meats would be great, and it's balanced with the acid from a combination of red wine vinegar and jarred giardiniera pickles. I like Marconi brand's hot giardiniera best; it's Chicago-style, packed in oil, and IMO no hoagie is complete without it.

1 PREP THE SHRETTUCE SLAW:

- Thinly slice **½ head iceberg lettuce** to turn it into shrettuce.

- Thinly slice **¼ red onion**.

- In a large bowl, combine the shrettuce, red onion, **¾ cup giardiniera, 2 ounces grated Parm, ¼ cup red wine vinegar,** and **a couple glugs of olive oil.** Season with **salt and freshly ground black pepper** and toss well to combine. Taste and add more red wine vinegar as needed until it's super bright and zingy—it should be more intense than a salad because it's going to be combined with bread.

2 TOAST THE HOAGIE ROLL (OPTIONAL[1]):

- Preheat your broiler or toaster oven. Split **2 hoagie rolls** in half lengthwise and toast them on their cut sides until golden brown.

3 ASSEMBLE:

- Swipe each side of the hoagie roll with **a light coating of Calabrian chiles** (especially if your giardiniera is mild).

- Divide **⅓ pound sliced mortadella, ⅓ pound sliced capicola,** and **⅓ pound sliced spicy soppressata** evenly between the hoagie roll bottoms, gently draping the meats on and folding as needed.

- Pile a generous amount of shrettuce slaw on top of the meats.[2]

- Finish each sandwich with the top of the hoagie roll and cut in half crosswise. If it looks particularly unwieldy, you can wrap the hoag in parchment paper or aluminum foil to help keep it together.

[1] This is not a necessary step, but if your hoagie roll feels particularly soft and spongy, toasting will help avoid sog-town. If your roll is quite sturdy, you can move on to assembly.

[2] You'll need more than you think. The sandwich will compress after you've added the top of the hoagie roll. You're ultimately aiming for a sandwich that is 50 percent meat and 50 percent slaw once it's sliced.

FRIED MORTY–D SANDO

GOES WITH: DILLY BEANS & BURRATA WITH FRIZZLED SHALLOTS
(PAGE 218), SALTED CITRUS SHANDY (PAGE 229)

MAKES 2

QUICK AS HECK!

DAIRY

● 2 slices provolone cheese

PROTEIN

● 6 ounces thinly sliced mortadella

PANTRY

● ⅓ cup mayonnaise, plus more for schmearing

● 2 tablespoons whole-grain mustard

● 2 pretzel buns

● Extra-virgin olive oil

● Pickled sport peppers or other whole pickled peppers, for garnish

I had my first fried bologna sandwich at Au Cheval in Chicago and was left utterly speechless. It was dripping in sauce, stuffed with house-made bologna and melted American cheese, and was easily one of the best sandwiches I've ever had. That's how the Fried Morty-d Sando was born. Unlike bologna, where the pork's fat and meat are blended smooth, mortadella has fat dotted throughout like a pork-fat mosaic. Dijonnaise is the perfect bracing condiment for this rich and fatty sandwich, and pickled sport peppers provide some acidic relief between bites. Also, they're pickles—sandos looove pickles.

1 MAKE THE DIJONNAISE:

● In a small bowl, stir together **a few heaping dollops of mayonnaise** and **a couple tablespoons whole-grain mustard**. CONDIMENTS ARE YOUR BFFL (PG 22) If you are a mustard freak, add more—the ratio of this condiment is totally up to you.

2 FRY THE MORTY-D:

● Heat a large cast-iron skillet over medium heat. Lightly schmear the cut sides of **2 pretzel buns** with mayonnaise. Cook, cut-side down, until golden and crisp, 3 to 4 minutes. Transfer each bun to a plate.

● Add **a glug of olive oil** to the skillet, along with **6 ounces thinly sliced mortadella,** spreading the slices out in the skillet—they don't need to lie flat; in fact, little voluminous piles are fun because some bits get crispy and others stay tender. Cook until crispy and brown underneath, 90 seconds. Flip each piece of mortadella and cook on the second side for 90 seconds.

● Stack the morty-d slices into 2 tall piles and top each with **a slice of provolone cheese**. Reduce the heat to low and cook until the provolone has melted, about 30 seconds.

3 BUILD:

● Slather the cut sides of the buns with Dijonnaise. Place a mortadella stack on each bottom bun. Cover with the bun tops and, using a toothpick, skewer **some pickled sport peppers** on top of each sando.

SPICED LENTIL BURGER WITH A VERY SPECIAL SAUCE

MAKES 4

GOES WITH: PICKLE-MARINATED FETA (PAGE 65), SIZZLED DOLMAS WITH YOGURT & BROWN-BUTTERED PINE NUTS (PAGE 54)

The thing I love about lentil burgers is that they know who they are. They aren't pretending to be meat. They're just lentil burgers, loud and clear. And they're absolute sponges for flavor. I've packed these with spices, lemon zest, dried mint, crumbled feta, and chickpeas. The very special sauce on top is not your usual burger special sauce, but it's exactly the right condiment for the job. You'll see.

PRODUCE

- 1 large white or yellow onion
- 3 garlic cloves
- 1 lemon
- 2 Persian cucumbers
- 4 handfuls of arugula, for serving

DAIRY

- 4 ounces feta cheese
- ½ cup plain whole-milk yogurt (not Greek)

PANTRY

- Kosher salt and freshly ground black pepper
- ½ cup brown lentils
- 1 tablespoon coriander seeds
- Extra-virgin olive oil
- 2 teaspoons ground cumin
- Red pepper flakes
- 2 tablespoons dried mint
- 1 (15.5-ounce) can chickpeas, undrained
- 5 tablespoons all-purpose flour, plus more as needed
- 2 tablespoons mayonnaise
- 4 brioche buns

1 DO SOME PREP:

- Bring a medium pot of water to a boil over high heat. **Salt** generously and add **½ cup brown lentils**. Cook until tender but not falling apart, 8 to 10 minutes. Drain and transfer to a large bowl.

- Finely chop **1 large white onion**. Smash and peel **3 garlic cloves**.

- Crush **1 tablespoon coriander seeds**.

- Using a peeler, peel strips of **zest from 1 lemon**. Thinly slice the strips lengthwise, then slice the strips crosswise to finely mince them.

2 MAKE THE PATTIES:

- In a medium skillet, heat **a couple glugs of olive oil** over medium-high heat. Add the onions, season with **salt and freshly ground black pepper** and cook, stirring occasionally, until softened and just beginning to turn golden, 8 to 10 minutes.

- Finely grate the 3 garlic cloves into the skillet. Continue to cook, stirring, until the garlic is softened and fragrant but not browned, 1 minute. Add the crushed coriander seeds, **2 teaspoons ground cumin**, and **a couple pinches of red pepper flakes**.

- Add **about 1 tablespoon dried mint**, crumbling it finely with your fingers as you go. Sauté for 1 minute. Transfer the onion mixture to the bowl with the lentils.

- Open **1 (15.5-ounce) can chickpeas** and pour ¼ cup of the liquid (aquafaba) into the lentils. Drain the rest of the liquid and measure out ½ cup of the chickpeas (no need to rinse—the starchy liquid is working in our favor here to help bind the burger). Add the chickpeas to the bowl with the lentils.

- Stir in **1 tablespoon olive oil** and about half of the minced lemon zest. Mash the mixture with a potato masher until the lentils and chickpeas are lightly smashed. Season to taste with salt and pepper.

- Add **5 tablespoons flour** and stir to incorporate. Squeeze a small handful of the mixture in your hands—it should hold together in a smooshed mass. If it crumbles, add **another tablespoon of flour**. Crumble **4 ounces feta** into the bowl and fold to combine.

- Form the mixture into four (4-inch-wide) patties. Chill on a small baking sheet for at least 10 minutes, or until ready to cook.

3 MAKE THE VERY SPECIAL SAUCE:

- In a medium bowl, combine **½ cup yogurt**, **2 tablespoons mayonnaise**, and the remaining chopped lemon zest. With your fingers, finely crumble in the remaining **1 tablespoon dried mint**. Season with salt and pepper to taste.

4 PREP THE BURGER ACCOMPANIMENTS:

- Split **4 brioche buns** in half. Heat a large cast-iron skillet over medium heat. Add **a small glug of olive oil** and swirl to coat the pan. Toast the buns in the pan (in batches if necessary and replenishing oil as you go) until golden and crisp, 1 to 2 minutes.

- Thinly slice **2 Persian cucumbers** lengthwise into planks.

5 COOK THE BURGERS AND BUILD 'EM:

- Raise the heat to medium-high. Add **1 tablespoon olive oil** and swirl to coat. Add the burgers (in batches as necessary) and cook, undisturbed, until golden and crisp on the outside, 3 to 4 minutes per side. Repeat with any remaining burgers, adding more oil between batches.

- Build your burgers on the buns, each with some of the very special sauce, some sliced cucumbers, and **a pile of arugula**. Squeeze some **lemon juice** over the arugula. Top and serve.

ARTY REUBEN

GOES WITH: SALTED CITRUS SHANDY (PAGE 229), CRISPY POTATO SKINS WITH FRIED HERB AIOLI (PAGE 226), SHOESTRING ONION RINGS WITH PEPERONCINI & YUMMY DUST (PAGE 217)

QUICK AS HECK!

I loooove a classic Reuben, but I suspect that has a lot more to do with the interplay of oozy, melty Swiss cheese, tangy sauerkraut, and creamy Russian dressing than it does with the hero meat itself, corned beef. Turns out I'm right, because this vegetarian version replaces the corned beef with crispy, smoky seared artichokes and still satisfies my Reuben craving (and then some). Sorry, corned beef, I still love you, but I'll see you in my hash.

PRODUCE

- 1 large garlic clove

DAIRY

- 4 slices Swiss cheese

PANTRY

- ½ cup mayonnaise, plus more for brushing
- 2 tablespoons ketchup
- 2 tablespoons prepared horseradish
- Kosher salt and freshly ground black pepper
- ⅔ cup sauerkraut
- 2 (10-ounce) jars marinated artichokes
- Extra-virgin olive oil
- 1½ teaspoons smoked paprika
- 4 slices rye bread

1 MAKE THE RUSSIAN-ISH DRESSING:

- In a small bowl, whisk together **½ cup mayonnaise, 2 tablespoons ketchup**, and **2 tablespoons prepared horseradish**. Season with **lots of salt and freshly ground black pepper**.

2 PREP THE ARTICHOKES AND KRAUT:

- Drain **⅔ cup sauerkraut**, squeezing out some of the liquid.

- Drain **2 (10-ounce) jars marinated artichokes**, then pat dry with paper towels. If the artichokes are whole, halve them; if they're already cut, you're all good!

- In a large nonstick skillet, heat **a few generous tablespoons of olive oil** over medium-high heat. Add the artichokes (arranging them cut-side down as much as possible) and cook until crisp and browned, about 4 minutes. Remove from the heat, stir in **1½ teaspoons smoked paprika**, and finely grate in **1 large garlic clove**. Transfer the chokes to a bowl and season with salt.

- Add the drained sauerkraut to the pan and cook over medium heat, stirring, just until warmed through, about 1 minute. Transfer to a small bowl.

3 ASSEMBLE AND COOK:

- Wipe out the skillet. Brush one side of **2 slices rye bread** with mayonnaise and the other with some of the Russian dressing. Place the bread, mayo-side down, in the skillet (still no flame here, just assembling in the skillet).

- Divide the artichokes between the bread slices, as well as the sauerkraut. Top each with **2 slices Swiss cheese**.

- Slather some Russian dressing on one side of **2 more slices rye bread** and mayo on the other side. Place on top of each sando, Russian dressing–side down.

- Turn the heat to medium and cook until golden brown on the bottom, 2 minutes.

- Carefully flip each sandwich and cook until golden brown on the second side and the cheese is melted, 1 to 2 minutes longer.

- Transfer to a cutting board and season the tops of the sandos with salt. Cut in half and serve hottttt!

BREAKFAST

I THOUGHT YOU SHOULD KNOW

BREAKFAST

THAT   I   RARELY   EAT   BREAKFAST

SMASHPATTY™ BREAKFAST SANDO

MAKES 2

QUICK AS HECK!

PRODUCE

● ½ white onion

● 2 handfuls of arugula

DAIRY

● 2 slices American cheese

● 1 tablespoon unsalted butter

PROTEIN

● 2 large eggs

● 6 ounces uncooked pork or plant-based breakfast sausage (loose or links)

PANTRY

● ¼ cup mayonnaise

● Hot sauce, such as sriracha, Cholula, Red Clay, etc.

● Kosher salt and freshly ground black pepper

● 2 English muffins, kaiser rolls, or brioche rolls

● Vegetable oil

GOES WITH: CRISPY POTATO SKINS WITH FRIED HERB AIOLI (PAGE 226), BLOODY MOLLY & MEECHY MARY (PAGE 259)

In this griddled breakfast sando, we're giving a sausage patty the Smashburger treatment. It gets smashed thin, covered in griddled onions, blanketed in American cheese, and then topped with a pile of hot sauce–marinated onions and spicy mayo. Basically, IT GOES OFF. To the veg heads in the house: This breakfast sando is also for you! Get your hands on some plant-based breakfast sausage and then proceed with the recipe.

1 DO SOME PREP:

● In a small bowl, whisk together **a couple big spoonfuls of mayonnaise** and **some hot sauce** to taste.

● Thinly slice **½ white onion** into paper-thin rings (use a mandoline if possible). Set half of the sliced onions aside. Toss the remaining sliced onions in a small bowl with **a big pinch of salt** and **a few dashes of hot sauce**.

● In a medium bowl, beat **2 large eggs** until no streaks remain and season with salt and **freshly ground black pepper**.

2 SMASH THE PATTIES:

● Divide **6 ounces uncooked breakfast sausage** (removed from the casings, if you're using links) into 2 piles. Using your hands, work the sausage together until it forms 2 homogeneous ball-shaped masses.

● Place the 2 sausage balls on half of a large piece of parchment paper, fold the parchment over them, and firmly smash down on each ball with the bottom of a heavy skillet to flatten them into 4-inch-ish rounds.

3 TOAST THE ENGLISH MUFFINS:

● Heat a large cast-iron skillet over medium heat.

● Lightly spread both sides of **2 English muffins** with some of the mayo–hot sauce mixture. Arrange them cut-side down in the skillet and toast, moving them around the skillet as needed, until golden brown, 3 to 4 minutes. Transfer to a plate.

4 COOK THE PATTIES:

● Raise the heat to high and add **a big glug of vegetable oil** to the skillet. Heat until you see wisps of smoke.

● Remove the parchment from one side of the patties and then flop the patties, one at a time, into the skillet. Peel the parchment back. (Work one at a time if the pan looks crowded.) Divide the raw sliced onions between them, topping each patty. Season the onions well with salt. Cook, undisturbed, until the patties are well caramelized underneath, 3 to 5 minutes. Flip the patties. Turn off the heat and place **a slice of American cheese** on each patty. Cover the skillet with a lid or overturned baking sheet to allow the cheese to melt and the onions to cook from the residual heat.

5 COOK THE EGGS:

● Heat a small nonstick skillet over medium-high heat. Add **1 tablespoon unsalted butter** to the skillet. Once the foaming subsides, add the beaten eggs.

● Working quickly with a heatproof rubber spatula, pull the eggs from the outside edges of the pan toward the center, tilting the pan to allow any raw egg to run toward the outside and continuing to push the eggs toward the center, until large fluffy curds have set in the center but are still slightly wet on top, 30 seconds (it's fast!). Remove from the heat.

6 ASSEMBLE:

● Slather more spicy mayo on the cut sides of the English muffins. Place a sausage patty on the bottom halves of the muffins. Divide the scrambled eggs between them. Add more hot sauce, if desired. Top with some of the pickled onions, **a small handful of arugula**, and the top halves of the muffins. EAT!

SWEET COTIJA & SESAME PANCAKES

SERVES 4 TO 6

GOES WITH: SAUCY, GLOSSY SPANISH EGGS (PAGE 208), TAHINI DATE SHAKE SMOO (PAGE 271)

DAIRY

- 1 cup plus 2 tablespoons whole milk

- 8 ounces Cotija cheese, plus more for serving

- 6 tablespoons (¾ stick) unsalted butter, plus more for serving

PROTEIN

- 2 large eggs

PANTRY

- 1 cup plus 2 tablespoons (135g) all-purpose flour

- ½ cup (69g) fine cornmeal

- ¼ cup plus 2 tablespoons (54g) toasted sesame seeds, plus more for cooking the pancakes

- 2 tablespoons baking powder

- Kosher salt

- ⅔ cup maple syrup, plus more for serving

- 2 teaspoons vanilla extract

I first tasted the brilliant combination of sweet sesame and Cotija cheese at Popoca, a Salvadorean pop-up in Oakland, California, run by chef Anthony Salguero. I was lucky enough to spend a full day alongside Anthony in his kitchen as he cooked through some of the menu for me. One of those dishes was his quesadilla, which, unlike the Mexican version, is a sweet sesame-crusted butter cake dotted with salty crumbles of Cotija cheese. The mind-altering taste explosion has stayed with me ever since. These sweet-salty, crispy-buttery cornmeal pancakes are an ode to that dish, but you should absolutely seek out Anthony's recipe for the traditional version.

1

- Preheat the oven to 300°F. Place a wire rack inside a rimmed baking sheet.

2 MAKE THE BATTER:

- In a large bowl, whisk together **1 cup plus 2 tablespoons (135g) all-purpose flour, ½ cup (69g) cornmeal, ¼ cup plus 2 tablespoons (54g) toasted sesame seeds, 2 tablespoons baking powder**, and **1 teaspoon salt**.

- In a small bowl, combine **1 cup plus 2 tablespoons whole milk, ⅔ cup maple syrup, 2 large eggs**, and **2 teaspoons vanilla extract**. Whisk until smooth.

- Add the wet ingredients to the dry, whisking until incorporated (do not overmix). Crumble **8 ounces Cotija cheese** and fold it into the batter with a rubber spatula, stirring to distribute.

3 COOK THE 'CAKES:

- Heat a nonstick skillet over medium-high heat. Add **a couple pats of unsalted butter** (don't be shy!), swirl to coat the pan, and when the foaming subsides, sprinkle enough **sesame seeds** on the skillet to lightly coat the bottom (about 1 tablespoon). Add a heaping ½ cup of the batter to the pan and sprinkle the top with another **smattering of sesame seeds**.

- Cook until golden brown on the underside, 2 to 3 minutes. Flip and cook, reducing the heat as necessary to prevent burning, until puffed and golden on the second side, 2 to 2½ minutes. Transfer to the wire rack and place in the oven to keep warm.

- Wipe out the skillet, replenish with more butter, and repeat with the remaining batter, keeping the pancakes warm in the oven between batches.

- Serve topped with butter, maple syrup, and a final sprinkling of Cotija.

EARL GREY & APRICOT JAM SCONES

MAKES 8

GOES WITH: MOLTEN OMELET (PAGE 264), BLOO SMOO (PAGE 271)

DAIRY

- 8 tablespoons (1 stick) unsalted butter, cold
- ⅓ cup heavy cream
- ⅓ cup crème fraîche

PROTEIN

- 1 large egg

PANTRY

- 2½ cups (300g) all-purpose flour, plus more for dusting
- ¼ cup (50g) granulated sugar
- 1½ teaspoons baking powder
- 1 teaspoon kosher salt
- ¾ teaspoon baking soda
- 3 Earl Grey tea bags
- ½ cup apricot jam, plus more for brushing
- Turbinado sugar, for sprinkling
- Flaky sea salt, for sprinkling

Poor scones, always overshadowed by their cousins, biscuits. Well, I've got news for you, son! Scones and biscuits are basically the same thing! Scones tend to have a crumblier crumb, thanks to the addition of an egg, and a slightly lower butter content, but otherwise, not so diff! I'm on a mission to reinstate the (not dry, not bland) scone, and I'm starting with these. They're flecked with Earl Grey tea and swirled with apricot jam—sweet and fragrant and, like most things, even better with butter.

1

- Position a rack in the center of the oven.

- Preheat the oven to 425°F. Line a rimmed baking sheet with parchment paper.

2

MAKE THE DOUGH:

- In a large bowl, whisk together **2½ cups (300g) all-purpose flour**, **¼ cup (50g) granulated sugar**, **1½ teaspoons baking powder**, **1 teaspoon kosher salt**, and **¾ teaspoon baking soda**. Cut open **3 Earl Grey tea bags** and add the tea leaves to the dry ingredients. Whisk to incorporate.

- Cut **8 tablespoons unsalted butter** into very small cubes. Toss to coat in the dry ingredients and begin to rub the butter into the flour mixture using the tips of your fingers. Working quickly so as not to warm the butter, continue massaging the butter into the dry ingredients, pressing and flattening the cubes to create a mixture that resembles coarse sand with some larger, pea-size pieces throughout. Transfer the bowl to the freezer while you whisk the wet ingredients.

- In a measuring cup or medium bowl, whisk together **1 large egg**, **⅓ cup heavy cream**, and **⅓ cup crème fraîche**.

- Remove the bowl from the freezer and gradually pour the wet ingredients into the center. Using a rubber spatula, begin stirring the dry ingredients into the wet, mixing until nearly no dry bits remain.

- Lightly flour your work surface. Dump the mixture onto the work surface and pat the dough, kneading 2 or 3 times if necessary to bring it together into a 10-inch square.

3

ADD THE JAM:

- Using a spoon or an offset spatula, spread **½ cup apricot jam** on top of the square, leaving a ¾-inch border on all sides. Using a bench scraper,[1] lift one side of the dough up and into the center. Repeat with the other side, so the two edges meet in the middle—pinching together as needed to seal the edge. Use your hands to shape the dough into a 4 × 8-inch rectangle—some of the jam may spill out. It's not going to be a totally clean process, but as long as you get close enough size-wise, you'll be golden.

4

CUT AND BAKE:

- Using a large, floured chef's knife, cut the dough into 8 triangles. Place them evenly spaced on the prepared baking sheet and transfer to the freezer. Chill until firm, at least 15 minutes. These can be covered well with plastic wrap and frozen for later. Just plan on baking the scones a bit longer when the time comes.

- Brush the tops of each with a little more apricot jam. (You can warm the jam on the stovetop or in the microwave, if it's very thick.) Sprinkle with **turbinado sugar** and a bit of **flaky sea salt**.

- Bake until the edges are golden brown and the scones are cooked through, 20 to 24 minutes. Let cool for at least 20 minutes before eating.

[1] In a pinch, you can use a large flat spatula, but a bench scraper will really shine here.

GRIDDLED CHORIZO & EGG STUFFED PITAS

MAKES 2

QUICK AS HECK!

PRODUCE

- 2 scallions

DAIRY

- ⅓ cup sour cream

PROTEIN

- 10 ounces fresh Mexican chorizo (not cured)[1]

- 2 large eggs

PANTRY

- ½ cup pickled jalapeños, plus their brine

- Kosher salt

- 2 pita rounds

- Extra-virgin olive oil

GOES WITH: BLOODY MOLLY & MEECHY MARY (PAGE 259), BIG-ASS LATKE (PAGE 230)

This is so much more fun (and portable, hello!) than a breakfast sandwich spilling out of its kaiser roll, egg yolk dripping down your wrists. We're stuffing Mexican chorizo inside a pita with eggs before we griddle it in a skillet so that all of those fatty juices soak into the pita while the exterior crisps. If that doesn't sell you on this, perhaps the pickled jalapeño sour cream will, and if still not, well, there are about ten more breakfast recipes in this book you could make instead.

1 MAKE THE JALAPEÑO SOUR CREAM:

- Finely chop **½ cup pickled jalapeños**. Stir them into **a few big dollops of sour cream**, along with **a splash or two of the jalapeño brine** to loosen it to a drizzle-able consistency. Season with **salt**.

2 STUFF THE PITAS:

- Thinly slice **2 scallions**.

- Remove the casings of **10 ounces fresh Mexican chorizo**.

- Using a pair of kitchen shears or a sharp knife, cut an X-shaped slit in the top of **2 pita pockets**, being careful not to cut the bottom layer of bread. This is the opening through which we will stuff the pitas, but we want the bottom layer to remain intact.

- Divide the chorizo between the 2 pitas, pressing it in between the top and bottom layer and using your fingers to stuff it in so that it covers most of the bottom of the pita, nearing the edges.

- Into a small bowl, crack **1 large egg**. Lift the flaps in the center of a pita and gently slip the egg inside. Season the egg with **salt** and scatter half the scallions over the egg. Gently close the flaps of the pita. Repeat with the remaining pita, egg, and scallions.

3 CRISP:

- In a large skillet, heat **a glug of olive oil** over medium heat. Brush the top of one pita lightly with olive oil. Place in the skillet, cut-side up, and cook until deeply browned and crisp underneath, 4 minutes.

- Using a large flat spatula, flip the pita in one swift motion and cook on the second side for 2 to 3 minutes.

- Flip again and cook for 1 to 2 minutes longer—the internal temperature of the sausage should be 155°F. But no worries if you don't have a thermometer: a total of about 8 minutes of cooking (from the start) will get you there. You'll start to see all the juices from the chorizo seeping out and soaking into the pita, saturating it. When the pita is crisp all over, transfer it to a cutting board. Season the top of the pita with salt. Repeat this process with the second pita.

- Cut each pita into quarters and serve with the jalapeño sour cream for drizzling/dunking/dipping.

[1] A few types of chorizo are commonly found in grocery stores, so be sure you've got the Mexican kind. It's a freshly ground sausage and must be refrigerated, whereas the Spanish variety is dry-cured and more along the lines of a spicy, smoky salami and is stored at room temperature.

COOK ALONG!

VIDEO

DRINK

BREAK

BLOODY MOLLY

MAKES 4

GOES WITH: CRISPY RICE EGG-IN-A-HOLE (PAGE 127), GRIDDLED CHORIZO & EGG STUFFED PITAS (PAGE 256)

- 3 cups tomato juice

- ¼ cup dill pickle brine, plus pickle spears for serving

- 3 tablespoons Worcestershire sauce

- 2 tablespoons Castelvetrano olive brine, plus olives for serving

- 2 tablespoons prepared horseradish

- 2 lemons

- 1 small bunch of dill (optional but highly encouraged)

- 2 tablespoons hot sauce, plus more as needed

- Kosher salt and freshly ground black pepper

- 4 celery stalks

- Ice

- 6 ounces tequila, gin, or vodka

- 1 (12-ounce) can Mexican lager, such as Modelo or Tecate

I used to be the type of girl who would wake up on Sunday and drive straight to the nearest Bloody. Then I realized that nine out of ten Bloodys I consumed left me unimpressed. So, this is a Bloody Molly—the way I make and drink them at home. Beyond the usual suspects (horseradish, hot sauce, Worcestershire), the base mix is loaded with fresh dill, pickle brine, and fresh lemon juice to balance and brighten the intensity of the tomato juice and topped with a splash of beer. ENJOY RESPONSIBLY!

1 MAKE THE BLOODY MOLLY MIX:

- In a large pitcher, whisk together **3 cups tomato juice, ¼ cup dill pickle brine, 3 tablespoons Worcestershire sauce, 2 tablespoons Castelvetrano olive brine, 2 tablespoons prepared horseradish**, and the **juice of 1½ lemons**.

- Finely chop **1 small bunch of dill** (if using). Stir into the tomato juice mixture.

- Add the **hot sauce** by taste. Start with a couple tablespoons and go from there, remembering that it will get further diluted, so if you want things really spicy, go heavy now.

- Season the mixture with **salt** and **tons and tons of freshly ground black pepper**. We're talking several teaspoons of it—this is an important element of the flavor of a good Bloody.

2 PREP THE GARNISHES AND SERVE:

- Cut the remaining **½ lemon** into wedges for serving.

- Cut **4 celery stalks** into sticks (an inch or two taller than the height of your glasses) for garnish.

- Combine a big handful of salt and lots of pepper on a small plate.

- Lightly run one of the lemon wedges around the rim of each glass. Dip the rim of each glass into the salt-and-pepper mixture to coat. Fill each glass with **ice**.

- Pour **1½ ounces tequila** into each glass. Top with the Bloody Molly mix, leaving about an inch or so of room at the top of each glass. Stir well to combine. Garnish each glass with some **olives, pickle spears**, celery sticks, and lemon wedges. Fill each glass to the brim with a splash of **Mexican lager**.

MEECHY MARY

My love for a Bloody Mary is rivaled only by Ben's love of a michelada, which is a little lighter, a little more chuggable, and heavenly on a hot summer day. He makes them better than anyone else I know, thus his well-earned nickname: The Meech. The great thing about his michelada recipe is that it uses my Bloody Molly mix as its base. To make one, rim each glass with a mix of Tajín seasoning and salt. Fill each glass with ice, then add the juice of ½ lime, a few generous dashes of Worcestershire, and some hot sauce. Stir in 2 ounces Bloody Molly mix and top with beer, leaving more on the side to keep topping up.

SESAME
BISCUITS WITH BLACK PEPPER– MISO GRAVY

[MAKES 8]

[GOES WITH: BLOODY MOLLY (PAGE 259), CRISPY RICE EGG-IN-A-HOLE
(PAGE 127), TAHINI DATE SHAKE SMOO (PAGE 271)]

PRODUCE

- 8 garlic cloves

DAIRY

- 16 tablespoons (2 sticks) unsalted butter, cold

- ¾ cup buttermilk, plus more for brushing

- 2 cups whole milk

PROTEIN

- 1 pound breakfast sausage

PANTRY

- ½ cup (71g) toasted sesame seeds

- 2½ cups plus 2 tablespoons (315g) all-purpose flour, plus more for dusting

- Kosher salt and freshly ground black pepper

- 1¾ teaspoons baking powder

- 1 teaspoon sugar

- ½ teaspoon baking soda

- 1 teaspoon toasted sesame oil

- Flaky sea salt

- 3 tablespoons white miso paste

- 1 tablespoon low-sodium soy sauce

My dad used to wake up at the ass-crack of dawn at least once a week to make biscuits for me before school (God bless ya, Dougie!). We ate them slathered in butter and raspberry jam, and it wasn't until I was about twenty-one that I had my first taste of Southern-style biscuits and gravy. MAN OH MAN did they hit different. Here you will find my highly nontraditional version, with sesame biscuits and a sausage gravy seasoned with miso and black pepper.

DO SOME PREP:

- Preheat the oven to 425°F. Line a rimmed baking sheet with parchment paper.

- Cut **12 tablespoons cold unsalted butter** into ½-inch cubes. Transfer them to a small bowl and chill in the fridge until ready to use.

MAKE THE BISCUITS:

- In a small bowl, place **a scant ⅓ cup toasted sesame seeds (45g)**.

- In a large bowl, whisk together **2½ cups (300g) all-purpose flour**, the remaining **3 tablespoons toasted sesame seeds (26g)**, **2 teaspoons kosher salt**, **1¾ teaspoons baking powder**, **1 teaspoon sugar**, and **½ teaspoon baking soda**.

- Add the chilled butter pieces to the dry ingredients and, using your fingers, pinch and smash the butter into the flour until the mixture resembles coarse sand with some larger pea-size pieces throughout.

- Make a well in the center of the flour mixture. Add **¾ cup buttermilk** and **1 teaspoon toasted sesame oil** to the well. Stir into the dry ingredients in circular motions until the dough comes together in large clumps.

- Using lightly floured hands, knead the dough a few times in the bowl to bring it together into a shaggy mass and incorporate any floury bits at the bottom of the bowl.

- Transfer the dough to a lightly floured surface. Knead a few times to form it into a more uniform mass and incorporate any last floury bits. You will still see some shagginess.

- Pat the dough into an 8 × 4-inch rectangle. Cut the rectangle into 4 equal squares. Stack the squares on top of one another (creating a tower) and firmly press down with your hands to compress them together. This will force them to develop flaky layers. Pat the dough back down into a 8 × 4-inch rectangle. Cut the rectangle in half lengthwise and then cut each half crosswise into 4 equal pieces to create 8 squares total.[1]

- Lightly brush the tops and bottoms of the biscuits with some buttermilk. Dip the tops and bottoms into the bowl of sesame seeds, transferring the biscuits to the prepared baking sheet as you do so. Sprinkle the tops with **flaky sea salt**. You will have some sesame seeds left; we'll get to those later!

- Bake the biscuits until golden brown on top, 18 to 22 minutes.

(CONT. ON PAGE 263)

[1] At this point, you can chill the cut biscuits overnight, covered lightly with plastic wrap, so they're ready to bake the next morning.

COOK ALONG!

VIDEO

SESAME BISCUITS WITH BLACK PEPPER– MISO GRAVY (CONT.)

MAKE THE MISO–BLACK PEPPER GRAVY:

● Thinly slice **8 garlic cloves**.

● Remove **1 pound breakfast sausage** from its casings.

● Heat a large cast-iron skillet over medium heat. Swirl in the remaining **4 tablespoons butter**. Once the foaming subsides, add the sausage, spreading it out in a layer in the skillet, and cook, undisturbed, until nicely browned underneath, 3 to 4 minutes.

● Flip the sausage and cook, using a wooden spoon to break it up into bite-size pieces as it cooks until browned on the second side, 2 to 3 minutes. Transfer to a plate with a slotted spoon.

● Reduce the heat to low, add the sliced garlic, **3 tablespoons miso paste**, and **lots of freshly ground black pepper**. Cook, stirring, until the garlic is fragrant but not browned, 30 seconds.

● Sprinkle the remaining **2 tablespoons (15g) all-purpose flour** over the skillet and stir to incorporate. Cook, stirring, for 1 minute.

● Gradually whisk in **2 cups whole milk** and **1 tablespoon soy sauce**. Raise the heat to medium and bring to a simmer. Adjust the heat as needed to maintain a simmer and whisk constantly until the gravy has thickened, 3 to 4 minutes. Return the cooked sausage to the skillet. Taste and adjust the seasoning as needed.

SERVE:

● On each plate, crack a biscuit in half, spoon some sausage gravy over it, and sprinkle with **flaky sea salt** and some of the remaining sesame seeds.

MOLTEN OMELET

GOES WITH: SESAME BISCUITS WITH BLACK PEPPER–MISO GRAVY
(PAGE 261), EARL GREY & APRICOT JAM SCONES (PAGE 255)

MAKES 2

QUICK AS HECK!

PRODUCE

- 1 small bunch of chives

DAIRY

- 2 ounces fontina cheese

- 1 heaping tablespoon sour cream

- 1 tablespoon unsalted butter, plus more for serving

PROTEIN

- 6 large eggs

- 3 ounces silken tofu (about ⅓ cup)

PANTRY

- Kosher salt and freshly ground black pepper

SPECIAL EQUIPMENT

- Blender

Brace yourself for the fluffiest, easiest, least-stressful, and most ooey-gooey omelet you've ever tasted/made/seen! Here's the secret: By blending silken tofu into the eggs, you create creamy, fluffy curds that retard browning and leave you with a perfectly blond French-style omelet that (I'm guessing) would impress Jacques Pépin himself. The molten interior is a mix of sour cream and fontina cheese that spills out as you cut in—and ohhhh mama, is it sensual. Use any melting cheese you'd like, though funky fontina does a pretty damn good job.

1 MAKE THE CHEESY CHIVE MIXTURE:

- Grate **2 ounces fontina cheese** on the large holes of a box grater. (You'll have about ½ cup.)

- Thinly slice **1 small bunch of chives**.

- In a small bowl, combine the fontina, chives, and **a heaping tablespoon of sour cream**. Season with **freshly ground black pepper** and stir well to combine.

2 GET YOUR OMELET ON:

- In a **blender**, combine **6 large eggs**, **3 ounces silken tofu**, and **2 big pinches of salt**. Blend until smooth. Pour into a glass measuring cup and knock it against the counter a few times to pop the air bubbles.

- Heat an 8-inch nonstick skillet over medium-high heat. Add about **½ tablespoon unsalted butter** to the skillet, swirling to coat. Add half the egg mixture to the skillet. Immediately reduce the heat to low and let set for 15 seconds.

- With a heatproof rubber spatula, begin to stir slowly, scraping the sides and bottom of the pan to create large, wet curds. Gently shake the pan to encourage the super-loose raw egg to pool into empty spots in the skillet. Continue stirring until the eggs are beginning to set but the top is still quite wet (the runny eggs should no longer fill the gaps when you stir), 1 to 2 minutes.

- Spoon half of the cheesy chive mixture on top, in a line down the middle. Now, NOT stirring at all, continue cooking over low heat until the cheese is nearly melted (it will finish melting as it sits later), 1 to 2 minutes more.

- Scrape around the sides of the pan with the spatula and shake to loosen the omelet. Slide the spatula underneath the bottom of the omelet closest to the handle side of the pan and fold it in half, leaving the folded side about 1 inch shy of the other edge. Place a plate right beneath the edge of the skillet and nudge the omelet out of the skillet and onto the plate, holding the handle of the pan with your dominant hand. When the edge of the omelet hits the plate, invert the pan, flipping the omelet out to create an enclosed, tri-folded packet. Let sit for 1 minute to allow the cheese to finish melting. For some shine and extra richness, immediately spread a small slick of butter on top before serving.

- Repeat with the remaining ingredients to make another!

COOK ALONG! AUDIO

COOK ALONG! VIDEO

PEACH HALVA BOSTOCK

GOES WITH: A STRONG CUP OF COFFEE AND A MOLTEN OMELET (PAGE 264)

QUICK AS HECK!

PRODUCE

- 3 medium stone fruit, such as peaches, plums, or nectarines

DAIRY

- 4 tablespoons (½ stick) unsalted butter, very soft

PROTEIN

- 1 large egg

PANTRY

- ⅓ cup tahini

- ¼ cup sugar

- 1 teaspoon vanilla extract

- ½ teaspoon kosher salt

- 6 (1-inch-thick) slices brioche

- ½ cup peach or apricot preserves

- 4 tablespoons halva

- Flaky sea salt

Bostock is a French pastry that repurposes day-old brioche, much the same way that almond croissants make use of day-old butter croissants. This version (an atypical one) is slathered in a quick homemade tahini frangipane (a paste of tahini, sugar, and eggs) and then shingled with fresh peaches and dotted with halva. The frangipane soaks into the brioche, creating a custardy layer beneath the stone fruit. You'll ultimately do very little prep for something that tastes like it just popped out of a French patisserie, and how often can you say that?

1 MAKE THE TAHINI FRANGIPANE AND CUT THE FRUIT:

- In a medium bowl, use a fork to whisk together **⅓ cup tahini**, **4 tablespoons very soft unsalted butter**, **¼ cup sugar**, **1 teaspoon vanilla extract**, and **½ teaspoon kosher salt**. Once the mixture is homogeneous, whisk in **1 large egg**.

- Cut the flesh off the sides of **3 medium peaches** in lobes and thinly slice the peaches, leaving them in tight order so you can fan them out (avo-toast style) on the brioche later on.

2 ASSEMBLE:

- Preheat the oven to 375°F. Line a large rimmed baking sheet with parchment paper.

- Arrange **6 (1-inch-thick) slices brioche** on the prepared baking sheet. Transfer to the oven and toast until golden brown on both sides, 3 to 4 minutes per side.

- Brush the tops of each piece of toast, edge to edge, with **1 tablespoon peach preserves**.

- Using a butter knife, evenly slather about 2 tablespoons of the tahini frangipane on top of the jam.

- Top each toast with about ½ sliced peach, fanning it out to expose the slices. Then brush with more peach preserves and crumble **a few teaspoons of halva** over each one.

3 BAKE AND SERVE:

- Bake until the frangipane has spilled over the sides slightly and set and is turning golden at the edges, 15 to 20 minutes.

- Top with **flaky sea salt** and serve warm.

DILLY MATZO BREI PANCAKES

SERVES 4

GOES WITH: BLOODY MOLLY (PAGE 259), BIG-ASS LATKE (PAGE 230), MONOCHROMATIC MELON SALAD (PAGE 85)

QUICK AS HECK!

PRODUCE

- 1 bunch of dill
- 3 scallions

DAIRY

- 3 tablespoons sour cream, plus more for serving
- 4 tablespoons (½ stick) unsalted butter

PROTEIN

- 6 large eggs

PANTRY

- 3 sheets of matzo
- Kosher salt and freshly ground black pepper

I grew up on matzo brei, which my dad made with eggs, matzo, and butter. But we're "more is more" people, so this matzo brei does not stop there. It gets loaded with scallions, dill, and sour cream and transformed into a stack of pancakes. Matzo brei brilliantly straddles the line between being both scrambled eggs and a pile of buttery carbs, which is the best of both, if ya ask me. If you still can't imagine them, just know this: these are pancakes for savory people!!!

1 MAKE THE MATZO BREI:

- Crush **3 sheets of matzo** with your hands into roughly 1-inch pieces. Place in a medium bowl and cover with **cold tap water**. Let sit for 5 minutes while you prep the rest.

- Finely chop **1 bunch of dill**, reserving some leaves for garnish.

- Thinly slice **3 scallions**.

- In a second medium bowl, whisk together **6 large eggs** and **3 tablespoons sour cream**. Whisk in the chopped dill and scallions.

- Drain the soaked matzo and press on it firmly to expel as much water as possible. Add the matzo to the egg mixture, stir to combine, and season well with **1½ teaspoons salt** and **lots of freshly ground black pepper**. Let the batter sit for 5 minutes.

FRY THE PANCAKES:

- Heat a large nonstick skillet over medium heat.

- Swirl in **1 tablespoon unsalted butter**. Once the butter is melted, scoop the matzo brei batter into the pan in about ⅓-cup portions, adding only as many as you can fit comfortably without overlap. Fry until golden brown underneath, 90 seconds. Using a spatula, flip the pancakes, add **another tablespoon of butter**, and cook on the second side until puffy and browned underneath, 90 seconds. Transfer to a plate, lightly season with salt, and cover to keep warm while you repeat with the remaining batter and butter.

3 SERVE:

- Serve the pancakes with another dollop of sour cream alongside, and garnish with the reserved dill.

SMOO

BREAK

Every so often, I find myself in a deep and unrelenting smoothie phase. It lasts a month or two, during which I make a smoothie a day, each one slightly different from the last. And then my palate fatigues, I remember that I'm actually a savory breakfast person, and the smoos fade, only to resurface a few years later. My MVP is this one with nutty tahini, frozen bananas, and dates, plus a big pinch of nonnegotiable salt to tone down that sweetness. My other favorite combo is blueberry-ginger, so when you go through your own BIG Smoo phase, I got you.

BLOO SMOO

- 1 cup cashew or almond milk
- ½ cup frozen blueberries
- ½ cup ice
- 1 frozen banana
- 1 large Medjool date, pitted
- 1 (1-inch) piece of fresh ginger
- ½ teaspoon vanilla extract
- Big pinch of kosher salt

TAHINI DATE SHAKE SMOO

- ¾ cup oat milk
- ½ cup ice
- 1 frozen banana
- 2 large Medjool dates, pitted
- 2 tablespoons tahini
- ¾ teaspoon vanilla extract
- ¼ teaspoon ground cinnamon
- Big pinch of kosher salt

For each, throw **all the ingreedz** in a **blender** and blend on high until thick and creamy! Serve immediately.

SALTY
COFFEE & PEANUT SLICE CREAM

SERVES 8

GOES WITH: TANGLED LEEK 'ZA (PAGE 121), PEPPERONI FRIED RICE (PAGE 103)

When I lived in Los Angeles's Chinatown for a few months, I became hooked on the cold brew with salty whipped cream from a Taiwanese pop-up called Today Starts Here. Think Starbucks Frappuccino, with a lot less sugar and a lot more salt. I went three, four times a week, and it remains the best coffee beverage I've ever had. This five-ingredient coffee ice cream loaf is an ode to it, and it's decidedly salty. If you can't brew coffee at home, hit up your local coffee shop and ask for four double shots, which should measure about ½ cup.

DAIRY

- 3 cups heavy cream

PANTRY

- ¾ cup whole coffee or espresso beans
- 1½ teaspoons kosher salt[1]
- 1 cup roasted, salted peanuts
- 1 (14-ounce) can sweetened condensed milk
- Flaky sea salt

SPECIAL EQUIPMENT

- Stand mixer

1 BREW THE COFFEE:

- Boil **1 cup water**. Coarsely grind **¾ cup whole coffee beans**. (You should have ¾ cup ground coffee—grind more if needed.) Place the grounds in a glass measuring cup. Add the boiling water and stir. Let sit for 8 minutes, stirring twice.

- Strain the coffee through a fine-mesh strainer into a bowl (or use a paper towel set inside a strainer, if you don't have one that's fine enough), pressing on the solids lightly with the back of a spoon to extract ½ cup coffee (add a little water if you don't have enough). Chill until completely cool, about 30 minutes.

2 PREP THE PAN:

- Line a 9 × 5-inch loaf pan with parchment paper, leaving a 2-inch overhang on both of the long sides. These little flaps will help you lift the semifreddo out of the pan once it's frozen. Place the loaf pan in the freezer.

3 WHIP THE CREAM:

- In the bowl of a **stand mixer**[2] fitted with the whisk attachment, place **3 cups heavy cream** and **1½ teaspoons kosher salt**. Beat on medium-high until stiff peaks form.

4 COMBINE AND FREEZE:

- Finely chop **1 cup roasted, salted peanuts**.

- Into a large bowl, pour **1 (14-ounce) can sweetened condensed milk**. Add the cooled coffee, including any sludgy bits that have accumulated at the bottom, and whisk until smooth. Spoon a big dollop of the whipped cream into the condensed milk mixture and gently whisk to combine. Repeat twice more with 2 more big spoonfuls of the whipped cream. Switch to a rubber spatula and, in one go, add all of the remaining whipped cream and all but a small handful of the chopped peanuts. Gently fold once or twice, just ever so slightly, to incorporate.[3]

- Scrape the contents of the bowl into the prepared pan. No need to smooth the top because some irregularity here is good and will make for a nice tall slice.

- Sprinkle the top with the reserved peanuts. Freeze until frozen, covering the loaf lightly with plastic wrap once it has just set, about 8 hours or overnight. (You can make the loaf up to 5 days in advance.)

5 SERVE:

- When ready to serve, rub your palms around the exterior of the pan to warm the sides. Gently lift the semifreddo out of the pan using the parchment paper flaps and transfer to a serving platter or cutting board. Remove the parchment paper.

- Cut the loaf into slices and sprinkle with **flaky sea salt**. Don't be afraid to let the slices sit for a minute or two before serving; they will only get creamier and less icy as they warm a bit.

[1] This recipe was tested with Diamond Crystal kosher salt. If you're using Morton or a finer sea salt, reduce the salt to 1 teaspoon, or else it'll be way too salty (there is such a thing).

[2] Alternatively, beat the cream and salt by hand, using a big whisk and a large bowl.

[3] Do not overmix! Streaks of visible cream are what we want here! Those ribbons of unincorporated whipped cream will become pleasantly salty bites and will be pretty when the loaf is sliced, too.

SUNKEN DRUNKEN APPLE CAKE

MAKES ONE 9-INCH CAKE

GOES WITH: SALTY COFFEE & PEANUT SLICE CREAM (PAGE 275),
MISO-BRAISED CHICKEN & LEEKS (PAGE 178)

PRODUCE

- 2 large navel oranges
- 1 (3-inch) piece of fresh ginger
- 3 medium firm apples, such as Pink Lady or Honeycrisp

DAIRY

- 8 tablespoons (1 stick) unsalted butter, at room temperature, plus more for the pan
- ½ cup sour cream

PROTEIN

- 2 large eggs

PANTRY

- 1 cup plus 3 tablespoons (143g) all-purpose flour, plus more for the pan
- ⅔ cup walnuts
- 1 cup plus 3 tablespoons bourbon
- 1 cup plus 1 tablespoon maple syrup
- ⅓ cup (32g) almond flour
- 2 teaspoons ground cinnamon
- 1 teaspoon baking soda
- 1 teaspoon kosher salt, plus more for the walnuts
- ½ teaspoon baking powder
- ⅔ cup (133g) sugar
- Flaky sea salt

SPECIAL EQUIPMENT

- 9-inch springform or round cake pan
- Food processor

This apple cake gets a double dose of booze—bourbon gets stirred into both the batter and the maple glaze. And while that's fun and all, the real stars of this show are the maple-y wet walnuts that get strewn over the surface of the cake, caramelizing into a nutty, crisp topping as it bakes. The apples will sink partially into the batter, but that's the whole point—the cake will keep them tender and moist. Be sure to use a cake pan that is at least 2 inches high or the batter will overflow like a shot of whiskey at last call.

1 GET READY TO BAKE:

- Position a rack in the center of the oven. Preheat the oven to 350°F.
- Cut **8 tablespoons unsalted butter** into small pieces and let sit at room temperature.
- Lightly grease a **9-inch springform pan** with butter and coat it in **flour**, tapping out any excess. Line with bottom of the pan with parchment paper round cut to fit.[1]
- Coarsely chop **⅔ cup walnuts** and set aside.

2 MAKE THE BOURBON MAPLE GLAZE:

- In a small saucepan, bring **1 cup bourbon** and **¾ cup maple syrup** to a simmer over medium heat. Cook, whisking constantly, until thickened and bubbling vigorously, 8 to 10 minutes. (You'll have about ½ cup glaze.)

3 MAKE THE BATTER:

- In a medium bowl, whisk together **1 cup plus 3 tablespoons (143g) all-purpose flour**, **⅓ cup (32g) almond flour, 2 teaspoons ground cinnamon, 1 teaspoon baking soda, 1 teaspoon kosher salt**, and **½ teaspoon baking powder**.
- In a **food processor**, pulse the butter, **⅔ cup (133g) sugar**, and the finely grated **zest of 2 large navel oranges** in long pulses until it starts to come together in one homogeneous mass. Finely grate **1 (3-inch) piece of fresh ginger** into the food processor. Add **½ cup**

sour cream, **2 large eggs**, the remaining **⅓ cup maple syrup**, and the remaining **3 tablespoons bourbon**. Pulse to combine. Scrape down the sides of the bowl, add the flour mixture, and pulse in a few 3-second pulses, scraping in between, until it forms a thick, homogeneous batter. Spread the batter evenly in the prepared springform pan.

4 PREP THE APPLES AND BAKE:

- Peel **3 medium firm apples** and cut them into quarters straight through the core. Slice off the core from each quarter so that the apples sit flat on your cutting board. Cut ⅛-inch slices across each quarter, taking care not to cut all the way through.[2]
- Arrange the apples in concentric circles on top of the batter, taking care not to press them in too firmly or they will sink into the cake. You may not need all of them. Brush the apples lightly with the bourbon maple glaze.
- Add the chopped walnuts to the remaining glaze, season with salt, and stir to coat. Sprinkle the walnuts over the cake. Reserve any leftover glaze. Bake until the cake is well browned at the edges and a toothpick inserted into the center comes out clean, 55 to 65 minutes. Let cool in the pan for at least 15 minutes. Release from the springform pan and let finish cooling on a wire rack.

5 SERVE:

- Just before serving, brush the apples with any remaining glaze and sprinkle the cake with **flaky sea salt**.

[1] You could also use a regular 9-inch round cake pan; just cut and serve out of the pan.

[2] You can place 2 chopsticks above and below the apple quarter to anchor it and prevent your knife from cutting all the way through the apple to the cutting board.

BLACK SESAME RICE PUDDING BRÛLÉE

SERVES 8

GOES WITH: A GLASS OF AMARO, A CUP OF TEA

DAIRY

- 4 cups heavy cream
- 1 cup whole milk

PROTEIN

- 7 large eggs

PANTRY

- Kosher salt
- ½ cup long-grain white rice
- ¼ cup black sesame seeds
- 1¼ cups sugar
- 2 heaping tablespoons tahini
- 1 tablespoon vanilla extract
- 1½ teaspoons ground cinnamon
- ¾ teaspoon ground cardamom

SPECIAL EQUIPMENT

- 9-inch round cake pan

I am a sucker for black sesame desserts, and this one is no exception. Think of this as the love child of creamy rice pudding and classic crème brûlée . . . and then some. Tahini and black sesame seeds provide a nutty background flavor for this light-as-clouds spiced custard. It may look intimidating, but really all you're doing is boiling some rice, whisking together eggs and cream, and letting it gently cook in the oven. The final touch is a layer of crackly sugar on top that requires no fancy culinary torches or specialty equipment—just a baking sheet and your oven's broiler.

1 DO SOME PREP:

- Position one rack in the bottom third of the oven and remove any other racks. Preheat the oven to 325°F.

- Place a **9-inch round cake pan** into a deep skillet that fits the pan and still has some room around it. This will be your bain-marie setup.[1]

- Bring a small pot of water to a boil and season with **salt**. Add a **generous ½ cup long-grain white rice**, stir, and boil until nearly tender but still slightly undercooked, about 8 minutes. Drain. Transfer the parcooked rice to the cake pan.

- In a mortar and pestle or resealable bag with a rolling pin, coarsely crush **¼ cup black sesame seeds**.

2 MAKE AND BAKE THE PUDDING BRÛLÉE:

- In a medium saucepan, combine **4 cups heavy cream** and **1 cup whole milk** and cook over medium-low heat, stirring occasionally, just until it comes to a bare simmer. Turn off the heat.

- While the cream mixture heats, in a large bowl, whisk together **6 large egg yolks** and **1 large egg**. (Reserve the whites for another use.)

- Whisk in **¾ cup sugar**, **2 heaping tablespoons tahini**, **1 tablespoon vanilla extract**, **2 teaspoons salt**, **1½ teaspoons**

ground cinnamon, **¾ teaspoon ground cardamom**, and the ground black sesame seeds.

- While whisking continuously, slowly stream the hot cream mixture, a little at a time, into the bowl. Once the mixture in the bowl seems to have reached the same temperature as the mixture in the pot, begin to pour with more gusto.[2]

- Pour the hot custard over the rice in the cake pan. Carefully transfer the skillet to the oven. Fill a vessel with a pour spout with **hot tap water** and fill the skillet until the water comes about three-quarters of the way up the sides of the cake pan.

- Bake until the custard is set but still quite jiggly, 38 to 42 minutes. Remove from the oven, let cool at room temperature for 20 minutes, then transfer to the refrigerator until cold, at least 4 hours.

- Position a rack at least 6 inches from the broiler. Preheat the broiler.

- Sprinkle the baked custard with the remaining **½ cup sugar** and shake the pan from side to side to distribute the sugar in an even layer. Set the pan on a rimmed baking sheet under the broiler. Watch carefully, rotating the sheet if necessary to encourage even browning, until the sugar melts and becomes deeply caramelized, 2 to 6 minutes, depending on the strength of your broiler. Remove from the oven and either chill again until cold or serve immediately!

---

[1] A bain-marie is a French term for a hot water bath. Cooking a custard like crème brûlée in a pan of hot water ensures that it cooks evenly and gently.

[2] This is called tempering, and it ensures that the eggs don't go into shock and scramble when they come into contact with the hot cream mixture.

MAPLE RICOTTA MUNCHKINS

MAKES 12 TO 15

GOES WITH: SALTY COFFEE & PEANUT SLICE CREAM (PAGE 275), HOT SAUCE–BRAISED SHORT RIBS WITH WINTER SQUASH (PAGE 149)

QUICK AS HECK!

PRODUCE

- 1 orange

DAIRY

- 1 cup (227g) fresh whole-milk ricotta cheese

PROTEIN

- 1 large egg

PANTRY

- Canola oil, for frying (about 6 cups)
- ½ cup (60g) all-purpose flour
- 1½ teaspoons baking powder
- Kosher salt and freshly ground black pepper
- 2 tablespoons granulated sugar
- 3 tablespoons maple syrup
- ½ teaspoon vanilla extract
- ½ cup (56g) powdered sugar

I've never been much of a doughnut fan. A controversial take, I know. But before you throw this book into the ocean (please don't do that, it would really upset me), know that I've never said no to a Munchkin. It's something about their perfect bite-size shape. These aren't really doughnuts, anyway—ricotta cheese gives them an ethereal, fluffy texture that takes them to an entirely different doughnut plane of existence. Let's go there together, shall we?

1 GET YOUR OIL GOING:

- Fill a large Dutch oven or heavy-bottomed pot with enough **canola oil** to achieve a depth of 1½ inches. Set over medium heat and heat to 375°F, checking periodically with a thermometer.

2 PREP THE DOUGHNUT BATTER:

- In a medium bowl, whisk together **½ cup (60g) all-purpose flour**, **1½ teaspoons baking powder**, and **¼ teaspoon salt**.

- In another medium bowl, whisk together **1 cup (227g) ricotta cheese, 1 large egg, 2 tablespoons granulated sugar, 1 tablespoon maple syrup, the zest of 1 orange**, and **½ teaspoon vanilla extract**.

- Fold the dry ingredients into the wet ones with a rubber spatula until the batter is thick and well combined.

3 FRY:

- Line a rimmed baking sheet with paper towels and set a rack inside the sheet.

- When the oil has reached 375°F, use 2 large spoons or a small ice cream scoop to drop heaping tablespoons (about the size of a golf ball) of batter into the oil—enough to fill the pot without overcrowding. Fry until the doughnuts rise to the surface, the bubbling begins to mellow out, and the doughnuts are deeply golden brown, 4 to 6 minutes. They will likely flip themselves as they fry, but if not, encourage them to do so by gently nudging them with a slotted spoon.

- Transfer to the wire rack to cool slightly. Repeat with the remaining batter.

4 GLAZE:

- In a medium bowl, whisk together **½ cup (56g) powdered sugar**, the remaining **2 tablespoons maple syrup**, a good pinch of salt, and **lots and lots of freshly ground black pepper**. Add a squeeze of **juice from the orange** to thin the glaze to a drizzle-able consistency.

- When the doughnuts are no longer piping hot, dip them into the glaze, rolling them around to coat. Transfer to a plate and eat while still warm, if poss!

PISTACHIO, BROWN BUTTER & HALVA CHOCOLATE CHUNK COOKIES

MAKES 12 LARGE COOKIES

GOES WITH: A COLD GLASS OF MILK!

DAIRY

- 10 tablespoons unsalted butter

PROTEIN

- 1 large egg

PANTRY

- ¾ cup (90g) raw, shelled pistachios

- 4 ounces (112g) dark chocolate (not chips)

- ½ cup plus 2 tablespoons (120g) packed dark brown sugar

- ⅓ cup (66g) granulated sugar

- 1 tablespoon vanilla extract

- 1 cup (120g) all-purpose flour

- 1 teaspoon kosher salt

- ½ teaspoon baking soda

- 3 ounces (85g) halva[1] (preferably pistachio-flavored)

- Flaky sea salt

SPECIAL EQUIPMENT

- Food processor

[1] Halva can be found in the international section of most grocery stories or Middle Eastern markets.

The thing that makes these cookies so special is the way they linger between the sweet and savory. They are loaded with finely ground pistachios, studded with halva (a Middle Eastern sweetened sesame confection), and bound together by deeply nutty browned butter. If you're a chocolate hater like me (not that I expect any of you are), you can leave out the chocolate chunks and still have a truly exceptional cookie in front of you.

1 PULSE THE PISTACHIOS:

- Place ¾ cup (90g) raw, shelled pistachios in the bowl of a food processor and pulse several times until chopped but not yet finely ground. Scoop out and set aside 2 to 3 tablespoons of the chopped nuts (we'll use those later on for the cookie tops). Continue pulsing the pistachios in long pulses until very finely ground, about 1 minute.

2 BROWN THE BUTTER:

- Cut 10 tablespoons butter into 1-inch pieces. Place in a medium saucepan over medium heat and cook, stirring the pot every minute or so, until the butter has turned very foamy and bubbling but not yet browned, about 6 minutes.

- Quickly add the finely ground pistachios and cook, stirring constantly, until they smell very nutty and are golden brown and the butter has browned, 2 to 3 minutes more. The nuts should no longer be bright green and the butter around them should be deeply speckled with brown.

- Using a rubber spatula, scrape the brown butter mixture into a large bowl. Add 1 ice cube to the butter and let the ice cube melt and the butter cool for 10 minutes (it will foam up again momentarily).

3 MAKE THE COOKIE DOUGH:

- Chop 4 ounces (112g) dark chocolate into irregular ¼-inch to ½-inch chunks.

- To the cooled butter, add ½ cup plus 2 tablespoons (120g) packed dark brown sugar, ⅓ cup (66g) granulated sugar, 1 large egg, and 1 tablespoon vanilla extract. Whisk vigorously until well combined and thickened, about 1 minute.

- Add 1 cup (120g) all-purpose flour, 1 teaspoon kosher salt, and ½ teaspoon baking soda, and stir well with a spatula or wooden spoon until combined and a sticky dough forms.

- Add half of the chopped chocolate along with 2 ounces (57g) halva, crumbling it lightly with your fingers as you add it. Gently stir to combine. Cover the top of the dough with plastic wrap and refrigerate at least 3 hours and ideally overnight. The longer you chill the dough, the deeper and more complex the flavor of the cookies will be, so, if you can, plan ahead!

4 SCOOP, TOP, AND BAKE:

- Preheat the oven to 375°F. Line 2 baking sheets with parchment paper.

- Using a 2-ounce ice cream scoop (or large spoon), scoop out 12 equal portions of dough, rolling them into a rough ball shape.

- Working one at a time, dip the tops of the dough balls into the reserved chopped pistachios, then place them on the baking sheets about 2½ inches apart.

- Dot the tops of each cookie with a few more big shards of the reserved chocolate chunks and another crumble or two of halva, pressing lightly with your fingers to encourage the chunks and crumbles to adhere.

- Bake, rotating the baking sheets from top to bottom and front to back after about 8 minutes, until the cookies are browned at the edges and no longer wet on top, 12 to 14 minutes total.

- While still warm, sprinkle the cookies with flaky sea salt. Once cool enough to handle, transfer to a wire rack to finish cooling. Store the cookies in an airtight container to make them last longer!

COOK ALONG!

AUDIO

SPICED PEANUT SHORTBREAD

MAKES ABOUT 25

GOES WITH: MAPLE RICOTTA MUNCHKINS (PAGE 280), RAMEN NOODLES WITH SHROOMS & SOY BUTTER (PAGE 128), SPICED LENTIL BURGER WITH A VERY SPECIAL SAUCE (PAGE 245)

DAIRY

- 8 tablespoons (1 stick) unsalted butter, at room temperature

PROTEIN

- 1 large egg white

PANTRY

- 1¼ cups (178g) roasted, salted peanuts
- 3 tablespoons turbinado sugar
- Kosher salt and freshly ground black pepper
- 1 teaspoon flaky sea salt
- 1¼ cups (150g) all-purpose flour
- ¼ cup (50g) granulated sugar
- ¾ teaspoon ground cardamom
- 1 teaspoon vanilla extract

SPECIAL EQUIPMENT

- Food processor

A food processor is gonna be your best friend here because you'll use it to pulverize the peanuts that coat the outside of these slice-and-bake cookies and then use it again (psst, don't wash it) to build the cookie dough. These cookies are part peanut butter cookie, part buttery shortbread cookie, part holiday spice cookie. They've got an incredibly deep, warm flavor thanks to the black pepper, cardamom, and flaky sea salt flecked throughout. Nothing but great things to say about them, really.

1 MAKE THE CRUNCHY COATING:

- In a **food processor**, process **1¼ cups (178g) roasted, salted peanuts** until the peanuts are very finely chopped and resemble coarse graham cracker crumbs. Transfer ⅓ cup of the peanut crumbs to a large dinner plate, leaving the remaining peanuts in the food processor. To the dinner plate, add **3 tablespoons turbinado sugar, 1 tablespoon freshly ground black pepper**, and **1 teaspoon flaky sea salt** and mix to combine. Set aside.

2 MAKE THE COOKIE DOUGH:

- Add **1¼ cups (150g) all-purpose flour, ¼ cup (50g) granulated sugar, ¾ teaspoon ground cardamom**, and **¾ teaspoon kosher salt** to the food processor. Pulse to combine.

- Cube **8 tablespoons unsalted butter** and add it to the food processor, along with **1 teaspoon vanilla extract**.

- Process until a dough forms, scraping down the sides of the bowl with a rubber spatula as necessary, 1 to 2 minutes. The mixture will eventually form a ball around the blade.

- Transfer the dough to a work surface and roll it into a fat log. Set the log of dough in the middle of a large piece of parchment paper and fold the bottom half of the paper over the dough. With the log lying horizontally, place the edge of a bench scraper or ruler on top of the folded portion of the paper, pushing up against the dough. Using one hand to pull the bench scraper toward you and the other to pull the bottom piece of the parchment away, push and pull until the dough becomes an even log 2 inches in diameter and 9 inches long.

- Roll up the dough in the parchment paper and transfer to the refrigerator to chill until very firm, at least 1 hour.

3 ROLL, SLICE, AND BAKE:

- Position racks in the upper and lower thirds of the oven. Preheat the oven to 325°F. Line 2 rimmed baking sheets with parchment paper.

- Unwrap the chilled dough and cut it crosswise into thirds.

- Place **1 large egg white** in a small bowl. Working with one-third of the dough at a time, brush the exterior with egg white. Roll it in the crushed peanut mixture, firmly pressing, and sprinkling all sides to get as much coating as possible onto the exterior of the dough.

- Using a sharp chef's knife, slice the log into rounds ¼ inch thick. Place the rounds ½ inch apart on the prepared baking sheets. (They won't spread much at all.) Sprinkle the tops with any remaining sugar-spice mixture.

- Bake, rotating the baking sheets from top to bottom and front to back halfway through, until lightly golden brown on the edges and undersides, 14 to 17 minutes. Let cool completely on a wire rack before eating.

OOEY-GOOEY CARROT CAKE

OOEY-GOOEY

PRODUCE

- 1 pound carrots (6 to 8 medium)

DAIRY

- 1¼ cups (284g) sour cream
- 8 tablespoons (1 stick) unsalted butter
- 1½ tablespoons whole milk
- Vanilla ice cream, for serving

PROTEIN

- 4 large eggs

PANTRY

- ¾ cup (149g) vegetable oil, plus more for the pan
- 8 ounces Medjool dates (½ cup)
- 3¼ cups (390g) all-purpose flour
- 1 tablespoon plus 1 teaspoon ground cinnamon
- 1 tablespoon baking powder
- Kosher salt
- ½ teaspoon freshly grated nutmeg
- ¼ teaspoon ground cloves
- 1½ cups (298g) granulated sugar
- 1¼ cups packed (267g) dark brown sugar
- 3½ teaspoons vanilla extract
- 1½ cups (192g) walnuts

If the name didn't already make it clear, this is what happens when you marry a classic carrot cake (my all-time favorite) with a St. Louis–style ooey-gooey butter cake. It's got a tender, moist, lightly spiced crumb and a ridiculously gooey brown sugar and butter topping in place of cream cheese frosting, which I guarantee you won't miss. This is for those of you who eat raw cookie dough out of the fridge and prefer desserts underbaked in a good way.

1 **DO SOME PREP:**

- Position a rack in the center of the oven. Preheat the oven to 350°F.

- Grease a 9 × 13-inch baking dish with **vegetable oil**.

- Coarsely grate **1 pound carrots**. Pit **8 ounces Medjool dates** and slice crosswise roughly into thirds.

 MAKE THE CAKE BATTER:

- In a medium bowl, whisk together **2½ cups (300g) all-purpose flour**, **1 tablespoon plus 1 teaspoon ground cinnamon**, **1 tablespoon baking powder**, **1½ teaspoons salt**, **½ teaspoon freshly grated nutmeg**, and **¼ teaspoon ground cloves**.

- In a large bowl, add **¾ cup (149g) vegetable oil**, **¾ cup (149g) granulated sugar**, and **¾ cup packed (160g) dark brown sugar**. Add **3 large eggs** and **2 teaspoons vanilla extract** and whisk to combine.

- Add the dry ingredients to the wet ingredients in 3 additions, alternating with **1¼ cups (284g) sour cream**, beginning and ending with the dry ingredients.

- Add the grated carrots. Using your hands, coarsely crush **1½ cups (192g) walnuts** directly into the bowl. Stir to incorporate.

- Transfer the batter to the prepared baking dish and smooth the top with an offset spatula.

3 **MAKE THE OOEY-GOOEY AND BAKE:**

- In a medium pot over medium-high heat, melt **8 tablespoons unsalted butter**. Remove from the heat and whisk in the remaining **¾ cup (149g) granulated sugar** and remaining **½ cup (107g) brown sugar**. Add the remaining **¾ cup (90g) flour**. Stir to combine. Add **1½ tablespoons milk**, **1 teaspoon salt**, and the remaining **1½ teaspoons vanilla extract**. Stir to combine. Add the remaining **1 egg** and the sliced dates and stir to distribute.

- While still warm, spread the ooey-gooey over the top of the batter.

- Bake until the cake is golden brown on the edges and a toothpick inserted into the lower, cakey part of the baking dish comes out clean, 45 to 55 minutes. The ooey-gooey toward the top should remain slightly, uhhh, ooey-gooey.

- Let cool in the pan for at least 30 minutes. Cut the cake into squares and serve topped with **vanilla ice cream**.

 # RUFFLE PIE

GOES WITH: HALLOUMI, CUKE & WALNUT SPOON SALAD (PAGE 81), ONE-POT CHICKEN MUJADARA (PAGE 194), SAUCY, GLOSSY SPANISH EGGS (PAGE 208)

DAIRY

- 12 tablespoons (1½ sticks) unsalted butter
- 1¾ cups (398g) whole milk
- 1 cup (227g) heavy cream

PROTEIN

- 4 large eggs

FROZEN

- 10 ounces phyllo dough (about twelve 12 × 17-inch sheets), thawed

PANTRY

- ¼ cup plus 2 tablespoons (74g) sugar, plus more for sprinkling
- ½ cup plus 2 tablespoons (210g) honey
- 1 tablespoon ground cinnamon
- 1½ teaspoons vanilla extract
- 1¼ teaspoons ground cardamom
- Kosher salt
- ½ teaspoon freshly grated nutmeg
- ¼ teaspoon ground cloves
- ⅔ cup raw, shelled pistachios and/or walnuts
- Flaky sea salt

Stop!! If you saw this pic and immediately started to get overwhelmed, hang on a sec. Here is a pie that is about seven billion times more impressive looking than it is difficult to execute. Taste-wise, it lands somewhere between baklava and French toast, making it the dessert you can end one day with and start the next one in front of. Buttered swirls of (store-bought!) phyllo dough get baked until deeply golden and crisp and then bound together by a light-as-air spiced milk custard. The finished pie gets drenched in honey and chopped pistachios. Make this for the holidays, make this for brunch, make this on a random Saturday . . . Whatever you do, MAKE IT!

1 BAKE THE PHYLLO BASE:

- Preheat the oven to 350°F.

- In a small saucepan, melt **12 tablespoons unsalted butter** over medium heat until just melted but not browned.

- Lightly brush a 12-inch cast-iron skillet with some of the melted butter to coat.

- Place **10 ounces phyllo dough** on a work surface and cover with a kitchen towel.

- Working with 1 sheet of phyllo dough at a time, lightly brush one side with melted butter. Swiftly scrunch the shorter sides of each sheet toward each other to create a loose, ruffled length of dough (it will look like a drawn curtain). Roll into a loose spiral (it will look like a rosebud). The goal is to keep the phyllo sheets loose and airy (see the photo for reference!). Transfer the phyllo spiral to the prepared skillet and repeat with the remaining phyllo sheets, placing each coil next to the other but not so close that they are scrunching the folds of pastry.

- Lightly sprinkle the tops with **sugar**.

- Bake until deeply golden and crisp, about 45 minutes. Remove from the oven and let sit until the cast-iron pan is just warm to the touch, at least 1 hour.

2 MAKE THE CUSTARD:

- In a large bowl, combine **4 large eggs, ¼ cup plus 2 tablespoons (74g) sugar, and ¼ cup (84g) honey.** Whisk until smooth. Add **1¾ cups (398g) milk, 1 cup (227g) heavy cream, 1 tablespoon ground cinnamon, 1½ teaspoons vanilla extract, 1¼ teaspoons ground cardamom, 1¼ teaspoons kosher salt, ½ teaspoon freshly grated nutmeg, and ¼ teaspoon ground cloves.** Whisk to combine.

- Transfer the custard to a large measuring cup and pour it into the pan, aiming for the crevices and between the ruffles of the pastry, not on top of the pastry itself.

- Return the pan to the oven to bake until the custard is just set and very puffed, 32 to 38 minutes.

3 HAVE YOUR BAKLAVA MOMENT:

- Finely chop **⅔ cup raw, shelled pistachios and/or walnuts.** Scatter on top of the pie.

- Warm the remaining **¼ cup plus 2 tablespoons (126g) honey** in a small saucepan just until pourable. Using a pastry brush, drizzle and lightly brush the tops of the ruffles with the honey. Sprinkle lightly with **flaky sea salt** and cut the pie into slices to serve.

COOK ALONG!

VIDEO

SALTED MALTED BANOFFEE TRIFLE

SERVES 8

GOES WITH: A CUP OF COFFEE, A POT OF TEA

PRODUCE

- 5 large ripe bananas

DAIRY

- 3 cups heavy cream
- 8 tablespoons (1 stick) unsalted butter
- ½ cup sour cream

PANTRY

- ½ cup plus 2 tablespoons packed dark brown sugar
- 2 tablespoons red or white miso paste
- 1½ teaspoons vanilla extract
- Kosher salt
- 1½ cups Grape-Nuts cereal (8 ounces)
- ⅓ cup plus ¼ cup malted milk powder[1]
- 2 tablespoons granulated sugar

SPECIAL EQUIPMENT

- Stand mixer

This might be the ultimate *More Is More* dessert. I've taken a classic American dessert, banana cream pie, and mashed it up with a classic British one, banoffee pie (a cream-topped banana-and-toffee dessert), but the fun did not stop there. The sweet-salty crumble is made of Grape-Nuts for extra-nutty crunch (s/o to the '90s), the toffee sauce reinforced with miso paste for a deeper savory note, and the whipped cream flavored with malted milk powder! The effect is a multi-textured, banana-toffee trifle that hovers between salty and sweet and is-that-cereal-milk, and I'm telling you, it is absolutely hypnotizing. You can make one big trifle to be shared among friends or a bunch of individual ones, depending how communal you're feeling.

1. MAKE THE MISO-TOFFEE SAUCE:

- In a medium saucepan or skillet, combine **1 cup heavy cream**, **½ cup packed dark brown sugar**, **4 tablespoons unsalted butter**, and **2 tablespoons miso paste**. Place over high heat and whisk to combine. When the mixture begins to boil, reduce the heat as needed to maintain a lively boil and cook, whisking frequently, until the mixture has darkened a few shades and thickened, 5 minutes. (Set a timer!)[2]

- Remove from the heat and stir in **1½ teaspoons vanilla extract** and **½ teaspoon salt**. Transfer to a heatproof bowl and chill in the refrigerator until cold.

2. MAKE THE GRAPE-NUT CRUMBLES:

- In a medium skillet, melt the remaining **4 tablespoons unsalted butter** over medium heat. Once the butter is melted, add **1½ cups Grape-Nuts** and cook, stirring often, until sizzling and a shade darker, about 2 minutes. Stir in **¼ cup malted milk powder**, **2 tablespoons granulated sugar**, and **¾ teaspoon salt** and cook, stirring, for 1 minute to marry the flavors. Let cool.

3. WHIP THE CREAM:

- Pour the remaining **2 cups heavy cream** into the bowl of a **stand mixer** fitted with the whisk attachment.

(You can also use electric beaters or, if you're up to it, a large whisk and a big bowl.) Beat the cream until lofty but not quite holding peaks. Add the remaining **⅓ cup malted milk powder**, **2 tablespoons dark brown sugar**, and a large pinch of salt. Continue to beat until soft peaks form. Do not overbeat. Beat in **½ cup sour cream** just until incorporated.

- Scoop out about ½ cup of the whipped cream and fold it into the chilled toffee sauce, gently stirring and folding with a spatula to incorporate. This will lighten the sauce a bit.

4. ASSEMBLE:

- Thinly slice **5 large ripe bananas** on a bias.

- Choose your assembly vessel: either 8 (8-ounce-ish) glass cups or ramekins or one larger glass baking dish or bowl—anything will work, really, though if you don't use something glass, you won't be able to see the layers.

- Layer the elements in the following order, making 2 layers: Grape-Nuts crumbles, toffee sauce, bananas, whipped cream, repeat. End with a big dollop of whipped cream, spreading it to cover the bananas. Transfer to the refrigerator and chill for at least 1 hour and up to 1 day before serving.

- Serve by the big scoopful if you made one large one, or individually if not.

[1] Malted milk powder can be found in the baking aisle of most large American grocery stores—Nestlé Carnation and Ovaltine both make great versions.

[2] The bubbles will appear larger and less viscous, and the toffee sauce should reduce to 1¼ cups. Take a measurement after about 4 minutes to see how fast the mixture is reducing. You don't want to over-reduce because the resulting toffee will be too thick.

ORANGE CREAMSICLE POPPY CAKE

PRODUCE

- 2 oranges (preferably blood)

DAIRY

- 1¾ cups (397g) sour cream

PROTEIN

- 3 large eggs

PANTRY

- ½ cup (100g) neutral oil, such as canola or vegetable, plus more for the pan

- 1½ cups (180g) all-purpose flour

- 2 teaspoons baking powder

- 2 teaspoons kosher salt

- 1 cup plus 2 tablespoons (223g) granulated sugar

- 1 tablespoon vanilla extract

- ⅔ cup plus 2 tablespoons (114g) poppy seeds

- ¼ cup (29g) powdered sugar

SPECIAL EQUIPMENT

- Blender

Loaf cakes are the ultimate lazy person's dessert, and I love them not because I'm lazy (I certainly am not!) but because I am a very busy lady and rarely have time for anything more complicated! This one is reminiscent of the orange Creamsicle ice cream pop I ate growing up and swirled with a rich filling of poppy-flecked sour cream. You'll use two bowls, one whisk, and a ton of poppy seeds, and the cake will be in the oven in mere minutes.

1

- Preheat the oven to 350°F. Grease a 9 × 5-inch loaf pan and line with parchment paper, leaving a couple inches of overhang on both long sides.

2 MAKE THE BATTER:

- In a medium bowl, whisk together **1½ cups (180g) all-purpose flour**, **2 teaspoons baking powder**, and **1½ teaspoons salt**. Set aside.

- In a large bowl, finely grate the **zest of 2 oranges** into **1 cup plus 2 tablespoons (223g) granulated sugar**. Mix well with your fingers to massage the zest and sugar together. Whisk in **3 large eggs** until combined, then add **¾ cup (170g) sour cream**, the **juice of both oranges**, **½ cup (100g) neutral oil**, and **1 tablespoon vanilla extract**.

- Whisk the flour mixture into the wet mixture until incorporated but not overmixed. Set aside.

3 MAKE THE POPPY SWIRL:

- In a **blender** or spice grinder, blitz **⅔ cup (96g) poppy seeds** until finely ground. Transfer to the bowl you used for the flour mixture. Add the remaining **1 cup (227g) sour cream**, **¼ cup (29g) powdered sugar**, and the remaining **½ teaspoon salt**. Whisk until smooth. Set aside.

4 ASSEMBLE AND BAKE THE CAKE:

- Transfer half of the cake batter to the prepared pan and level it with a spatula. Dollop half of the poppy cream into the center of the batter, trying to keep it away from the sides of the pan. Top with the remaining cake batter and dollop with the remaining poppy cream. Using a small offset spatula or the handle of a tablespoon, swirl the poppy cream and batter in about 5 small swirls, using a scooping motion to bring the batter to the surface and sink some poppy cream into the batter.

- Scatter the remaining **2 tablespoons (18g) poppy seeds** over the top.

- Bake until the center of the cake has a slight spring when touched and a toothpick inserted into the center comes out clean (aside from a few clinging poppy seeds), 50 to 55 minutes.

- Let cool until you are able to handle it. Remove it from the pan using the overhanging parchment and let finish cooling on a wire rack. Slice and serve!

PUMPKIN-CANNOLI CHEESECAKE CAKE

MAKES ONE 9-INCH CAKE

GOES WITH: PIÑACILLIN (PAGE 89), A GLASS OF SHERRY

PRODUCE

- 1 orange
- 1 (2-inch) piece of fresh ginger

DAIRY

- 1 pound fresh whole-milk ricotta cheese

PROTEIN

- 4 large eggs

PANTRY

- 1 cup (198g) vegetable oil, plus more for the pan
- 1¼ cups raw, shelled pistachios (6 ounces)
- 1½ ounces crystallized ginger
- 2 cups plus 2 tablespoons (421g) sugar
- 2½ cups plus 2 tablespoons (315g) all-purpose flour
- 2 tablespoons vanilla extract
- 2 teaspoons kosher salt
- 1 tablespoon ground cinnamon
- 2 teaspoons ground cardamom
- 1 teaspoon baking powder
- ½ teaspoon freshly grated nutmeg
- ½ teaspoon baking soda
- 1 (15-ounce) can pumpkin puree

SPECIAL EQUIPMENT

- 9- or 10-inch springform pan

COOK ALONG!

VIDEO

I like to think this version of the pervasive pumpkin bread is a major upgrade—it's topped with a creamy ricotta cheesecake layer that tastes like the filling of a great Italian cannoli. My pumpkin cake (it's a cake, let's just admit it) doubles down on ginger—there's both freshly grated ginger in the batter and crystallized ginger in the cheesecake filling, because why settle for just one expression of fall's quintessential ingredient when you can have two?!

 DO SOME PREP:

- Position a rack in the center of the oven and preheat the oven to 350°F.

- Lightly grease a **9-inch springform pan** with **vegetable oil**. Line the bottom with a round of parchment paper cut to fit if you'd like to more easily transfer the baked cake to a plate or cake stand to serve. Grease the parchment.

2 MAKE THE CANNOLI CHEESECAKE TOPPING:

- Coarsely chop **1¼ cups raw, shelled pistachios**. Set aside 2 handfuls for sprinkling later on. Transfer the remaining pistachios to a large bowl.

- Finely chop **1½ ounces crystallized ginger** (you should have ¼ cup).

- Using a vegetable peeler, remove the **zest of 1 orange** in strips. Thinly slice them lengthwise. Now thinly slice the strips crosswise to finely chop.

- Add the orange zest and crystallized ginger to the pistachios, along with **1 pound ricotta cheese, 2 large eggs, ½ cup plus 2 tablespoons (124g) sugar, 2 tablespoons (15g) all-purpose flour, 1 tablespoon vanilla extract**, and **1 teaspoon salt**. Whisk vigorously until smooth. Set the ricotta mixture aside for now.

 MAKE THE BATTER:

- In a medium bowl, whisk together the remaining **2½ cups (300g) all-purpose flour, 1 tablespoon ground cinnamon, 2 teaspoons ground cardamom, 1 teaspoon baking powder**, the remaining **1 teaspoon salt, ½ teaspoon freshly grated nutmeg**, and **½ teaspoon baking soda**.

- Finely grate enough of the **2-inch piece of fresh ginger** to measure 1 heaping tablespoon. Add that to a large bowl, along with the remaining **2 large eggs**, remaining **1½ cups (297g) sugar, 1 (15-ounce) can pumpkin puree**, and remaining **1 tablespoon vanilla extract**. Whisk until smooth. Add **1 cup (198g) vegetable oil** and whisk until incorporated. Add the dry ingredients in 2 batches, stirring just until no floury bits remain.

4 ASSEMBLE AND BAKE:

- Scrape the batter into the prepared pan and smooth the top. Add the ricotta mixture on top and spread it to the edges in an even layer. Scatter the reserved pistachios over the top.

- Bake until a toothpick inserted into the center of the cake layer comes out clean, 1 hour to 1 hour 15 minutes. Remove the pan from the oven and let cool for at least 20 minutes. Run a knife around the edges of the springform pan to loosen it. Release the cake from the pan, place on a wire rack, and let cool before slicing. Store any leftovers in the refrigerator—the cake's great cold, too!

BIG FAT THANKS

There are a mill-bajill people who have touched this book in a very tangible way, but before I get to any of that, a thank you to every chef, sous chef, line cook, prep cook, dishwasher, manager, bartender, host, server, barback, busser, home cook, grocery clerk, delivery person, colleague, friend, or family member who has ever fed me, and in doing so contributed to this life full of deliciousness that I am so blessed to live.

And now some very specific, highly personal thanks:

To the team at Clarkson Potter, who yet again believed in me enough to make this book happen. And especially to my editor, Jenn, for helping me create something bigger and better than I could on my own.

To my agent, Nicole, for sticking with me for another round, for being the baddest bitch I know, and for always having my back.

To mi Nora, who gave EVERYTHING and then some in working on the recipes for this book. This book would be half as delicious had you not been involved in it, and as I've said a million times, I trust and respect no one's palate more than yours.

To my creative team—Jen, Taylor, Christopher, Eli, Jake, Jasmyn, Stephanie, and the whole team at PlayLab. Y'all have yet again made all my visual dreams a reality and then some. I love every minute that we work together, I trust your creative brains entirely, and I cannot wait to make beautiful books with you till the end of time.

To Ben Persky/Baign, thank you for devoting all of your time to shaping my career for me, with me, and alongside me. Thank you for the relentless

embarrassment and constant giggles, and for making this bonkers-ass hustle wayyyy more fun than I ever knew it could be. I promise to do everything I can to make it worth your while someday.

To Beggs, for helping me find a voice for this book that somehow sounds more like me than my own voice alone. Thank you for "getting" it and getting me.

To Becky, for keeping this ship afloat, ensuring I don't lose my marbles, and always going above and beyond the call of duty.

To Sara Tane, my incredible recipe tester, for diligently cooking through each and every recipe in this book, oftentimes more than once!

To my parents, Momma and Dougie, for letting me be entirely me since day one. Your unwavering support and enthusiasm for every detail of my life, both career-wise and personally, does not go unnoticed. (Some might say I'm spoiled. I say that's good parenting.)

To my brudder, Addle Skiddadle, and his gf, Sam, for knowing and caring more about my work and the creation of this book than should ever be required of siblings, and for always being there at the drop of a text to help me bring this crazy vision to life.

To Tuna, an absolutely perfect and extra-long wee, who brings unbridled childlike joy to my world every single day, and regularly causes me and my thirty-seven-year-old husband to squeal.

To sweet baby Joans and my lover girl Matisse, for making me look way too good on the cover of this book and in the pages throughout. Nothing brings me more joy than the seamless intersection of work and friendship.

To Evan, Noah, Jamie, and the whole team at Salt for creating audio and video experiences for this book that are far more sophisticated than I ever thought they could be.

To allll the rest of my friends who ALWAYS let me feed them, cook for them, get them drunk, and photograph them. I ask a lot of you, and you always show up. Many of you are newish to my life, but the friendships have felt lifelong since day one. Y'all are fucking epic, and you make my life tick.

And lastly, but my God not leastly, to my sweet, generous, loving, bighearted, committed, supportive, <ins. all other positive adjectives here> husband, Ben, who lives and breathes this grind with me, who always goes above and beyond for me, who selflessly puts my dreams before his own, and who always, always, ALWAYS ensures that I feel the LOVE.

KISSING BOOTH

INDEX

recipes